The Master Musicians Series

21-4-77

MUSSORGSKY

Series edited by
Sir Jack Westrup, M.A., Hon.D.Mus.(Oxon.), F.R.C.O.
Professor Emeritus of Music, Oxford University

THE MASTER MUSICIANS SERIES

MUSSORGSKY

by
M. D. Calvocoressi

Completed and revised by Gerald Abraham

*With eight pages of plates
and music examples in the text*

London
J M DENT & SONS LTD

Made in Great Britain
at the
Aldine Press · Letchworth · Herts
for
J. M. DENT & SONS LTD
Aldine House · Albemarle Street · London

First published 1946
Revised edition 1974

ISBN: 0 460 03152 x

To my dear friends
MARY and RALPH LUCAS
in warm affection

INTRODUCTION

IT is ironical that this book on Mussorgsky should have been left by its author as Mussorgsky left all but one of his operas; some parts completed, others sketched, some not even begun. Fortunately this is not the big definitive work on Mussorgsky to which Calvocoressi devoted so many years of his life; that lies in a Paris safe, awaiting the day when conditions will make its publication possible. When that day comes it may be found that some of its judgments and conclusions differ from those that have had to be supplied here by another hand; hence it is doubly necessary to make clear what in the present volume is Calvocoressi's own and what has been added.

The author had finished Chapters I, II, III, IV, V and XI in all essentials, though with numerous lacunae—varying in length from a single word to a whole paragraph—which I have had to fill. Throughout the book my additions, sometimes necessarily lengthy, are enclosed in square brackets. Chapter VI existed only in fragments, and the bulk of it is mine. For Chapters VII, VIII and IX only the section dealing with *The Marriage* had been completed by the author, but thanks to the courtesy of the editors of the *Monthly Musical Record*, the *Musical Times* and *Musical Opinion*, I have been able to construct most of the long and very important sections on *Boris* and *Khovanshchina* from various articles the author had contributed to those journals; for the sections on *Oedipus, Salammbô, Mlada* and *Sorochintsy Fair* I am solely responsible. Chapter X is entirely mine, and I have compiled the list of works and bibliography.

1946   GERALD ABRAHAM

▼

NOTE TO THE REVISED EDITION

Ten years after the original appearance of this book Calvocoressi's 'big definitive work on Mussorgsky,' rescued from its Paris grave by Francis Poulenc, was duly published. It did not, however, supersede the smaller volume. (Both of course superseded the deplorable English version (1919) of Calvocoressi's pioneering book in French.) Calvocoressi had parted with his manuscript in 1938 and by the time he came to write the torso of the present book in 1944 further information had come to light. A quarter of a century later still, the student of Mussorgsky has the help of Alexandra Orlova's invaluable compilation, *Trudi i dni M. P. Musorgskskovo*, an almost day-by-day documentation of his life and work, and can consult the original full score of *Night on a Bare Mountain*, to say nothing of sources of less importance.

In this revised edition I have corrected and brought up to date not only the main text but also the bibliography and list of works.

1974   G. A.

CONTENTS

ILLUSTRATIONS

Between pages 56 and 57

CHAPTER I

CHILDHOOD AND YOUTH (1839–62)

In a little village, at that time named Karevo, but, a hundred years later, renamed Mussorgsky in commemoration of the event, Modest Mussorgsky was born, on 9th/21st March 1839.[1]

The genealogy of the family harks back to Roman Vassilievich Monastïrev, nicknamed Mussorga (said to have meant 'the back-biter'), who lived in the fifteenth century and was a descendant of Prince Yury Fedorovich Smolensky, of the lineage of St. Vladimir. Roman's grandson Ivan was the first to bear the family name Mussorg-sky (which also appears in other forms: Mussorgskoy, Musserskoy, Mussorsky). The correct pronunciation always was that which stressed the first syllable. The wrong one, with the stress on the second, originated in Poland.

Early in the seventeenth century his descendants had settled in the Pskov government and become well-to-do landowners. Modest's grandfather, Alexey Mussorgsky (1758–182?), married one of his serfs, Irina Egorovna. In the light of the composer's great love and understanding of the people, a few biographers ascribe importance to the fact that a proportion of peasant blood flowed in his veins. There is one reference to the fact in a letter from Mussorgsky to Golenishchev-Kutuzov: 'What could you expect from the grandson of an aristocrat landowner and one of his serfs?'—obviously an allusion to a mild joke which the two shared.

Alexey's only son, Peter, married the daughter of another well-to-do landowner, Julia Chirikova, of whom we have no information except that she was romantic and highly strung, wrote sentimental doggerel and played the piano well. Modest was the youngest of their four sons; the first two died in babyhood, the third, Filaret, born in 1836, died in his sixties, surviving Modest by twenty years or so.

[1] The first date is the Russian old-style one, the second the equivalent reading in our own calendar. Soviet Russia has adopted the new style; as a rule, old-style dates alone are given hereafter, except in Appendix A.

Karevo was an old-world village in the Toropets district, Pskov government, in the heart of the country some three hundred miles south of St. Petersburg, south-west of the Valday table-land—a region of fertile plains, lakes, rivers, marshes and age-old forests. The Mussorgsky estate at that time covered over forty square miles, and the manor house stood on a hill [commanding a beautiful view over Lake Zhistsa]. Karatïgin, who published all the above information, visited Karevo in 1910. By that time the house had been pulled down, and one of its wings rebuilt on another site. He was profoundly impressed by the character and atmosphere of the scenery; he says that

No doubt the beautiful, spacious surroundings, fraught with memories of long-past events, historical and legendary, in which Mussorgsky spent the first ten years of his happy childhood and which he visited many a time in later years, played a big part in the forming of his mind and imagination. They are the source of both the realistic and the mystical elements in his nature. They account for the live, multiform, highly poetic quality of his realism, for the realistic tinges perceptible here and there even in his most mystical ideas, and also for the mystical undercurrents that now and then make themselves felt, unexpectedly, in his most realistic ventures.

On Mussorgsky's years of childhood we have no information except that which he provided in a short autobiographical note—or rather in three unfinished rough drafts of it, one in Russian and two in very bad French. It is not known whether he ever went further with it.

Here is a translation of the part of the Russian draft that concerns the early years. Passages appearing here and there in the French that supplement or correct the Russian are quoted in footnotes.

Modest (Petr) Mussorgsky. Russian composer. Born 16th March 1839, in the Toropets district, government of Pskov.[1] Under the influence of his nurse, he became familiar with the old Russian tales.[2]

It was mainly his familiarity with the very spirit of the life of the people that impelled him to extemporize music before knowing even the most elementary rules of piano playing. His mother gave him his first piano

---

[1] Karatïgin discovered in 1911 that the real date of his birth was 9th March (21st).

[2] Tout enfant, il veillait peut-être des nuits, de là vient naître la passion de dire au monde le tout de l'homme, pour l'incorporer en formes musicales.

lessons.[1] He made such progress that at the age of seven he was able to play small pieces by Liszt; and at eleven, at a party in his parents' home, he performed in front of a large audience a big concerto by Field. His father, who worshipped music, decided to develop his ability, and his musical education was carried on under Herke at Petersburg. This teacher was so pleased with his pupil that he made him play, at the age of twelve, a concert rondo by Herz at a charity affair given at the house of Mrs. Ryumin, a lady-in-waiting. The success and the impression created by the young musician's playing were so great that Herke, although an exacting taskmaster, presented him with a copy of Beethoven's Sonata in A flat major. At thirteen, young Mussorgsky entered the school of the cadets of the Guards and was honoured by particularly gracious notice on the part of the late Emperor Nicholas. At that time he composed a small piano piece which he inscribed to his comrades. This was published by his father with Herke's help. It was the gifted young musician's first published composition. At the school he associated much with the religious instructor, Father Krupsky, and succeeded, thanks to him, in acquiring a deep knowledge of the very essence of old church music, Greek [2] and Catholic. At the age of seventeen, he entered the Preobrazhensky regiment. One of his brother officers, Vonlyarsky, introduced him to the great composer Dargomïzhsky, at whose house Mussorgsky became acquainted with the leading representatives of musical art in Russia, C. Cui and M. Balakirev.[3] With the latter the nineteen-year-old composer studied the whole history of the evolution of musical art, by means of actual examples, and with strict systematic analysis of all the capital works of European composers in their historical sequence, and through sedulous playing of these works [with Balakirev] on two pianos. Balakirev introduced him to the family of one of the greatest experts in Russian art, the famous critic Stassov . . . soon afterwards Mussorgsky made friends with another gifted composer who is now a well-known professor at the Petersburg Conservatory, N. A. Rimsky-Korsakov. Intimacy with this small group of talented musicians and also with a wide circle of scholars and writers such as Lamansky, Turgenev, Kostomarov, Grigorovich, Kavelin, Pisemsky, Shevchenko and others, greatly stimulated the young composer's mind and gave it an earnest, strictly scientific turn.

---

[1] . . . leçons durant il n'a pu supporter ce qu'on lui prescrivait. Néanmoins . . .

[2] Luthérienne-protestante.

[3] Le grand cœur et le grand esprit de Balakireff ont fait ressusciter Moussorgsky pour aller 'à large pâture.'

Mussorgsky proceeds to describe his further career, using many laudatory epithets, mentioning among other things the 'triumphant success' of *Boris Godunov*, and stating that the two operas *Khovanshchina* and *Sorochintsy Fair* are 'now going through the press.'

This autobiography was accepted at its face value by Mussorgsky's first biographer, Stassov, and by all subsequent writers, even long after its untrustworthiness in certain vital respects had been denounced by several Russian commentators. As we now know, Mussorgsky had written it for Riemann, who was preparing the first edition of his musical dictionary, and had sent circulars to all European composers, inviting them to contribute particulars. Mussorgsky wrote his autobiography at a time when he was ill, struggling to finish his operas *Khovanshchina* and *Sorochintsy Fair,* and when he was seeing the one opera of his which had been performed and won him a measure of fame, *Boris Godunov,* ruthlessly mutilated in performance and gradually dropping out of the repertory. Small wonder that when writing for a foreign editor, he wished to show himself and his compositions in the best possible light.

Viewed in this light, this autobiography becomes a very pathetic if not a trustworthy document. The story of his childhood may be substantially true, but it may also be very much embellished. We have no means of checking it. But we know for certain that in the year 1880 neither of the two operas *Khovanshchina* and *Sorochintsy Fair* was anything like going through the press: Mussorgsky died without having finished either of them. We also have evidence that Father Krupsky was incapable of imparting to anybody a deep knowledge of the very essence of old church music, because he himself was no specialist. He told an inquirer on the matter that he had done nothing but give young Mussorgsky a few works by Bortnyansky and other equally modern Russian composers to study. This evidence was published as early as 1881 in the *Russky Muzïkalny Vestnik*, but escaped notice; and the result was that the critics after Stassov have stressed the beneficial influence on young Mussorgsky of his 'thorough studies of the old church music, Greek and Latin.'

It was in August 1849 that Mussorgsky's father (concerning whose personality and relations with his sons we have no information beyond the one short reference in the autobiography) took the two boys to

St. Petersburg. He intended them, as was usual [in the Mussorgsky family], for an army career. They were two years at a preparatory school [with a 'crammer'], then Filaret entered the school for Cadets of the Guards and Modest followed him in 1852. On the years of his boyhood we have a small amount of independent information, consisting of a few recollections jotted down by Filaret for Stassov, and one or two indications given in a catalogue of works which Modest compiled in 1871 for Lyudmila Shestakova, Glinka's sister. We also have from the pen of Nikolay Kompaneisky, a composer and critic who passed through the cadet school a few years later, and eventually became a close friend of Modest's, a description of the school and of life in the Preobrazhensky regiment to which Modest was gazetted in 1856:

> The embryo cadets considered study below their dignity. This view was shared by the head of the school, General Sutgov, who, whenever he saw Mussorgsky working at his desk, would say to him: '*Mon cher*, what kind of an officer will you make?' The general objected to his pupils' drinking vodka like the common people, or coming back to the school on foot when they were drunk. But he was genuinely proud when a carriage and pair would bring back any one of them who had been overcome by the fumes of champagne. This was the sowing. The life in the regiment was the harvest. The young officers' favourite occupations were dancing, gambling, drinking and expedient love-affairs with titled ladies or wives of wealthy merchants.

One shudders when one thinks of the gentle, sensitive, country-bred boy spending six whole years of his adolescence in such surroundings.[1] According to the recollections of Alexandra Molas, another close friend of Mussorgsky's and, in later years, Rimsky-Korsakov's sister-in-law, he was fond of talking of his early childhood in the country, but not of his later youth. Apparently, during his military career, he was for a time under the influence of dissolute comrades, and ruined his health for life. In all likelihood, but for

[1] Kompaneisky's article appeared in 1906 [in the *Russkya Muzïkalnaya Gazeta*]. It remained overlooked by biographers for many years. In Russia, Findeisen alone (in the *Year-book of the Imperial Theatre* for 1911) referred to it in pre-Revolution days. It is mentioned neither in French biographies nor in the German biographies by Riesemann and Wolfurt.

his father's having planned for him, as was usual in their class, a military career, he would never have become a dipsomaniac, and the whole course of his life would have been different. Filaret's note tells us little except that his brother did well at school, always was in the top ten, studied history and German philosophy diligently, was popular with his schoolfellows and played the piano a good deal. Herke taught him nothing about the theory of music. One para-graph is worth quoting in full:

In his childhood, youth and maturity, he always evinced a deep love for the people and peasants. He held that the Russian muzhik was a real human being (a monstrous error) and in consequence he endured losses and poverty cheerfully. This love for the peasants compelled him to take up work in 1863 as a clerk in the civil service.

Here is the portion of the account written by Mussorgsky [for Lyudmila Shestakova] in 1871 that refers to the early years:

MUSSORGSKY. The first composition, published, to the author's regret, by Bernard in 1852, was *Porte-Enseigne Polka,* inscribed to his comrades of the Cadet School. He was then thirteen years old.
1856. Attempt to write an opera after Victor Hugo's *Han d'Islande.* Nothing ensued, or could ensue (the author was seventeen).[1]
1858. Scherzi: (1) B flat major, performed in 1860 at a concert of the Russian Music Society, A. Rubinstein conducting. (2) C sharp minor (for piano—unpublished), songs.
1859. Nervous disorder. Cure at the Tikhvin waters. I composed *Kinderscherz* (going through the press).
1860. I exercised my brains.
1862. I set my brains in order and stocked them with valuable knowledge.

No particulars of the nervous disorder he mentions are available, so that it is impossible to tell whether it was a consequence of regi-mental hard drinking. It occurred not in 1859, but in 1858, shortly after he had resigned his commission. From the moment he left the

---

[1] This is the only mention Mussorgsky made in writing of the 'attempt.' Stassov must have received from him verbal particulars, for he states: 'Mussorgsky had planned to write the libretto himself.'

army he strove hard, and for years successfully, to resist the habit, which, however, broke out in 1864–5 and again in 1873, when it finally established its hold on him.

However scanty the data are, a fairly distinct picture emerges from them: that of an attractive, dandified, rather affected youngster, whom his musical gifts made popular in society. (Besides playing the piano brilliantly, he could sing pleasantly and he was a clever amateur actor.) Borodin, who met him for the first time in 1856, gave Stassov a graphic pen‑portrait of him:

[A smallish, very elegant, dapper little officer: brand‑new, close‑fitting uniform; shapely feet; delicate, altogether aristocratic hands. Elegant, aristocratic manners, conversation the same, somewhat through his teeth, interspersed with French phrases, rather affected. Some traces of foppish‑ness, but very modest. Unusually polite and cultured. The ladies made a fuss of him. He sat at the piano and coquettishly throwing up his hands, played excerpts from *Trovatore, Traviata,* etc., very pleasantly and grace‑fully, while the circle around him murmured 'Charmant! Délicieux!' and so on.]

But there was nothing to show that he would ever be more than a gifted dilettante, and after having turned out the *Porte‑Enseigne Polka* (the only work of his that his father, who died in 1853, ever saw), he does not seem to have given a thought to composition—except for his vague *Han d'Islande* scheme—until 1857, when, a brother officer having introduced him to the composer Alexander Dargomïzhsky, he got his first glimpse of the musical world of St. Petersburg.

Those were momentous days. Russia, for the first time in her history, was becoming a music‑producing nation. With Glinka's operas *A Life for the Tsar* (1836) and *Ruslan and Lyudmila* (1842), and also his instrumental works, a national Russian style, originating partly in Russian folk‑music, partly in the music of the East, had come into being. Dargomïzhsky's *Rusalka,* produced in 1856, had aroused interest among the younger progressively minded musicians. Balakirev had started on his career and was soon to become the leader of a progressive‑nationalist group whose other members were César Cui, Mussorgsky, Borodin and Rimsky‑Korsakov. On the other hand, Anton Rubinstein, the great pianist, who in his capacity as a composer was as conservatively minded as he was prolific, was hostile to national tendencies in music, regarding them as antagonistic to musical culture and to the very spirit of the art. In 1859 he founded the Russian Music Society, and in 1862 the St. Petersburg Conservatoire, the first institution of its kind in Russia. The court and aristocracy were not interested in the new music, which they found too plebeian in character—'cabman's music,' they called it. On the side of the nationalists were Vladimir Stassov, a keen art-lover and a combative critic, and his brother Dimitry, an excellent and active musician, as influential as Vladimir, although less in the limelight.

At Dargomïzhsky's house and at other meeting-places of Mussorgsky's new friends a good deal of music was performed at the piano and discussed; especially Berlioz's, Liszt's, Schumann's, Dargomïzhsky's and Glinka's. There was also much talk about the ideals and achievements of the members of the circle. All this impressed and fascinated Mussorgsky deeply. He decided to become a composer, and that very year he asked Balakirev to teach him composition. He was very fortunate (and so a few years later were Borodin and Rimsky-Korsakov) to find him willing to do so. Whatever his shortcomings as a teacher of theory and technique may have been (Rimsky-Korsakov, in his memoirs, complained bitterly and most unfairly [1] of his methods of tuition), he was a splendid adviser and animator. With his knowledge, his infectious courage and enthusiasm, he was the very man of whom the budding Russian composers stood in need. He would have been of great use to them even if the country had not been entirely devoid of resources for their technical education—of schools, teachers and text-books in the Russian language. He is hardly to be blamed for not having acquired knowledge not available at that time in the country. On the contrary, he is to be admired for having learnt as much as he did. The notion of learning the processes of composition from the study of actual works, new in his time, has made great headway since. His far-reaching intuition led him to direct his pupils towards the works of Liszt, from which so many composers, from Wagner onwards, have learnt so much, and to Beethoven's last quartets, [then greatly neglected. One

[1] On this question, see Andrey Rimsky-Korsakov's preface to the third and subsequent editions of his father's memoirs.

8

of the works he gave Mussorgsky to study in 1857 was Beethoven's second Symphony].

To Mussorgsky Balakirev was far more than a teacher. Borodin and Rimsky-Korsakov, when, aged twenty-six and twenty-one respectively, they became his pupils, were men of poise and experience, with a good background of family and social connections. Mussorgsky, when he came to him, at the age of eighteen, was still very callow and inexperienced. Alone in St. Petersburg with his mother and brother, and having formed no really close friendships in his regimental and social circles, he stood badly in need of an intimate friend whom he could trust and confide in even on the most private, personal subjects. And such a friend Balakirev turned out to be, at least for a time, until he became disappointed with Mussorgsky's outlook and musicianship.

But even then Mussorgsky continued to trust and respect him, despite the many clashes that took place between them, as is shown by the following excerpts from a letter to him of October 1859:

Less than two years ago I was tormented by a cruel disease: mysticism, coupled with cynical thoughts on God. I was able to hide it from you, but you must have noticed the repercussion on my music. I suffered terribly and became morbidly sensitive. Then (perhaps because I found distractions; perhaps because I indulged in fantastic dreams) this mysticism decreased; and my brains having reverted to normal working order, I took measures to extirpate it altogether. I have partly succeeded by now.

As regards my attitude to you; from the very outset I always looked up to you. Whenever we had an argument, I could feel how lucid and firm you were. I may have felt angry with myself and with you, but I realized you were in the right. Only my wounded pride made me obstinate. You know how soft my nature is. You know I am liable to associate with unworthy people. But I never ceased to keep watch on myself, and I gradually learnt my lesson. I am deeply indebted to you for your watchfulness. Later, I understood you thoroughly and grew strongly attached to you. I found in you echoes of my own thoughts, at times their very germ.

Another letter, dated 10th February 1860, gives further particulars of his health, mental and physical:

Thank God, I am getting better after cruel, very cruel sufferings, physical and mental. Do you remember, two years ago, one summer day, we had been reading *Manfred* together and I felt so electrified by the sufferings of that

9

lofty nature that as I was seeing you home, I suddenly exclaimed: 'Oh! would I were Manfred.' (What an infant I was!) Now fate has fulfilled that wish. I am thoroughly 'Manfredized,' my soul has killed my body. Now, I must resort to all manner of antidotes. Dear Mily, I know you love me. For God's sake, in our conversations, strive to curb me, help me to keep myself in hand.

These letters seem to show that the nervous disorder of 1858, although partly an aftermath of the regimental hard drinking, was, in the main, the beginning of a double crisis of pubescence, mental at first and later definitely physical. A portion (not translated here) of the one of 10th February contains a very frank confession. Mus-sorgsky then goes on:

Entertainments, peace of mind, gymnastics and swimming will be my salvation. Yesterday my brother and I went to see the ballet *Pâquerette*, a very delightful ballet despite Pugni's abominable music. It created a strange impression on me, affecting me quite morbidly. When I lay down to sleep, I had most perturbing dreams, but so sweetly impassioned, so intoxicating that [I could easily have died]. Fortunately that was the end of my sufferings. I am now far better—or at all events, quite calm. I didn't intend to tell you all this; but as I started writing to you, I thought of you affectionately, and without my being aware of it I poured out the whole confession.

This brings us to the question of his loves and his sexual life, which has exercised a few of his biographers. All that is known on the subject can be set down in a few lines.

He was never interested in expressing in music the emotions of love. This fact, coupled with his horror of marriage (vouched for by his friends and by various utterances in his letters), has given rise to the notion that those emotions were foreign to him. Yet Karatïgin, in the course of his investigations at Karevo, heard a story of his having been, as a youth, in love with a cousin of his, and unpublished letters from Stassov to Findeisen state that he was infatuated for a time (probably in 1859–60) with a brilliant society woman, Marya Shilovskaya, and later with a young opera singer, A. Latïsheva. We also know that later still he bore a great—and probably platonic —love to Nadezhda Opochinina, whose memory he commemorated in his admirable *Epitaph* of 1875. But this is all that can be said concerning his affection for women. A native delicacy prevented his ever touching upon such a subject in his letters or conversation. A similar feeling, on another plane, led him to shun unclean topics. Once he confessed to Balakirev (letter of 19th January 1861) that he had 'sunk into the mire in an affair with a woman'; but he gave no details. In another letter he expressed his dislike of certain coarse jokes in which Stassov had been indulging.

It was shortly after becoming Balakirev's pupil that Mussorgsky resigned his commission (5th July 1858). At that time the only compositions he had to his credit were the *Porte-Enseigne Polka*, republished in 1947; a song, *Where art thou, little star?* very charming and thoroughly Russian in colour in its first version with piano accompaniment (1857), far less attractive in a version with orchestral accompaniment (1858), the manuscript of which bears the naïve inscription: 'My little song, transcribed for orchestra by myself—first attempt at orchestration'; and a *Souvenir d'enfance* for piano. His other compositions up to the end of 1860 consist of instrumental pieces prescribed by Balakirev by way of exercise, notably, in 1859 two piano sonatas [in E flat major and F sharp minor, practically no trace of which remains] and in 1860 two movements of another [in C major for piano duet, published in 1939]; a few songs, two Scherzi (1858), one in B flat major orchestrated with Balakirev's help, the other in C sharp minor for piano, [which was transposed down a semitone and inserted in the duet Sonata just mentioned;] *Ein Kinderscherz*, also for piano (1859–60) and a mediocre *Impromptu passionné*, inspired by Herzen's novel *Who is to blame?* He also started work [on what he himself described more than once as music to Sophocles's *Oedipus*, but which seems really to have been an opera based on the tragedy *Oedipus in Athens* by V. A. Ozerov].

In the spring of 1859 Mussorgsky paid a visit to his friends the Shilovskys at their country home, Glebovo, near Moscow; a magnificent manor on a hill top, he wrote to Balakirev,

with a lovely English garden—a kind of park—and a farmhouse opposite. All very beautiful, which is only as should be, the Shilovskys being sinfully wealthy. He and his wife are perfect hosts.

Thence he went to Moscow, which impressed him deeply. 'The Kremlin!' he wrote,

the wonderful Kremlin! As I drew near I could not repress a feeling cf awe. St. Basil the Blessed affected me so deeply that it seemed to me as though at any moment a boyar of ages past might appear in his long coat and tall hat. In the Cathedral of the Archangels I paid homage to the tombs of the old tsars. Rambling through the streets, I remembered the saying: 'Every Muscovite bears a peculiar imprint.' As regards the simple people, I agree: nowhere else could such beggars and rogues be found. I felt as though I was moving in another world, in the far-away past. Look here: you know I was a cosmopolitan, but now I feel reborn—everything Russian is close to me.

The year 1860 was marked by an auspicious event: [Mussorgsky made his public début as a composer on 11th/23rd January, when his orchestral Scherzo in B flat major was played with some success at a sympony concert of the newly founded Russian Music Society, Anton Rubinstein conducting].

From May to August, he [again] stayed with the Shilovskys at Glebovo, where he fell ill. Back in Petersburg, in September, he wrote to Balakirev:

You will be glad of the change that has taken place within me, and is, without a doubt, clearly reflected in my music. My mind is stronger, concerned with realities and free from mysticism at last. My last mystic outpouring is the *andante* B flat minor chorus for *Oedipus*. Thank God I am cured, dear Mily, thoroughly cured.

The letter mentions several new compositions, none of which has reached us. Nor is there any trace of two movements [of a Symphony in D major] (*andante* and *scherzo*) on which, according to another letter, he started work at the beginning of 1861, in Moscow, where he was the Shilovskys' guest and made new friends, students and other young people. He enjoyed talking music with them and playing to them Beethoven, Schubert and Schumann. Balakirev, [as soon as] he heard of this, rebuked him for mixing with inferior people, whereupon he flared up in defence of himself and his friends:

Since I am fond of associating with people of limited intelligence, perhaps my own intelligence is limited. Ustimovich, however, is a fine mature personality, he has knowledge and talent; Shchukarev is wise and has a trained and original mind . . . your letter is the outcome of misguided spite: it is high time you ceased regarding me as an infant who has to be held in leading-strings. Such is my reply to your letter—an impetuous reckless letter, but one for which I thank you: I was fearing that you were not going to write to me at all.

Neither that year nor in 1862 did Mussorgsky compose anything except a brief *Alla marcia notturna* for orchestra, the manuscript of which bears the note 'Exercise in instrumentation—lesson on Wednesday' (which suggests that he was receiving, or about to receive, [additional] tuition from some instructor, whose name remains unknown); and also a first draft, for piano, of an *Intermezzo* to which he gave its final orchestral form later. He had, it is true, many worries on his mind. On 19th February/3rd March 1861 an imperial decree ordering the emancipation of the serfs was promulgated, which seriously affected the circumstances of landowners. He spent a good deal of time trying to devise measures to cope with the situation.

In April [the choral Temple scene from *Oedipus* was performed at a concert in the Marinsky Theatre, under Constantine Lyadov, father of the future composer of *Baba-Yaga, Kikimora* and *The Enchanted Lake*].

Throughout the year the situation remained very much the same. Mussorgsky spent most of his time in the country, thinking, planning and taking stock:

I see that although I never shirked, I have accomplished but very little, because of my Russian laziness. I have no particular faith in my talent, but I do not mistrust it. I will and shall work to the full measure of my strength: but I am still trying to discover a line of work in which I can be really useful. (Letter to Balakirev.)

This confession reveals a Mussorgsky very different from the one of whom, two years earlier, Balakirev had written to a friend: 'Mussorgsky looks well and cheerful. He has composed an *Allegro* and thinks he has done a good deal for art generally and for Russian art in particular.'

13

CHAPTER II

DEVELOPMENT (1863–6)

THE music Mussorgsky composed up to 1863 shows no sign of personality: none of the characteristics of his mature style is to be found in it, nor does it reveal any inclination towards the realism that was to be one of the most distinctive features of his later works. Neither does it appear that any particular kind of music, or the music of any one composer, stirred his imagination and ambitions more than any other. Of this he was fully aware: 'I am still seeking a province in which I can do useful work,' he wrote to Stassov. The notion of writing dramatic music appealed to him. But although, when visiting Moscow, he had felt reborn a true Russian and been fascinated by both the relics of the past and the beggars and rogues he saw in the streets, his experiences there did not suggest any music to him, or even plans for compositions.

What is it then that led to his finding himself? The beginning of the change is to be traced back to the year 1863, when having, as he says in another document, 'set his brains in order,' he started life as one of a small community of young men, all of them intent upon new ideas and especially new ideals. The names of the other members of this community do not matter, because none of them ever achieved anything in life, and we have no means of ascertaining exactly what kind of people they were. But what is of interest is the clue Mussorgsky gives us in his autobiography when he speaks of the writers and scientists who contributed to the maturing of his mind. Those writers and thinkers, as well as others whom he mentions in his letters, must have had a far more direct influence upon his progress than any composer could have had. Later, in a letter to Stassov, Mussorgsky complained that whereas he often heard painters or writers express live ideas, musicians, to his knowledge, never did anything of the kind. This, I think, is another important clue.

Let us try to think what kind of live ideas may have come to Mussorgsky from his contact with his writer friends. The history of

Russian thought and literature at the period is that of the steady growth of a keen interest in the people and their life and fate, and also in true-to-life or realistic methods in art. All the men whom Mussorgsky mentioned had something to do with that [type of] art. Grigorovich, Turgenev, Pisemsky, were among the first Russians to introduce simple people, serfs, in fiction, describing them with warm sympathy and understanding. Lamansky was a lecturer on the history of Russia, a keen believer in nationalism and a student of folk-lore. Kostomarov, the historian, strove, to quote from his own autobiography, above all things 'to give the first place in history to the life of the people in all its typical aspects.' Kavelin, who worked hard for the freedom of the serfs, published a long essay on Troitsky's book on German psychology. In that essay he endorsed Troitsky's view that 'the duty of psychology is the empirical study of psychological and physiological facts jointly,' in accordance with the methods of the English, not the German, psychologists. Mussorgsky was very fond of quoting Troitsky, in whose book we find expressed all the principles which Mussorgsky was to apply, very often in the same terms which he used in his letters to his friends.

Chernïshevsky, too, [was preaching against conventional definitions of beauty, against art for art's sake, and teaching that life was more important than art, the true function of which was to explain life and comment on it. 'That object is beautiful which speaks to us of life,' he wrote in his *Aesthetic Relationship of Art to Reality*.]

The germ of the idea of realism may have come to Mussorgsky from his early contacts with Dargomïzhsky. But he and the other members of the group, after having been fascinated awhile by Dargomïzhsky's *Rusalka* and his ideas of truth in art, ceased to find the atmosphere of his circle stimulating, dropped out of it and did not resume their relations with him until he had begun work on his last opera, *The Stone Guest,* by which time Mussorgsky's ideas and style had progressed considerably. The truth is that in those days he must have felt singularly isolated; from the moment when he set his heart upon his 'true to life' ideal, he could not find much to help him in the music of another composer, because the processes he would have required were not in existence. What he set out to do was entirely unprecedented. He had a great sensitiveness to intonations, to inflections, to colour and to the properties of chords and rhythms and a hundred other indefinable factors. The Russian critic Glebov has remarked that, had he been born fifty years later, the resources he required would have been available for him; but as things were, he had to make his own bricks as he went along, expending much energy in the process, proceeding empirically, and naturally falling, now and then, far short of perfection. The wonder is that he should have achieved so much and given us so much that was not only of seminal, but of lasting artistic value.

This his friends could not realize. They were interested in him, but had no faith in him. Even Vladimir Stassov was not at first the trusted friend and adviser he was later to become. In his biography he said: 'I first met Mussorgsky in 1857, and we forthwith became great friends.' This is not the whole truth. He may have liked Mussorgsky from the first (and as a matter of fact could not help it, for most people found him very likable), but he had no high opinion of him. In 1863 he wrote to Balakirev: 'I have no use for Mussorgsky. His views may tally with mine, but I have never heard him express an intelligent idea. All in him is flabby and dull. He is, it seems to me, a thorough idiot.' To which Balakirev replied: 'Yes, Mussorgsky is little short of an idiot.' Only in the late sixties did Stassov's views change. Balakirev's never changed, but he was a good friend to Mussorgsky for many years, and in time things adjusted themselves. Mussorgsky became a great admirer of *The Stone Guest,* and remained very grateful to Balakirev for his tuition. But, as a composer, he developed unaided and owes surprisingly little to the influence of his brother musicians.

Very rightly he stressed, in the last paragraph of his autobiography, the fact that neither by the character of his compositions nor by his ideas of music did he belong to any of the existing musical circles. All the evidence we have, internal or circumstantial, confirms the notion that it was under the influence of the writers mentioned above that he formed his conception of musical realism and his own solution of the problems it set. Naturally there can be no question of alleging that that influence helped him to evolve his musical style; but it goaded him into inquiring more and more searchingly into the properties of all the elements he used, whether rhythms, patterns or harmonies, and made him realize that nothing but going straight for the means of expression he wanted, however unusual they happened to be, would do.

According to the *Encyclopaedia Britannica* realism, in art, is opposed to idealism in various senses. The realistic artist is either (1) he who prefers to describe ugly things and bring out unpleasant details; or (2) he who deals with individuals, not types; or (3) he who goes in for matter-of-fact, everyday subjects instead of more stimulating and poetic ones; or (4) he who tries to show facts and express feelings exactly as they are, without adornment, romantic distortions, exaggeration or over-emphasis. Of these four definitions, the last is the only reasonable and useful one. The first is the most absurd. If realism consists in keeping as close as possible to reality, it will not lay more stress on the unpleasant, ugly details than on any others. It will handle them all on the same plane, selecting those that are significant regardless of pleasantness or unpleasantness. It will exaggerate neither the beautiful nor the ugly. It consists in a maximum of veracity and specificness in suggestion and expression, together with a minimum of stylization. It is entirely a matter of outlook and processes: not of choice of subjects, or vision, but of treatment: not of impressions conveyed, but of methods of conveying them. In that sense the notion of realism in music is as old as opera, and even older. Long before opera came into being composers had begun to experiment in that direction, trying to capture characteristic attitudes, gestures and intonations, and to find close musical equivalents for them. This ambition had governed the experiments of the Florentine artists who, in the early seventeenth century, had created the *stilo recitativo*. And there are in Galilei's *Dialogues on Music Ancient and Modern* (1581), Caccini's *Nuove musiche* (1601), Monteverdi's letters and prefaces and the writings of Lully, Rameau and Gluck passages that express ideas similar to Dargomïzhsky's and Mussorgsky's—often in the selfsame words. Mussorgsky is unlikely to have known of Galilei, Caccini and Monteverdi; but as early as 1858 he was studying several of Gluck's operas including *Alceste,* [*Iphigénie en Aulide* and *Armide*]. The practical effects of the realistic principle on his style and methods will be considered in Chapter VI. Meanwhile, let it be noticed that the principle in itself may lead anywhere; it leads nowhere in particular. At best it prescribes the avoidance of artifices that make for formalization of all that it is neutral and conventional, of mechanical procedure, and so on. One might say that it is positive in what it prohibits rather than in what it prescribes. So it makes for discipline but not for narrow, ness. It is neither fertile nor sterile. It is worth exactly what the artist's practice is worth, neither more nor less. There is a world of difference between negative realism, which consists in avoiding all that would be non-realistic, and positive realism, which consists in discovering striking processes of evocation and expression—entirely a matter of creative imagination.

Mussorgsky spent the greater part of the spring and summer of 1863 at Toropets and Volok, trying hard, but with little success, to solve the problem of the family estate. During his stay in the country he composed three songs, two of them, *We parted* and *The Harper's Song*, lyrical and the third, *King Saul*, of which two very dissimilar versions exist, dramatic. *But if I could meet thee again* is rather tame; so is one of the two versions of *King Saul* (see Chapter VI), but the other version and *The Harper's Song* (from Goethe's *Wilhelm Meister*) belong to the best of Mussorgsky's early output. These three songs constitute the whole of his output for that year. On his return to town he joined a 'commune' of young men; and owing to his straitened circumstances he entered government service, becoming a clerk in the Ministry of Communications. Yet at that very time he began to plan an opera *Salammbô*, based on Flaubert's famous novel [which had been published in France only the year before and appeared serially in the Petersburg *Otechestvennïe Zapiski* in 1863. *Salammbô* was one of the books read by the 'commune'—probably in translation.]

The year 1864 was not more productive. Again, as it happens, Mussorgsky turned out three songs and nothing else, apart from the not inconsiderable amount of work he did on *Salammbô*; but all three are of importance and deserve to be regarded as the first proofs he gave of having reached artistic maturity. *Night* is a beautiful example of his lyrical vein at its best. *Kalistratushka* (which bears the sub-title 'a study in the comic') is the first in date of his peasant character, sketches—a thoroughly characteristic one showing full command of the vernacular style, which Mussorgsky had exploited but little since the day when he composed *Where art thou, little star? The wild winds blow* is an impressive romantic tone-picture of a kind seldom to be found in his output. In tone it recalls *On the Dnieper*. Many features of his mature style are noticeable in it.

During 1865 he continued working on *Salammbô* and composed four unimportant piano pieces and two songs: one, *The Outcast*, pompous and feeble; the other, *The Peasant Lullaby*, one of his very finest.

The death, that spring, of his mother, whom he dearly loved, was a terrible blow to him. His grief led to an outburst of the dipsomania he had successfully resisted so far, a crisis of delirium tremens following. He was taken to his brother's home, made a good recovery and was able to resume work in January 1866.

During the first half of the year he did some more work on *Salammbô*, [the scene of the priestesses dressing Salammbô in wedding garments and the war song of the Libyans], but he soon lost interest in it and gave it up for good. Karatïgin suggests that it was because he realized its many shortcomings, its lack of unity of style, the conventional and neutral character of its musical exoticism, and soon Findeisen [writing in the *Year-book of the Imperial Theatres*] expresses a similar opinion:

He must have felt the inadequacy of his technique, which landed him into difficulties from which he could not extricate himself. Much of the music was of a conventional operatic kind, and Russian rather than Eastern in colour, suggestive of Moscow rather than of Carthage. So that later, when he decided to use portions of it in *Boris Godunov*, these fell into place quite naturally.

Kompaneisky's recollections provide further confirmation:

Once I asked him why he had given up *Salammbô*. He gazed at me intently, then, with a grin, and a wave of the hand, retorted: 'It would have been no use: Carthage would have fallen to the foe.' After a pause, he added in an earnest tone: 'We've had enough of the East with *Judith*.[1] Art is no game, and time is valuable!'

He had already proclaimed, more than once, his unwillingness to

---

[1] Serov's opera of that name.

write eastern music. In later years, when he used eastern elements, it was either in purely lyrical music (*Hebrew Song*) or dance-music (the Persian dances in *Khovanshchina*).

A scheme which seems for years to have been lurking in the background of his mind may have contributed to divert his thoughts from *Salammbô*. On Christmas Day 1858 he and his brother, with a few friends including Balakirev, had outlined a plan for a three-act opera, *St. John's Eve*, after Gogol—probably by way of a joke, because the scheme was never mentioned again. But in September 1860 Mussorgsky gleefully informed Balakirev that he had been commissioned 'to set to music a whole act of Mengden's drama *The Witch*,' depicting a witches' sabbath on St. John's Night—again a perplexing piece of news, because there is no further evidence of the commissioning, nor can any trace be found of a tragedy by Mengden entitled *The Witch*. But suddenly, in 1866, mention of 'witches' in another form—that of a tone-poem—occurs in two of the three letters he wrote to Balakirev: 'I have started outlining the witches.[1] Got into trouble. Satan's journey does not please me yet' (20th April). 'I am longing to discuss the witches with you' (14th August). One cannot help wondering why this subject, so different from those which he tackled earlier and after, fascinated him so strongly. Possibly the reason is to be found in the letter he wrote to friends after having finished his score, and especially one to Rimsky-Korsakov of 5th July 1867:

All your favourite bits came off splendidly in the scoring. In the Black Mass there is a bit in B minor (the witches glorifying Satan), thoroughly foul and barbarous. In the sabbath matter original calls are heard over trills in the strings and piccolo on B♭, and there is a harmonic tug-of-war: G minor leading to B flat major alternates with G flat major leading to B flat minor with loud F sharp minor chords continuously interrupting. The form is rather original. . . . The effect of outbursts of obscene music in the key of E flat minor is very funny. The whole thing is fiery, brisk, close-knit without German transitions. [In my opinion *St. John's Night* is something new, and ought to produce a satisfactory impression on any thinking musician.]

[1 From its position in the letter it is impossible to say whether Mussorgsky means 'the witches' quite simply or *The Witches* capitalized as a title; in the next letter 'the witches' are definitely not capitalized.]

The same delight is expressed in the less technical description he gave to his friend Professor Nikolsky:

> My *St. John's Night on the Bare Mountain* (a far better title than *The Witches*) is, in form and character, Russian and original; and I want to feel sure that it is thoroughly in keeping with historic truth and Russian folk tradition—otherwise it would not be good enough. I wrote it quickly, straight away in full score without preliminary rough drafts, in twelve days. It seethed within me, and I worked day and night, hardly knowing what was happening within me. And now I see in my sinful prank an independent Russian product, free from German profundity and routine, and, like my *Savishna*,[1] grown on our country's soil and nurtured on Russian bread.

Nowhere else in Mussorgsky's writings do we see him exulting, as he does here, over the purely musical aspects of a work of his. All this might have been written by a determined partisan of art for art's sake, by a composer concerned exclusively with music as an end in itself, and not as a means. So it should be obvious that the attraction lay, for him, in the opportunity it gave him for music-making—and we may say, despite the detailed programme he had devised and the stress he had laid on historical accuracy and keeping close to national tradition, music-making without ulterior purpose. No less obviously, he no longer felt cramped (as, rightly or wrongly, Findeisen supposes he did while at work on *Salammbô*) by any inadequacy in his technical equipment.

That same summer he planned another tone-poem, *King Podébrad of Bohemia*. In a letter to Rimsky-Korsakov he gave a fairly circumstantial outline of his plan, with a few musical examples,[2] but he soon gave up the idea, and never again did he plan an instrumental composition of any importance except, in 1874 for a special reason, the *Pictures from an Exhibition*.

The story of the fate of *St. John's Night on the Bare Mountain* will be told in due course. It was never performed during Mussorgsky's lifetime; so he never heard the original and telling harmonic effects he had imagined and set down with such gusto, but which greatly shocked Balakirev and Rimsky-Korsakov. The disappointment

---

[1] For *Savishna* see next chapter.   [2] See pages 178-9.

must have been bitter, but, again, his new works and new plans must have helped him to forget about it. By 1867 he had reached full maturity; and it is chiefly upon the music composed during the next few years that his fame rests. The neglected *Night on the Bare Mountain* at least served the purpose of helping him to test the ground under his feet: it played its part in the pattern of his musical career.

CHAPTER III

MATURITY (1866–8)

LET us now hark back to 1866, an important year in more ways than one. Especially important were the new friendships Mussorgsky made. So far all the letters of his that are extant were to Balakirev, except for a solitary one of 1863 to Cui; and there is no reason to suppose that he had other correspondents outside his family.[1] But from 1867 onwards, while his letters to Balakirev grew fewer, he kept up a fairly regular correspondence with two friends he had made in 1866: Lyudmila Shestakova (Glinka's sister) and Vladimir Nikolsky. Lyudmila Shestakova (1816–1906) [had got to know Balakirev through her brother and the Stassovs, and at one time he had given piano lessons to her daughter. When this daughter died in 1863 Mme Shestakova isolated herself from the musical world for nearly three years, but] in the late sixties and after, her house was a favourite meeting‑place of musicians and music‑lovers interested in the new Russian music. 'Her sincere admiration for Mussorgsky's talent meant much to him, and he repaid her with deep affection and rever‑ ence,' [wrote Andrey Rimsky‑Korsakov in the notes to his great edition of Mussorgsky's letters, continuing thus:]

His worship of Glinka's music, and their common admiration for the great singer Petrov and his gifted wife (also a singer) were further bonds between them. Later, with the breaking up of Balakirev's circle, the gradual inroads of alcoholism which estranged from him even his closest friends and the financial difficulties which were ever besetting him, Mus‑ sorgsky stood more than ever in need of gentle genuine kindness and maternal solicitude. All this he found in her.

The friendship with Nikolsky (1836–83) was to prove fruitful in many ways. Nikolsky was a professor of literature at the Petersburg University and a Pushkin expert. So they had many interests in

[1] Except possibly Nadezhda Opochinina; there is, however, no evidence [that they corresponded].

common. By nature they were well fitted to enjoy each other's company both in work and in play. They also indulged in the same forms of humour: Nikolsky's jocular mannerisms of style and diction found a ready echo in Mussorgsky's letters to him and to others. [One of Mussorgsky's musical jokes played on him will be described in Chapter VI.] It was he who gave Mussorgsky the idea of deriving an opera libretto from Pushkin's play *Boris Godunov,* and no doubt he helped a good deal [in working out the scenarios of both versions. We know, for instance, that he suggested the ending of the second version with the so-called revolution scene near Kromy, instead of with the death of Boris.]

Of the songs Mussorgsky composed in 1866 some are insignificant; but *Hopak, Darling Savishna, The Seminarist* and a first version of *On the Dnieper* (entitled *Yarema's Song*; the version that has reached us was composed in 1879) are of high value. But, as already mentioned, he had given evidence of maturity as a song composer in the foregoing years. The series of the character songs which are his most original contribution to the song repertory begins in 1864 with *Kalistratushka,* a thoroughly representative example, although one in which the significance of the portrayal is the result of an apt choice of melodic patterns—real song patterns, as distinct from the realistic intonation and delivery of *Savishna* or *The Seminarist*. *Night* (1864) was the first of his great purely lyrical songs, culminating in the set *Sunless*; the *Peasant Lullaby* the first of those tragic peasant songs of his that to this day remain unique of their kind; and *King Saul* (1863) in its first version, although not a masterpiece, is a good example of his dramatic vein.

In December Mussorgsky was promoted to the rank of assistant head clerk. The practical advantage to him was not great, for government clerks' salaries were meagre. Still, the step augured well; and his dismissal from the service in April 1867, owing to a reduction in the staff of his department, must have come as a great shock to him. He consoled himself with the thought that he would have more time for composition. His musical imagination was continuously gathering speed. His orchestral works for the year have already been mentioned. At the end of 1866 or the beginning of 1867 he set for chorus and orchestra a translation of Byron's *The*

Destruction of Sennacherib, which was performed on 6th March at one of Balakirev's Free School of Music concerts.

Shortly after his dismissal Mussorgsky went to Minkino, his brother's country house, where he stayed until November, hard at work most of the time. In August he paid a visit to Petersburg and probably had [arguments] with Balakirev on the subject of *St. John's Night on the Bare Mountain,* which Balakirev flatly refused to consider for performance. On the other hand, made aware, for the first time it would seem, of the precarious state of Mussorgsky's finances, Balakirev must have shown his concern and offered help with a warmth that went far towards soothing Mussorgsky's indignation, as is shown by the letter he wrote from Minkino on 24th September: [1]

Your friendly injunction is so strongly put that to ignore it would be to transgress against my kindest friends. . . . Your message is so warm, so sincere, that I must show my gratitude by deeds, not by mere words. Were I without food or hope, my reply would be such as could be expected from a human being at bay. But, as things are, I have no right to frighten my friends and to mislead them. Their concern is most precious to me. My means have shrunk, it is true, but not to such an extent as to prevent me from supporting myself. Please set your mind at rest and reassure all my kind friends. The change in my circumstances, really, has affected me but slightly, and for a short time. I can adjust matters by staying in the country a month longer; and I intend to apply for a new appointment after the new year, when staff [changes] take place [in all the ministries].

My spleen was not the outcome of the autumn in the country or of my financial situation: it was an author's spleen. I'm ashamed to have to confess it, but it is the truth. I was embittered by your attitude in the matter of my witches. I considered, consider and shall continue to consider my work satisfactory. Coming after various minor independent compositions, it is the first big independent thing I have to show. The spleen has passed now, as most things have a way of doing. I realized it was the kind of thing authors have to put up with; and now I have another work in hand. The pine-laden breeze stimulates me wonderfully. But, dear friend, whether you agree to perform my witches or not, whether I hear

---

[1] When first published (in *M. P. Mussorgsky, Letters to M. A. Balakirev* (*1857–72*), Petrograd, 1915) this letter was said to have been written in 1862 —whence a number of problems and misinterpretations. Andrey Rimsky-Korsakov was the first to rectify the error, in his edition of the letters (1932).

them or not, I shall alter neither the general plan nor the treatment, which are thoroughly in keeping with the content [i.e. the subject] of the work, and honestly carried out, without sham or plagiarism. Every author remembers the mood in which he worked; and that feeling, or memory, helps him to abide by his own standards. I accomplished my task to the best of my ability. But I shall considerably alter the percussion, which I have misused. Write to me as often as you have the leisure to do so, express your positive opinions, and then we can discuss them. I embrace you warmly and offer you my heartfelt thanks for your sincere message, which has greatly cheered me and invigorated me. My greetings to all those who love me.

All the songs he composed that year, except the soul-stirring, wistful *Hebrew Song,* which is a setting of a few lines from the *Song of Songs,* and *Gathering Mushrooms,* one of his most impressive and mordant character songs, laden with hatred and passion, are in a cheerful, light-hearted vein. Two are sheer comedy: *The Ragamuffin,* a lively evocation of a young rascal gleefully baiting an old woman, and *The He-Goat,* telling the tale of a girl who fled in terror from an ugly, bearded goat, but was delighted when an ugly, bearded old man wooed her. (This must have given Ravel the idea of his partsong *Nicolette,* the subject of which is the same.) *The Classicist* (a musical pamphlet) is a capital lampoon on the reactionary critic Famintsïn. *The Magpie* is fantasy pure and simple, a delightful bit of scintillating humour; *The Garden by the Don* a charmingly poetic little idyll; and *The Feast* describes a peasant festival. Mussorgsky also devoted a good deal of time to the preparing of piano transcriptions of Beethoven quartets for performance at the Saturday meetings of his friends the Opochinins. So he really was quite buoyant. He had another satisfaction: in the course of the year, although still smarting under his twofold disappointment, the publisher Johansen brought out three of his songs, *Savishna, Hopak* and the less interesting *Tell me why* of 1858. [These were] the first of his compositions, except the *Polka* of 1852, to appear in print.

It is not clear whether Balakirev displayed any further interest in *St. John's Night on the Bare Mountain.* The only indication to that effect occurs in a short note from Mussorgsky (1867—exact date uncertain) telling him that the score of the work was, at the time, in

Rimsky-Korsakov's hands. And there is nothing to show that Rimsky-Korsakov thought well of it. A sentence in a letter of his of 6th October, 'I thank you for having ceased to chafe, dear friend, it is far better thus,' may refer either to Mussorgsky's annoyance with Balakirev or to a fresh outburst of author's spleen, provoked by some utterance of Rimsky-Korsakov's. There is no telling which.

During the first months of 1868 Mussorgsky composed *The Orphan* and *Eremushka's Lullaby*, which belong, like the songs of 1867, to the best of his song output; also a slight but charming *Child's Song*. He orchestrated the accompaniments of *Hopak* and *Night*. In February *Hopak* and *The He-Goat* were sung for the first time in public. In the course of the year Johansen published *The Feast, Gathering Mush-rooms*, the *Hebrew Song* and *The He-Goat*. In December Mussorgsky was appointed assistant head clerk in the Forestry department in the Ministry of Imperial Domains. By that time two capital events had taken place: in June he had set to music the first act of Gogol's comedy *The Marriage*, and a few months later he had started work on the opera *Boris Godunov*. The news of the latter undertaking aroused sufficient interest for the Russian Music Society to announce, in the prospectus of its forthcoming season, the performance of 'excerpts from Mr. Mussorgsky's opera *Boris Godunov*.'

As already mentioned, the Balakirev group had long ceased frequenting Dargomïzhsky's house. But they mustered round him again when it became known that he was setting Pushkin's play *The Stone Guest* as it stood without altering a single word, [converting it into an opera] which was to conform to his ideal, often proclaimed, of music that would express exactly what the words expressed—plain truths without the slightest concession to operatic usage or reigning fashions. The Balakirev group eagerly followed the progress of the work and were deeply impressed by it. At the readings that took place Mussorgsky used to sing the parts of Leporello and Don Carlos, and whereas he had [previously] never missed an opportunity to deride Dargomïzhsky in his letters to his friends, he [now] became one of his enthusiastic admirers. He inscribed to him his *Eremushka's Lullaby* and also *With Nurse*, a particularly fine application of his own realistic methods at their subtlest and most expressive (possibly com-posed under the influence of Dargomïzhsky's new venture), the dedication reading: 'To the great teacher of musical truth, A. S. Dargomïzhsky.'

At those meetings Mussorgsky made two new friends, the sisters Purgold, both of them excellent musicians: Alexandra, a singer (she married, in 1872, Nikolay Molas), and Nadezhda, a pianist and composer (she married, in 1872, Rimsky-Korsakov, and soon afterwards gave up composition). They were the life and soul of the readings, the one taking charge of all manner of female parts and the other doing so well at the piano that Mussorgsky used to call her 'Our excellent orchestra.' Nadezhda, in later years, gave the following description of Mussorgsky in 1868:

His personality was so exceptional that after having seen him even once it was impossible to forget him. He was of medium height, well built, had beautiful hands, a fine head of wavy hair and rather big, slightly bulging, light grey eyes. His features were ugly, especially the nose which was red (owing, he used to explain, to having been frostbitten once on parade); eyes expressionless and lack-lustre.[1] His face was neither mobile nor expressive. It gave the impression that he concealed a mystery within himself. His manners were exquisite, aristocratic; one felt he was a cultured man of the world. He made an impression on us both, and his singing delighted us. He had a not big, but pleasant baritone and a subtle sense of all shades of feeling and expression. His interpretations were simple, sincere, free from exaggeration and affectation. He excelled in both lyrical and dramatic parts and in comedy and humour. He also was a splendid pianist. He hated routine, not only in music, but in all things. He avoided plain commonplace words. The style of his letters was peculiar, piquant and witty. Later it became—especially in his letters to V. V. Stassov—laboured and unnatural.

Opinions of the quality of his voice vary, but all agree on the excellence of his interpretation and also of his piano-playing. Had he cared to take the trouble, Cui said, he could have equalled Anton Rubinstein. Kompaneisky expresses the same opinion and also mentions his wonderful musical memory (which enabled him to play long stretches of music heard or read but once) and his gift of improvisation, which others too have praised: Lapshin [was told by an eye-witness] of his improvising, at a meeting held on 4th February

---

[1] Alexandra, on the contrary, says 'his eyes were wonderful.'

28

1881, in commemoration of Dostoevsky (who had died a week before), a dirge 'conceived in the same spirit as that in [the death scene of] *Boris Godunov.*'

As regards the style of his letters, Nadezhda's son, Andrey Rimsky-Korsakov, in his edition of Mussorgsky's letters, has pointed out that it reflects a jocular practice more or less common to several members of the group, notably Nikolsky, who was fond of indulging in elaborate, stilted archaisms, and a certain Nikolay Borozdin, the chartered jester of the group, whose quips in later days were often ascribed to Balakirev and others with a view to discrediting them: so that to regard it as illustrating a significant twist in his mental make-up (as Lapshin did and others after him) is hardly justifiable. [But however uncertain the light thrown on the constitution of Mussorgsky's mind by the literary style of his letters, their value to the student of his aesthetic views is incontestable.]

A letter of 15th August 1869 to Rimsky-Korsakov, from which a passage referring to *The Marriage* will be quoted farther on, is of capital importance. Rimsky-Korsakov, engaged in composing his programme-suite *Antar*, had written to him:

The third movement, *Power*, ends with the main theme and the Antar theme in D major, a brief coda following. I shall start the fourth, *Love*, with a few introductory bars based on

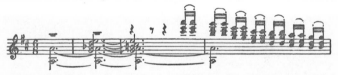

which will call to mind the Ruins and the Kingdom of the Peri in the first movement, and make a pleasing and effective link between the D major end of the third and the D flat major of the fourth. Balakirev will dislike *Power* because it is not a long *allegro* with plenty of symphonic working-out. But, after all, working out is not always desirable and suitable.

The reply was:

I object to your introductory bars to *Love*; in my opinion, to start outright, without preamble of any kind—as you had done before—is more artistic, simpler, more genuine. Is it true indeed that aesthetic taste, after the pompous key of D major has been asserted, calls for the A given by the French horns in order to introduce the melancholy, pathetic D flat major? It is you who say such things, you, the Glinka of aesthetics (do not blush)! Now what could be more poetical, after the *forte* in D major, *pomposo*, with which your *Power* ends, than the wistful D flat major, straightway, without any preparation?

If you feel you like the allusion to the Ruins and the Peri, why not go the whole hog and preface each section with an introduction built upon the motive of the Ruins and that of the Peri? Think how absurd *that* would be. I think that the simpler and more straightforward things are, the better. *Revenge,* without preparation; *Power* likewise: but for *Love,* you wish to borrow from the Germans! I disagree, and I think I am justified. Remember the ending of your *Sadko;* and learn that after the C sharp minor and D major in *Antar,* the key of D flat major carries your hero straight into the clouds, into the world of Houris and Peris where his mind is cleansed and appeased and elevated. O preparations, how much that was good has been ruined by you!

As regards symphonic working-out, let me tell you this: you seem to be appalled because you wrote *à la* Korsakov and not *à la* Schumann. But pray consider that a Russian mess of minced meat and herbs is as execrable to a German as his favourite *Milch-Suppe* or *Kirschen-Suppe* is to us (yes, I know, comparison is no argument!). In short, symphonic working-out, considered from the point of view of technique, is a German product. . . . The German, when thinking, starts by analysing, and then proceeds to demonstrate. Our Russian brother demonstrates forthwith, and subsequently may amuse himself with analysing. When at Borodin's home you showed me *Love,* you had indulged in no preparations, and now you begin to do so.

But enough on that point. Let me, dear Korsinka, tell you that the act of creating carries in itself the laws of beauty, whose tale is told by inner criticism, not outer; and whose consequences are determined by the artist's instinct. Where either of those two elements is lacking, there can be no artistic creation. For artistic creation implies both, and the artist is a law unto himself.

Such was the stage Mussorgsky's evolution had reached at the time, when, one fine day, Dargomïzhsky jocularly suggested that he should try his hand at setting, on the same lines [as *The Stone Guest*], Gogol's comedy *The Marriage,* and Cui seconded the suggestion in all earnestness. It appealed strongly to Mussorgsky, who set to work at once. From Shilovo, where he spent the summer months [of 1868], he wrote to Cui:

Guided by your remarks and Dargomïzhsky's, I have succeeded in considerably simplifying what I had shown you. I have devised for Podkolessin a jolly good orchestral phrase, which will prove most useful in the proposal scene. It crops up for the first time in his talk with Stepan, thus:

A mere fragment of a theme, you see. The whole theme will appear in the third act only when Podkolessin has decided to get married. It lends itself splendidly to evoking his stupid perplexity. I have found an amusing exit for Stepan. I am working on the second scene. I feel it is good and interesting. Podkolessin's bearish antics at the end of the scene are curiously dealt with. On the whole, this first act [might serve as an essay] in *opéra dialogué*. I should like to finish it quickly and then we can sit in judgment.

Tell your dear wife that the scene with the marriage-broker came off well. She will be glad. I appreciate her interest in my rash undertaking. Throughout I try as hard as I can to note down clearly those changes in intonation which crop up in human conversation for the most futile causes, on the most insignificant words, changes in which lies the secret of Gogol's humour.

The whole act, in vocal-score form, was finished within twenty-seven days from the start. Upon its completion he wrote to Rimsky-Korsakov, on 30th July:

I have been surveying my first act. It is, I feel, carried out interestingly enough; but who can tell? I've done my best, and you will judge. If you forget all operatic traditions and admit the principle of musical discourse carried out in all simplicity, *The Marriage* is an opera. If I have managed to render the straightforward expression of thoughts and feelings as it occurs in ordinary speech, and my rendering is musicianly and artistic, then the deed is done.

It will be for you to judge. I've done my best, and I willingly deliver myself into my tormentor's hands.

And to Lyudmila Shestakova, the same day:

I am thinking of the second act . . . and also observing the peasants around me. This may come in useful later. How many fresh, racy aspects, hitherto overlooked by art, in the Russian people! A few scraps of what life brought to me I have turned into musical imagery for the benefit of those whom I love and who love me [viz., in the songs]. If God grants me health and strength, I shall have a lot to say—but after *The Marriage* is finished. I have now crossed the Rubicon. *The Marriage* is a cage in which I have to remain imprisoned until I have learnt my lesson. . . . What I should like to do is to make my characters speak on the stage exactly as people speak in everyday life, without exaggeration or distortion, and yet write music which will be thoroughly artistic.

A fortnight later he made further significant references to *The Marriage* in letters to his friends. To Nikolsky:

I have composed a whole act of musical prose and limned four characters. I think this act is good; but what about the other three? I know they will have to be good, but not whether they can be. Anyhow, I must finish the job, and then judge.

To Cui:

I am thinking things out for the second act, but have not yet started the writing. I feel that I must wait until the tradespeople-like character of this act, and that of the new people who appear in it, come out in colours as adequate as those I succeeded in finding for Kochkarev and Fekla. A good many of my ideas are taking shape.

To Rimsky-Korsakov:

The second act is shaping, but I am not actually composing the music. The time has not yet come for that. Patience! Otherwise I might lapse into uniformity of inflection—the worst of sins under the circumstances.

A private performance of the act at Cui's house, with Mussorgsky as Podkolessin, Dargomïzhsky as Kochkarev, Alexandra Purgold as Fekla and Nadezhda at the piano, left the audience with mixed impressions. According to Rimsky-Korsakov:

Everybody was amazed at Mussorgsky's undertaking, delighted with his skilful characterization and with many features in his recitatives, but baffled by many peculiarities of the harmony. . . . Stassov was in raptures.

Dargomïzhsky said that Mussorgsky had gone rather far. Balakirev and Cui considered the work a mere curiosity, with a few interesting features in the declamation.

According to Nadezhda [Purgold], Dargomïzhsky ['laughed till he cried and was enthusiastic about the wit and expressiveness of this music.']

Borodin, in a letter to his wife, records his impressions thus:

An extraordinarily curious, paradoxical achievement, teeming with novelties and with humorous points; but, as a whole, a failure—impossible in practice.

As may be seen, Mussorgsky was disappointed in his hopes. Not one of his friends, except Stassov and Dargomïzhsky, liked *The Marriage*. For the first time the fact was brought home to him that he could not hope for much comprehension on the part of his brothers-in-arms and advisers. How clearly he must have realized it, and how deeply he must have felt it, is shown by the fact that from that moment on it is almost exclusively in his letters to Stassov or to women friends that confidences as to his plans and sidelights on his work are to be found. It is unlikely, however, that this lack of response had much to do with his decision not to continue *The Marriage*. Various reasons, some of them far-fetched and others illogical, have been adduced to account for this decision. Rimsky-Korsakov, in his preface to the published edition of the first act (1908), says:

Mussorgsky may have recognized this to be an experiment which need not be carried further. I am also convinced that had he reverted to it later, he would have smoothed down many things in the music—which, as it stands, contains much that no *fastidious ear* could accept.

Others also hold that if he did not continue *The Marriage*, it was because he was dissatisfied with it in some way or other. One biographer, Kurt von Wolfurt, thinks that a sentence in a letter of January 1872 from Mussorgsky to Alexandra Purgold provides an explanation. But this view rests upon an unaccountable miscon-struction. Both in the *Russkaya Muzïkalnaya Gazeta,* where the letter first appeared, and in the complete edition of the letters the sentence reads:

I know the Gogol subject [which you suggest] well. I thought of it two years ago, but it is not in keeping with my chosen path—it contains too little of big, simple-hearted Mother Russia.

Wolfurt mistranslates it thus:

A few years ago I worked at Gogol's *Marriage*, but the attempt led to no result on the path struck by me: it contained too little of Mother Russia in her full, primitive grandeur.

It is inadmissible that Mussorgsky, however casual he may have been in matters of dates, should have erred so grossly as to the time when he worked on (and not merely 'thought of') *The Marriage*, and inadmissible that Alexandra Purgold, who had taken part in the performances of the first act, should have suggested the subject to Mussorgsky over three years later.

Karatïgin may be nearer the mark when he writes:

At times this remorseless naturalism is carried so far that it becomes a mere curiosity and burlesque. The suitor, 'who cannot help lying,' is depicted in emphatically 'false' combinations of notes. The composer imitates in sound the felicities of married life described by Kochkarev: the barking of the pet dog, the canary's song, the noisy children, who, Koch-karev says, will be not two or three in number, but six, whereupon the music echoes the forecast with two quavers, a triplet of semiquavers and a sextuplet. However much we admire the extraordinary power of in-vention displayed, and appreciate single points in this highly skilful achieve-ment . . . we are justified in saying that Mussorgsky himself judged his music quickly and rightly. He wrote one act and left it at that. He was most sensitive to inner falsity, which he would discover—even in the province of realism—where most people would never dream of suspecting artifice.

It is unlikely that any one would notice the two-three-six effect unless on the look-out for evidence on which to base special pleading. It does not stand out. It is not sharply differentiated from the context. Nor are the 'barking dog' and 'canary' effects. Even if they all were, it would not matter much. This is comedy, after all. The whole score is there to prove that Mussorgsky did not rely on them, or need them. He used a few but took them in his stride, expecting, quite reasonably, his audiences to do the same, and not to lose their sense of humour and sense of proportion. In 1873 he presented the manuscript of the work to Stassov, whose former contemptuous attitude had turned, from the moment of his first contact with *The Marriage,* into one of enthusiastic admiration and faith. The letter accompanying the gift said:

On the occasion of your birthday, I asked myself how best to please my dear friend. The answer was: by making him a present of my very self. Accept my early work on Gogol's *Marriage.* Examine it, compare it with *Boris Godunov,* and you will see that what I give you is, irrevocably, my own self. I am convinced that to connoisseurs *The Marriage* will reveal much as to my musical audacities. And you know how great a store I set by it.

One can hardly imagine him writing in that strain if he had detected in his music a taint of 'inner falsity.' Yet such is the opinion, too, of Andrey Rimsky-Korsakov, based mainly on the composer's declaration that *The Marriage* was a cage in which he had to stay until he had learnt his lesson. 'But,' Andrey Rimsky-Korsakov continues,

this labour gave a powerful impulse to the working of his mind and sharpened his faculties of observation. The tone of the letters he wrote at that time is manly and high-spirited. One feels that the cage-door may fly open at any moment and the artist step out in full possession of his power, ready to tackle a greater, more momentous task. It is the eve of *Boris Godunov.* The matter may well be left at that: whatever other reasons there may have been for his decision, it is natural that the notion of *Boris* should have driven everything else out of his mind.

CHAPTER IV

WORK ON 'BORIS GODUNOV' (1868–74)

THE period from the autumn of 1868, when Mussorgsky began *Boris Godunov,* to the end of 1869, when he finished it, is in strong contrast with the foregoing. We know very little of it. For the period from August 1868 to May 1870 no single letter of his is extant, except for one note to Balakirev on sundry trifling matters. As Andrey Rimsky-Korsakov pointed out, this may be accidental. On the other hand, there is no evidence that he told any of his friends anything about *Boris* or showed it to any one, except an unpublished [and inaccurate] letter of July 1869 from V. Stassov to his brother Dimitry, which says:

Mussorgsky has now finished *Boris.* Just before the end there is a narrative of Pimen as beautiful as the most beautiful scenes in the first two acts.

He worked continuously at white heat, finishing the vocal score in about eight months: the first three scenes by 4th November, 14th November and 5th December respectively. In the orchestral score three scenes are dated: the second 30th September 1869; the fifth 19th October 1869; the seventh and last 15th December 1869. [In this original form *Boris* consisted only of the scene in the courtyard of the Novodevichy Monastery, the Coronation scene, the scene in Pimen's Cell, the Inn scene, a shortened form of the scene in the Kremlin, a scene before the Cathedral of St. Basil and the death of Boris.]

Mussorgsky had settled comfortably in the home of his friends Nadezhda and Alexander Opochinin, circumstances having compelled his brother Filaret to sell his Petersburg home. Except for the work on *Boris* and the death, on 5th January, of Dargomïzhsky, the year 1869 was uneventful. In 1870 Mussorgsky composed four of the *Nursery* songs and *The Peepshow,* a large-scale lampoon on enemies of the [Balakirev] group: Zaremba and Famintsïn of the Conservatory, the critic F. M. Tolstoy (who used the pen-name 'Rostislav'), Serov, the composer, and the Grand Duchess Helena Pavlovna, patroness of the Russian Music Society. In July Mussorgsky submitted *Boris Godunov* to the committee of the imperial theatres and then began to cast about for another libretto. Stassov gave him a circumstantial plan for one [named *Bobïl* (*The Landless Peasant*)] based on Spielhagen's *Hans und Grete,* which he considered awhile, actually outlining music for an incantation scene in it (he used it later in *Khovanshchina*), and then gave up.

On the 10th February 1871 *Boris* was rejected by the committee, [which consisted of the conductors Nápravnik, Vojáček, Papkov and Betz, the violinists Maurer and Klamrodt and the double-bassist Ferrero]. Obviously the judges, apart from being startled by the unusual character of the music, were put off by the very idea of an opera consisting almost entirely of dialogue and choruses, and lacking all the traditional features of the genre: no parts for a prima donna and first tenor, none of any importance for a female voice at all, no arias or vocal ensembles, no love interest, no dancing—nothing but grimness and gloom except for the one scene of comedy at the Inn. They must have felt, too, that it contained much to which the State censorship would object. [Pushkin's original play had been passed for stage performance only in 1866, more than forty years after it was written, and then only on condition that the Inn scene and one other were not to be represented; and the first performance—or, rather, the performance of sixteen of the twenty-four scenes—had been given, in the Marinsky Theatre, as recently as September 1870.] A few months before, Mussorgsky's own *Seminarist* had been banned by the censor because of its irreverent character; in 1872 Rimsky-Korsakov was to have great difficulties with his opera *The Maid of Pskov* on account of its libretto, [which introduced Ivan the Terrible as a singing character].

Almost immediately after receiving the news [of the rejection] Mussorgsky started remodelling *Boris.* But whereas nobody, except probably Nikolsky, had intervened during the composition of the first version, he showed the second version to his friends as he went along and received from them plenty of advice. His first step was to cut out the portions that were most likely to offend the censor: the end of the first scene, showing the people indifferent to the instructions given by Boris's agents; in the third scene, Pimen's narrative of the murder, by order of Boris, of the heir to the throne; and the whole sixth scene, in which the people are seen on the edge of revolt. He added songs here and there, and especially to Scene iv, which he rewrote practically from end to end. He composed a whole additional act, which showed Dimitry the Pretender in Poland, plotting against Tsar Boris and wooing Princess Marina; and also a magnificent scene showing the people in revolt and the Pretender marching on Moscow, a scene of passing fierceness and vehemence and final desolation, which, at Nikolsky's suggestion, he decided to put at the end of the score, after the scene of Boris's death.

He seems to have been quite happy about it all, writing to Stassov, for instance:

The Jesuit has kept me awake two nights running. That's good! I like it when ideas keep seething thus [18th April]. The guilty Tsar Boris perpetrates an *arioso* of sorts; and according to the musicians' unanimous finding the aforesaid criminal *arioso* is altogether praiseworthy and keeps the ear busy enough; the words of the same were concocted by my own self [10th August]. I have the honour to inform your leniency that we subjected Pimen to curtailment, amended Grishka [that is, composed him afresh], and that the Corsican admiral proclaims that now the scene is momentous, and we hold the trumps. A rogues-and-vagabonds-scene is under consideration: novelty of novelties and all is novelty! Awfully jolly! [11th September].[1]

There can be no doubt, however, that here we have at work, jointly, Mussorgsky the inspired creator and Mussorgsky the amenable, all too prone to follow advice. How far, in each particular instance, the one and how far the other is hard to tell. There are artists (Stravinsky is a case in point, and so was, in a measure, Ravel) who incline, as soon as a piece of work is finished, to lose all interest in it and concentrate exclusively on the work to be done next. There is

---

[1] A mild attempt is made here to convey an impression of Mussorgsky's jocular style, referred to on p. 29. Grishka is the novice Grigory, afterwards Dimitry the Pretender. 'The Corsican admiral' was one of the nicknames bestowed upon Rimsky-Korsakov, who at that time was in the Navy. 'The Jesuit' is Rangoni, a character in the Polish act.

no lack [of evidence] that Mussorgsky too was inclined that way: for instance, his dropping *The Marriage* as soon as he had begun to think of *Boris*, and also his writing to Stassov, on 2nd January 1873, five weeks before the public performance of three scenes from *Boris*:

It is gratifying to think that when we are arraigned for *Boris*, we shall already be looking into the distant musical future, thinking of *Khovanshchina*, living *Khovanshchina*.

So it is no wonder that the second *Boris* should have affected his interest in the first. One easily realizes how thrilled he must have been while composing the Revolution scene. One can accept without too much boggling his excitement over the Jesuit scenes, although those do not rise to a very high level, the episodes and songs added to Scene iv [—the chiming clock, the nurse's song of the gnat, the clapping game and the parrot episode—] and the changes in the character of the essential parts of this scene (the tsar's monologue and his dialogue with Shuisky); but it is more difficult to understand his being so cheerful about cutting out the end of the opening scene and the narrative of the murder, however expedient it may have been to do so in order to placate the censor. Truth to tell, not one of his friends had been quite satisfied with the first version—not even Stassov, who was to write later:

While moved to enthusiasm by the beauties of the work, all his friends (including myself) kept warning him that it was lacking in some essentials; and that however great its beauties, it might appear in certain respects unsatisfactory. But he would not believe us until it had been rejected by the committee—a decision whose ultimate effects were all to the good, since it compelled him to remodel his score.

This second *Boris* started in its public career unostentatiously, but speedily. As early as 5th February 1872 the Coronation scene was given at a Russian Music Society concert, under Nápravnik; and on 3rd April the Polonaise, after a few alterations suggested by Balakirev had been carried out, at a Free School of Music concert, Balakirev conducting. In April the work was submitted to the committee.

At the beginning of 1872 Gedeonov, the director of the imperial theatres, had conceived the curious idea of commissioning a fantastic, highly spectacular opera-ballet of his own devising, *Mlada* [of which the libretto was to be written by I. A. Krïlov, while] the score was entrusted to four composers: the first act to Cui, the second and third (which consisted almost entirely of pageantry and dances) to Mussorgsky and Rimsky-Korsakov jointly, and the fourth to Borodin. Mussorgsky and Rimsky-Korsakov, who since the autumn had been sharing a room, were able to divide the scenes allotted to them as they liked. The former's contributions were a processional march of princes [and priests], a vigorous and lively market scene, and for use in a fantastic scene in the third act a rearrangement, with added choral parts, of *St. John's Night on the Bare Mountain*. For other scenes he also used music from his early *Oedipus*.

Judging by the one letter he wrote to Stassov while engaged on *Mlada*, he did not enjoy his task. He complains of the senseless words, 'probably written at some time or other by somebody or other in a frenzy of delirium tremens,' of Gedeonov's treating the composers 'like so many casual labourers,' and foresees that the undertaking will end in the near future in a moral fiasco for the group. But the scheme collapsed before the end of the spring, and setting aside his *Mlada* music for future use if expedient (both the market scene and—probably with further alterations—the *Bare Mountain* found place in the comic opera *Sorochintsy Fair*), Mussorgsky was free to concentrate upon the notion of *Khovanshchina*, suggested to him by V. V. Stassov.

He may have thought of the subject as early as 1870, when he borrowed from Nikolsky books dealing with the history of the period; but certainly Stassov's intervention was the deciding factor. Many letters testify to his excitement and faith during that preliminary period:

When you come back, dear friend, all materials for our new opera will probably be collected. I have prepared a note-book and inscribed it *Khovanshchina,* a national musical drama.[1] On the first page I wrote a list of sources—nine of them—very nicely. I am swimming in information; my head feels like a boiler with a roaring fire underneath [13th July 1872].

[1] There is no foundation whatsoever for the allegation, in Riesemann's and Wolfurt's biographies, that he had given or even thought of giving the same sub-title to *Boris Godunov*. All manuscripts, including rough drafts of the title-page, have the sub-title 'opera' (see Lamm edition, preface,

To Vladimir Vassilievich Stassov, on dedicating to him *Khovanshchina*:

I don't care, nor is there any reason why I should, that there are no instances of dedicating works as yet non-existent. There is in my heart no fear that would lead me to defer the dedication and look back. I wish to look ahead. There is nothing absurd in my saying: 'I dedicate to you my own self and the whole period of my life during which *Khovanshchina* will be composed.' I vividly remember living *Boris, in Boris*; and in my brain the time I lived in *Boris* has left precious, indestructible landmarks. Now a new work, your work, is seething, and I am beginning to live it. How many invaluable impressions, how many new lands to discover! Wonderful! So, I pray you, accept the essence of my tumultuous self, with the dedication of *Khovanshchina*—a dedication which you begot together with the work itself [15th July].

Art representing beauty only, in the material sense, is crude childishness, art in an infantile stage. The subtlest features of individual masses, the most searching investigation of those little-known regions and their conquest —such is the artist's true mission. 'To new shores!' Fearlessly, through tempest and over shoals and sunken reefs, 'to new shores!' In humanity in the mass, as in individuals, there are always subtle, elusive traits, that none has ever touched. To observe and study these by reading, observing, conjecturing, to probe it all to the core, and with it to feed humanity as with a health-giving food, never tasted before, there is a task for you, there is the joy of joys! In *Khovanshchina* we shall try, shan't we? my beloved prophet! [18th October].

A few days later the news came that *Boris Godunov* had again been rejected. It did not upset him much. According to his autobiography (there is no other information on the event) a reading of the whole *Boris* took place, shortly afterwards, 'before an enormous audience' which included Cui, the famous singer Petrov, [the soprano Julie] Platonova, [F. P.] Komissarzhevsky and Lukashevich, assistant director of the imperial theatres; and it was decided, then and there, to organize a public performance of three scenes (the Inn scene and the two scenes of the Polish act). This performance

p. xiii). This is worth noting, for it testifies to the fact that Mussorgsky regarded *Boris* as a drama of individual psychology; but *Khovanshchina* he wished to be his contribution to the fulfilment of the people's desire to come into being—whence the sub-title, 'a national drama.'

took place at the Marinsky Theatre on 5th/17th February 1873. Petrov sang Varlaam, Komissarzhevsky Dimitry and Platonova Marina. It was part of the programme of the chief stage-manager Kondratiev's benefit night. The press notices [1] all register a triumphant reception. Cui wrote, in the *St. Peterburgskie Vedomosti*: 'The success was enormous and complete; never, within my memory, had such ovations been given to a composer at the Marinsky.' He extolled the Inn scene to the skies. The music, he declared, was in the style of that of *The Stone Guest*, worthy of taking place beside Dargomïzhsky's work. It betokened a perfect understanding of stage requirements, it teemed with original humour, it was inspired and beautiful. He praised the Polish act with qualifications; but his wish to do full justice to it was manifest in every one of his carefully thought-out remarks. The *Peterburgskaya Gazeta* [noted that after the Inn scene the composer had to take six calls and observed that this was all the more remarkable] considering that Dargomïzhsky's *Stone Guest*, Cui's *Ratcliffe*, Serov's *Power of Evil* and Rimsky-Korsakov's *Maid of Pskov* (the first performance of which had taken place on 1st/13th January), although not altogether fiascos when first produced, had been received far from sympathetically. The anonymous writer went on to say that 'the composer had given us Gogol in music'— a curious but not altogether appropriate way of emphasizing the vernacular, racy character of the music, and one which must have pleased Mussorgsky.

Strange to say, the most laudatory article, after Cui's, was that of Laroche, who so far had been, and afterwards continued to be, one of Mussorgsky's most persistent detractors. He wrote (in the *Golos*):

I was astonished at the unexpected beauties of those three scenes. A lack of skill and knowledge is perceptible in them; but the spiritual power that breaks through outweighs the defects (unlike what happens in the composer's songs). The Inn scene and the scene by the fountain [struck me by the brilliant] musical and dramatic talent [manifest in them].

Others were openly hostile; notably Soloviev who, in the *Bir-*

[1] Quoted here from a survey by A. A. Khokhlovkina in the collection of essays on *Boris Godunov* by various authors published by the Russian Academy of Artistic Sciences in 1930.

zheviïe Vedomosti, while recording the enthusiasm of the audience, poured confused, not very relevant strictures on all the music except a few passages that he damned with faint praise. On the whole, Khokhlovkina concludes, the press notices strike a more favourable note than they did after the 1874 production. One of the consequences of the success was that a second performance of the scenes was forthwith arranged, but did not take place owing to Komissarzhevsky's indisposition. Another was that Bessel announced the forthcoming publication of the work and opened a subscription list.

The events of 1873, apart from work on *Khovanshchina,* were many and complex. Mussorgsky's bachelor establishment with Rimsky-Korsakov had ended the year before, on the latter's marriage with Nadezhda Purgold, and in June he formed a friendship with a young relative on his mother's side, Count Arseny Golenishchev-Kutuzov (1848–1913), who had just given up the civil service to devote himself to poetry; they later took furnished rooms together. At the end of June Vladimir Stassov, and also Dimitry Stassov and his family, had left for a journey through western Europe, Vladimir's plans including a visit to Liszt at Weimar. Liszt, to whom a pupil of his, Adelaïde von Schorn, had shown *The Nursery,*[1] had been greatly impressed by it; and the news had reached Mussorgsky through the publisher Bessel. 'Liszt,' Mussorgsky announced to Pauline Stassov, Dimitry's wife, 'is so delighted with my work that he intends to inscribe a little song to me.' And to Vladimir he wrote:

I should never have thought that Liszt, who is usually concerned with colossal subjects, could take my *Nursery* seriously and understand it. The children in it are pure Russian and smell strongly of their native soil. What will he say when he sees the printed score of *Boris*? Russian music is fortunate indeed to have the sympathy of such an ace as he. God grant him life, and perhaps some day I shall go to him—but not without you, dear friend. Just now I am fated to wither and turn sour in Chaldaean wastes, frittering my time away on work that others could do better without my help. It's hard! How many new worlds might be revealed to me in conversations with Liszt! How many unknown corners might come to our joint sight! [23rd July].

---

[1] See note on page 85.

Vladimir [Stassov] tried hard and repeatedly to persuade him to come to Germany forthwith and join in the expedition to Weimar, confuting all his alleged reasons for refusing (special office responsibilities; his chief's illness; work on *Khovanshchina* and other compositions, and so on) and arranging to provide forthwith the required funds. He was deeply concerned with Mussorgsky's condition. Early in June Mussorgsky had confessed to him that he was suffering from attacks of dementia, as had happened some years before, adding that he was drinking but little, although he enjoyed drinking. Disquieting rumours had reached [Stassov] from Russia.

His anxiety was fully justified. On 23rd July a dear friend of Mussorgsky's, Victor Hartmann, a painter and architect, died suddenly in Moscow. Mussorgsky had not known him very long, but the friendship, originating in many traits of nature common to the two, and in their great admiration of each other's talents, had ripened speedily. Mussorgsky's distress, as well as a feeling of increased loneliness during the absence of his closest friends, may have been one cause of his altogether losing hold of himself during that fateful summer [of 1873]. The craving for drink broke out, stronger than ever before. 'Many a time,' the painter Repin, another close friend of the Stassovs' and Mussorgsky's, says in his recollections,[1]

Vladimir Stassov, returning to Petersburg after a journey, had been compelled to rescue his friend from the utmost depths. It is incredible how this well-bred, cultured, witty, polished officer of the Guards, as soon as he was without Stassov, would break down, sell his furniture and clothes and go haunting the lowest taverns; how often Stassov, upon coming home, had to spend long hours hunting for him in one disreputable drinking-den after another! Even from abroad he was continuously bombarding all his close friends with requests for tidings . . . but nobody knew whither Mussorgsky had vanished.

What an effort it was for the unfortunate composer to resist his friend's pressing invitations is shown in his further correspondence:

I have to deny myself my innermost wishes, and the very essence of life, and stick to my scrap-heap. How much the meeting with Liszt would

---

[1] Quoted by Andrey Rimsky-Korsakov in *M. P. Mussorgsky : Letters and Documents.*

have meant! How many beautiful deeds could have been done! You will see Liszt. I was ready to ask you to take a letter from me to him, but even that would be wrong—what could it mean to him? And have I the right to take such a step? Better keep silence, for ever, like a Trappist. I have faith in my star. It seems impossible that I should not, some time or other, see the men of Europe. But if not, well, patience, patience—just as now. Your offer is as great as you yourself are. To go to see Liszt, with you, the money found by you for this special purpose; and it all collapses. No help! . . . Yet, one live, precious impression remains, so alive that I seem to see Liszt before me, to hear his voice, to be engaged in conversation with him; and this is no dream, nor is it hot-headed phrase-mongering! But for you I might never have felt so wrapped in Liszt, never have had this vision of him and observed him so intently. And when you return, do not remind me that I have not seen Liszt. Or rather, remind me again and again: at times good is born of a loathsome feeling and disgust begets salvation [6th July].

A month after writing these lines—an invaluable document which reveals the depths of his over-sensitive, fervid, tormented and yet triumphant soul—he closed the discussion with one sentence in a letter chiefly devoted to particulars of *Khovanshchina*: 'Yes: you are their king. Mussoryanin [a nickname he was fond of using] is a rascal. Why does he say nothing about Liszt? Well, it's IM-POSSIBLE.' He probably felt he was in no condition to risk a visit to Liszt; that even if he succeeded in pulling himself together he would remain at the mercy of a fresh outbreak.[1]

How he succeeded in regaining hold of himself is not known: but he did eventually. And on 21st October the news came that Gedeonov, in spite of the committee's vote, had decided to produce *Boris* without delay. Apparently his decision was due to the joint

[1] It would be futile to wonder what the consequences of a visit to Liszt might have been, had it taken place (as it well might have done) unmarred by any untoward happening. Robert Godet proclaims his conviction that they would have altered the whole course of Mussorgsky's life and the fate of his works. But this writer, of set purpose, minimizes and attempts to disprove (very ineffectually) Mussorgsky's dipsomania, and one feels he would have liked to deny it altogether. From the known facts it would seem that after the 1873 outbreak there could have been no arresting the progress of the evil.

efforts of Platonova and Lukashevich. A long, highly dramatic account given by Platonova years later in a letter to Stassov in which she claimed that she alone had compelled Gedeonov to give *Boris* by threatening not to renew her contract with him unless he did, had been given credence until evidence (first set out in *Mussorgsky : Letters and Documents*) was discovered that her narrative contained, besides a measure of truth, gross exaggerations and mis-statements of facts.

On 20th January 1874 Mussorgsky signed the usual petition to the director, asking him to admit *Boris* to the repertory, on a fee-per-performance basis. Upon acceptance (which was simply the notification of an accomplished fact) the opera was put in the 'first class,' which entitled the composer to a fee of one-tenth of two-thirds of the takings.

Meanwhile, Nápravnik having declared that he was too busy at that time to deal with the first rehearsals, these had been taking place under Mussorgsky. Then Nápravnik—who had already earned a reputation as 'a master of cuts'—decided to cut out the scene in the cell and, in Act II, the episodes of the parrot and the chiming clock, and here and there other bits too. According to Golenishchev-Kutuzov's *Reminiscences of Mussorgsky* the composer whole-heartedly approved, saying 'All that was impossible on the stage. Those friends of mine who blame me for agreeing' (this refers mainly to Stassov) 'don't realize that effectiveness on the stage is the standard by which a composer must go. Meyerbeer would mercilessly cut out whole pages; he knew what he was doing, [and he was right!']

It must not be forgotten that Golenishchev-Kutuzov had an axe to grind. He was a hide-bound conservative, who loathed realism and modern tendencies in art. He could not stand things such as the dialogue of the people in the opening scene of *Boris,* the vernacular songs in Act II, 'the innkeepers and impossible Jesuits, vagabond monks and simpleton,' or among the songs, *Savishna, The Orphan, The Peepshow, The Classicist, The He-Goat* and *The Seminarist*; and he was out to establish that it was Stassov who urged Mussorgsky to follow the wrong path, whereas, left to himself, the composer would have stuck to the right path.

Still, accepting his recollections, written a year after Mussorgsky's death, as accurate, we may safely assume that it was the amenable, docile Mussorgsky speaking, and not the inspired composer of the 'beautiful, all-important Cell scene.'[1] Indeed, the reference to Meyerbeer might well be an echo of words spoken by Nápravnik.

When, in 1876, the Revolution scene was cut out in turn, Goleni-shchev-Kutuzov said that although the scene was superfluous from the dramatic point of view, he for one regretted [its complete omission, as it contained such good music]. Mussorgsky retorted:

I don't! In that scene for the one and only time in my life I calumniated the Russian people: I showed peasants baiting a boyar, their prisoner. That was wrong: Russians may punish, may kill, but they do not mock and taunt their enemies.

This at least sounds spontaneous.

The first performance [of Mussorgsky's masterpiece] took place on 27th January/8th February 1874. The cast was:

BORIS	Melnikov
GRIGORY (the Pretender)	Komissarzhevsky
SHUISKY	P. Vassiliev
PIMEN	V. Vassiliev
VARLAAM	Petrov
MISAIL	Dyuzhikov
MARINA	Platonova
FEODOR	Krutikova
THE HOSTESS	Abarinova
XENIA	Raab
RANGONI	Palechek
THE NURSE	Schröder
SHCHELKALOV	Sobolev

Nápravnik conducted and the settings were designed by Shish-kov and Bokharov, both of whom enjoyed a high reputation. According to reports[2] settings and costumes were of the sumptuous-conventional type, well up to average but no more.

It was a triumphant success. Only the old-school opera-goers,

[1] See footnote on page 42.

[2] Summarized in Appendix II of the volume *Mussorgsky: Articles and Materials*, published under the editorship of Y. Keldïsh and V. Yakovlev. (Moscow, 1932.)]

—the melomaniacs, as they were called—being shocked by the 'absolute lack of music,' did not share in the general enthusiasm. Mussorgsky had to take, it is said, about thirty calls. Only one incident marred [his triumph]: four young women had planned to have a wreath presented to him on the stage. But they did not comply with the regulations stipulating that such tributes should pass through the administrative channel; and the wreath had to be handed to him behind the scene by an assistant. The donors protested in the press, laying the blame on Nápravník. Mussorgsky, greatly upset, and fearing that the fate of *Boris* might be affected, wrote to Nápravník dissociating himself from the affair, and to the editor of the paper in which the protest had appeared, declaring that it was at his own request that the wreath had not been handed to him in public.

The press notices, with one exception, were decidedly unfavourable.[1] In the *Birzhevïe Vedomosti* Soloviev, without any attempt at critical discussion, inveighed mercilessly against the greater part of the opera and damned the remainder with faint praise. The work, he concluded, should have been entitled 'a cacophony in five acts.' Rapoport, in the *Russkaya Mïsl*, said he could not understand the success. *Boris* did not constitute a step forward. Mussorgsky lacked neither originality nor power, but these gifts were stifled by his fondness for resorting to 'impossible means.' The Revolution scene was 'a chaotic and feeble imitation of Serov's orchestral methods.' Strakhov, in the *Grazhdanin*, after finding fault with every single thing in the opera, summed up: 'He has talent, but this remains sterile for lack of artistic ideas . . . the outcome is unimaginable chaos.' Famintsïn (so [cuttingly satirized] in *The Classicist* and *The Peepshow*) prefaced his article (which appeared in Bessel's *Muzïkalny Listok*) with the ominous adage: 'La grammaire est l'art de parler et d'écrire correctement.' Most of the music he found 'disorderly, formless, shameless.' It created, he alleged, a heavy, unhealthy, murky atmosphere. The scoring was comparatively good, the recitatives really good. Reharmonized and, in parts, rescored, the opera would prove acceptable, despite its coarse realism; the composer had struck a praiseworthy direction.

[1] Quotations mainly from [the article by Khokhlovkina already referred to.]

Criticism of 'Boris'

In the *Muzïkalny Svet* two articles appeared. One, by Makarov, said that *Boris* contained but little music, did not constitute a step forward and was in many respects inferior to the operas of Serov and Dargomïzhsky; the other, signed 'Orphey' (the pseudonym of a certain Mikhnevich), that it successfully embodied a new tendency and that Mussorgsky had done well in the scenes [in which] the people [are the protagonists] and at certain dramatic moments, although not so well in the lyrical scenes. Regretting, it would seem, the impulse that had prompted him to forget his set standards and to speak well of the scenes given in 1873, Laroche, in the *Golos,* was merciless. He had always looked askance at Mussorgsky, while acknowledging that there were a few good things in his music: 'amid the frantic orgy of hideous, distorted sounds,' he had written with reference to the songs, 'here and there a good idea, a felicitous bit of declamation, a scrap of real melody, a fine sequence of three or four chords crop up, testifying to feeling and talent.' To this line of thought he now reverted:

The clique had consisted of imitators so far. With Mussorgsky it becomes original, genuinely creative. He is, however, a product of extreme immature liberalism. Lack of technique renders him incapable of using his ideas to good purpose. He has devoted much time and labour to studying orchestration; why did he not do the same with harmony and counterpoint? His imagination is impotent. He entirely depends on the piano; deprived of it, he would forthwith cease to be a composer.

Laroche's chief concern was to compare Mussorgsky with Dargomïzhsky, Serov or even Gounod, always to Mussorgsky's disadvantage. The recitatives in *Boris* were, he alleged, feeble shadows of Dargomïzhsky's, 'beyond even liberalism, formless, lawless in their melody, their harmony, their rhythms.'

In short, all those critics were prejudiced in some way or other: 'Laroche's standard was the musical experience of the past; Famintsïn's the letter of musical rules; Soloviev's analogies and resemblances,' comments Khokhlovkina. This, on the whole, was only to be expected, even though the reception of the three scenes might have led [Mussorgsky] to hope for [more intelligent appreciation]. But César Cui's notice in the *Peterburgskie Vedomosti* was a painful surprise.

49

He still praised, up to a point, and warmly, but mingled sharp and indeed often malicious censures with the praise. He deplored Mussorgsky's immaturity, his inability to develop his ideas, his self-satisfaction and lack of critical sense; his hasty methods, 'similar to those whose deplorable results were patent in the music of Messrs. Rubinstein and Tchaïkovsky'; the 'meagre musical contents' of the Cell and the Fountain scenes; the patchy, disjointed recitatives, the jumble of ill-assorted ideas 'owing to which the music now and then degenerated into sheer pot-pourri.' But what wounded Mussorgsky most of all was the reference to the wreath incident:

I wish I could shed a few sympathetic tears over the 'few ladies' who, deputizing for the public, were thwarted in their purpose. But, alas! I can't. I'm glad the wreath was not presented in public; for, unless blinded by self-esteem, a young composer to whom such a tribute would be proffered at the first performance of his first opera, before it was known how the opera would impress the real public, could but forthwith long to sink into the bowels of the earth. I am glad, too, that Mr. Mussorgsky felt no such longing, for it would have deprived us of a gifted composer with a great future—the road to which, however, is not through wreaths, as it is for circus-riders.

All this coming from a champion of modern tendencies and a close friend of Mussorgsky's, was a godsend to hostile critics, and they gleefully made capital of it. Cui with his article had become, Soloviev remarked, 'the Brutus of the clique.' In the long run, he did *Boris* more harm than even Laroche. 'What a horrible article!' Mussorgsky wrote to Stassov.

No educated man should dare to sneer thus at women. Shame on him! The tone of the article is odious. Why this [foolhardy] attack on the composer's alleged self-esteem? Fools have little of that humility which has never deserted me, nor ever will so long as I have brains in my head. Self-esteem! Immaturity! Hasty methods! whose? I should like to know. You often told me that you feared for *Boris* on account of Cui: the event has proved you right.[1]

Only the notice in the *Peterburgsky Listok,* signed 'Foma Pizzicato' (the pen-name of a young critic, Baskin, who later made his mark),

[1] Some time before, Stassov had written to Balakirev that nothing could dissuade Mussorgsky from trusting Cui 'blindly and stupidly.'

anticipated in several respects the verdict of posterity. He praised the originality and breadth of conception and execution, the composer's versatility and power in his evocations of the life of old Russia, in the crowd scenes and, above all, in his rendering of the tsar's psychology. 'Dramatization in vocal music,' he continued,

could go no farther. Mussorgsky has proved himself to be a philosopher-musician, capable of expressing with rare truth the mind and soul of his characters. He also has a thorough understanding of musical resources. He is a master of the orchestra; his working-out is fluent, his vocal and choral parts are beautifully written.

These views must have struck most readers as the outcome of an ultra-liberal tyro's lack of experience, or maybe sheer perversity. Many years were to elapse before they found endorsement. It is unlikely that at the time they carried weight with anybody; but they must have afforded Mussorgsky a measure of consolation.

The public, anyhow, continued to enjoy *Boris*. Nine further performances took place in the course of the year, with very satisfactory takings. But after that a drop came. Owing probably to the disfavour with which court, society and musical circles looked upon the work, it was given only twice in 1875; then, in much mutilated form, twice in 1876, five times in 1877, once in 1878, once in 1879 and once in 1881 (nine months after Mussorgsky's death). After that it was shelved [until 1896, when it was revived in Rimsky-Korsakov's first revision, not only very drastically cut, but with its musical substance seriously altered. The nature of these changes will be discussed in a later chapter].

CHAPTER V

THE LAST PHASE (1874–81)

APART from the production of *Boris Godunov,* the events of 1874 were few. A surprising one is that Mussorgsky suddenly started planning a comic opera on a Ukrainian subject, after Gogol's tale *Sorochintsy Fair.* This would be, he wrote to Karmalina, a singer who had provided him with old chants for use in *Khovanshchina,* a wise husbanding of his creative powers: 'two heavyweights such as *Boris* and *Khovanshchina* consecutively might be too much. Moreover, I shall be dealing with new types, a different setting and different natural traits.' Another reason was that it provided an opportunity for writing a worthy leading part for his dear friend, the Ukrainian bass Petrov.

Had he but known it, he was laying up endless trouble for himself. It might have been better if after discarding the notion because, he explained to Karmalina (10th April 1875), 'a Great-Russian could not successfully masquerade as a Ukrainian and master all the shades and peculiarities of the melodic contours of Ukrainian speech,' he had kept to his decision. By the time he again changed his mind (1875), he had not yet settled a definite plan for the libretto of *Khovanshchina,* but was unwisely trying to build it up as he went along and new ideas came to him for it. And for the *Fair,* too, he followed the same disastrous policy, the outcome being in both cases a tremendous waste of energy and hopeless confusion.

The other labours of the year were settings of poems by Golenishchev-Kutuzov: the wonderful song cycle *Sunless.* Also a grim ballad, *Forgotten,* inspired by Vereshchagin's painting showing a dead body on a battlefield; the set of piano pieces, *Pictures from an Exhibition* (his most important instrumental work after *St. John's Night on the Bare Mountain*), composed on the occasion of a memorial exhibition of Hartmann's works; and *Epitaph,* a deeply moving tribute to the memory of Nadezhda Opochinina, who had died, at the age of fifty-three, on 29th June.

Epitaph is (except, in a measure, *Sphinx,* which will be mentioned presently) the only one of Mussorgsky's works in which he directly expresses his own feelings, and also the only written document we have that reveals his feelings for the dearest of his women friends and in all likelihood the only woman he ever really loved. There is in his correspondence but one mention of her,[1] and no letter from him to her is known. Probably this love was the secret garden of his soul, which he kept inviolate and would not reveal even to his intimates.

[During 1875 Mussorgsky 'worked manfully at *Khovanshchina* once more,' as he told Lyubov Karmalina, and] composed three of his magnificent *Songs and Dances of Death.*[2] The fourth, *The Field-Marshal,* followed in 1877, but the set appeared only after the composer's death; [he had indeed planned four other numbers: the death of a monk, a gloomy fanatic who dies in his cell to the sound of a bell tolling in the distance, the death of a political exile, returning home, who is drowned within sight of his native land, the death of a young woman remembering her love and her last ball, and *The Warrior Anika and Death.* In December of the same year he composed] *Sphinx,* a song of a peculiar order written in peculiar circumstances.

Some time before, being more than ever financially straitened[3] and hopelessly in arrears with his rent, he had returned home one night to find himself locked out and his possessions put outside. After wandering several hours through the streets, he thought of [an old friend, Paul] Naumov, and to him he repaired for shelter.

[1] To Balakirev in 1869: 'I was unable to see Nadezhda Petrovna, for she never receives visitors before two.'

[2] Mussorgsky's original idea was to call the cycle *She*—Death personified.]

[3] Apart from the pittance he earned as a clerk, he received from Bessel, from January 1874 to December 1875, 500 rubles of the 600 agreed upon for the publishing rights of *Boris,* and another 15 presumably for the *Sunless* set (in 1871–2 he had received 186 rubles and 50 kopeks, for various works). He was also [—as appears from a letter of November 1876—] entitled to certain moneys from property at Karevo. To this should be added the regulation fee from the imperial theatres for the performing rights of *Boris.* It is true that 1875 marked the beginning of a period when works of his appeared more frequently on programmes, and he was in greater request than ever as an accompanist; but this did not increase his resources.

He was made welcome, given [a home], and in Naumov's house he spent the next few years. Paul Naumov, a retired naval officer, was gay, mercurial, fond of music and the theatre, and a *bon vivant,* although not (as suspected by Mussorgsky's right-thinking friends, who looked askance at him because of the life he led) a drink addict. He had separated from his wife and was living with her sister, Marya Kostyurina. Mussorgsky was very fond of them, and also of the third member of the household, Paul's son Sergey. Resenting the tongue-wagging of which he knew Marya to be the subject, he composed, and inscribed to her, *Sphinx,* a song in which he himself is heard, rebuking the backbiters:

There she stands, [motionless], silent. How dare you brand her with reproach? Keep silence, too, and hear the hammer-blows that fall upon your hearts of stone.

He made no attempt to have this published. It appeared only in 1911.

During the winter of 1875–6 Mussorgsky was busy helping to prepare the celebration of his beloved Petrov's golden jubilee, which took place on 21st April 1876, the famous singer appearing as Susanin in a gala performance of Glinka's *A Life for the Tsar.* Afterwards he continued *Khovanshchina* and started on the composition of *Sorochintsy Fair. Khovanshchina* progressed considerably and to his entire satisfaction. Towards the end of the year he wrote to Stassov:

To-day my desire is to prophesy, and what I foretell is the melody of life, not the melody of classicism. I am at work on human speech. With great pains I have achieved a type of melody evolved from it. I have succeeded in incorporating the recitative into melody (except, of course, for dramatic movements, when anything, even interjection, may be used). This type I should like to call well-thought-out, justified melody. My work rejoices me. Some day the unexpected, ineffable song will arise against classical melody, intelligible [at once] to one and all. If I succeed, it will be a triumph, and succeed I must. I wish to carry out experiments in a few scenes. There are foretastes in Marfa confiding her grief to Dosifey, and also in *The Fair.*

The episode in *Khovanshchina* (Lamm edition, pp. 210–13) is built on a beautiful, frankly melodic theme [1] and the themes of two songs previously sung by Marfa, with short stretches of recitative of the kind ordinarily used by Mussorgsky in between: so the 'foretastes' are not easy to detect. It is equally difficult to surmise which parts of *The Fair* composed or outlined in 1876 he had in mind. His work on it so far must have consisted mainly in planning and sketching: for, as with *Khovanshchina*, he went ahead without having written out a libretto. And in the songs he composed in 1877 (five settings of poems by Alexey Tolstoy, and one of a poem by Golenishchev-Kutuzov) there is nothing to justify their being regarded as experiments in the same direction. Mussorgsky's new discovery, therefore, is to be regarded as a dream that never [materialized]. Except for those songs, *The Field-Marshal* and the choral *Jesus Navin* (a re-arrangement of the chorus of Libyans in *Salammbô*), he did little that year but a certain amount of work on *The Fair*, [though in April—after the group of songs and before the resumption of work on *The Fair*—he actually began to note down Khirghiz, trans-Caucasian and other melodies for yet another opera, *Pugachevshchina*]. During the summer he vanished, and for weeks his friends remained without tidings of him. In the autumn Stassov wrote to Rimsky-Korsakov: 'Mussorgsky has composed a lot of rubbish for *The Fair*, but he is discarding it.'

Petrov's death (2nd/14th March 1878) was a terrible blow to Mussorgsky, and the craving for drink, which one cannot help suspecting had asserted itself the foregoing summer, again took hold of him. In April Stassov, realizing that he stood in danger of losing his official post, practically his only source of income, approached Terty Filippov, a state controller, whose keen interest in music, especially folksongs, had brought him in close contact with Bala-kirev, Rimsky-Korsakov and Stassov himself, and who had a great admiration for Mussorgsky, asking him to procure a transfer for the unfortunate composer to his own department. The situation was

[1] The main theme of César Franck's *Prélude, Aria et Final* is all but identical with it: a noteworthy example of coincidence, for Franck cannot have known *Khovanshchina,* and it is most unlikely that Mussorgsky knew a Bach violin sonata in which a prototype of the theme is to be found.

indeed grave, as shown by Lyudmila Shestakova's writing to Stassov in August:

> Mussorgsky came to see me several times running, in an appalling con-
> dition. In order to spare him whilst protecting myself, I wrote to him, as
> gently as I could, asking him not to call on me when suffering from what
> he calls his nervous disorder. Yesterday my dear Mussinka appeared, per-
> fectly correct, and promised never to distress me again. We shall see. I am
> sorry for him indeed: he has in him so much that is good.

Shortly before, at her house, Mussorgsky had met Balakirev for the first time after [six or seven] years, and Balakirev's impression had been excellent. 'He showed no trace of vaingloriousness,' he wrote to Stassov.

> On the contrary, he listened modestly and earnestly to what was said
> to him and did not protest at all when told it was needful to be conversant
> with harmony, and that he would do well to [have] lessons [with] Rimsky-
> Korsakov. I was delighted. He took from me his score of *The Witches*
> [i.e. the *Bare Mountain*] in order to remodel and amend it. That's good,
> for there are beautiful and powerful things in it, and it would be a pity if
> it remained in its present disorder.

So that when Stassov, more anxious than ever, urged Balakirev to help in devising some means of rescue, he willingly joined in the appeal to Filippov; and in October Mussorgsky was transferred to the Control department.

This was only a makeshift, the work being temporary and poorly paid; but it helped to keep the wolf from the door. And, sanguine as ever, he hoped to finish *Khovanshchina* soon, so [confidently] that in January 1879 it was announced that he was about to submit it to the committee of the imperial theatres. Yet he did very little work on it that year, part of which was taken up by an unexpected and welcome adventure: Darya Leonova, who had appeared as the hostess in the Inn scene of *Boris* in 1873, engaged him to join her in a concert tour through central Russia and the Crimea.

She was at that time fifty years of age. She had scored many successes in Russia and abroad, in opera and afterwards on the concert platform. Although past her [prime], she was still popular with the public at large. Mussorgsky was delighted with the

MUSSORGSKY'S BIRTHPLACE

MUSSORGSKY AS A YOUNG MAN IN OFFICER'S UNIFORM

MUSSORGSKY IN 1874

STAGE SET FOR THE 'STRELETSKAYA SLOBODA' SCENE IN 'KHOVANSHCHINA'

THREE BARS FROM THE OPERA 'SOROCHINTSY FAIR' (GYPSY SONG) IN
MUSSORGSKY'S HAND

From Vladimir Stassov's Collection

A PAGE FROM THE ORIGINAL MANUSCRIPT OF 'BORIS GODUNOV'

PORTRAIT BY REPIN, PAINTED IN HOSPITAL JUST BEFORE
MUSSORGSKY'S DEATH

scheme, according to Stassov. He expected from it, besides artistic success, 'a profit of at least a thousand rubles.' But Stassov was annoyed, holding that he would be 'cheapening himself and his comrades.' Balakirev was indignant. 'This is horrible,' he wrote to Shestakova. 'Could you not dissuade him? You would save him from playing a shameful part, and also from sharing Leonova's risky venture.'

In their over-eager solicitude they (and others with them) overlooked all that the tour would mean for their friend: not only fresh hopes at an all but hopeless juncture, but a change of surroundings and the enjoyment of seeing regions new to him and natural scenery to the beauties of which he was always most sensitive.

The tour lasted from the end of July to nearly the end of October; concerts were given at Poltava, Elizavetgrad,[1] Nikolaev (three), Kherson (two), Odessa, Sevastopol, Rostov-on-Don, Novocherkask, Yalta (two), Voronezh (three), Tambov (two) and Tver. The programmes consisted of excerpts from operas, Russian and others, and songs, mostly by Russian composers, but with one or two by Schubert and Schumann and some by unimportant composers such as Vitelyaro, Humbert, Kashperov and one [nominally] by Leonova herself (a Valse-Caprice, *Après le bal*), [in the composition of which Mussorgsky himself seems to have had a hand]. Mussorgsky, who appeared as accompanist and soloist, was well represented. His contribution as soloist consisted of pieces by Chopin, pieces of his own and extemporized paraphrases of scenes from his operas.

Mussorgsky's descriptions of the tour to his friends teemed with enthusiasm; but the truth is that it was not a success, especially from the financial point of view. His enthusiasm was [aroused partly by] the warm welcome they were given on many occasions, [partly by] his feeling that 'the concerts were of importance as [a good artistic service to the good Russian people'] (letter to the Naumovs) and also by his rapturous enjoyment of the scenery:

Nikolaev is lovely, with the river Bug running through it, its luxuriantly green banks, the far-off hills around it and countless windmills showing up against the sky-line. At sunset the colours of waters and hills are

---

[1] Now Pervomaysk.

magnificent. At Kherson, on the unruffled waters of the Dnieper, the re-flection of the great trees spreads afar from the banks over the widest stretches and pools. In the light of the lilac-rosy afterglow of the rays of the moon and Jupiter, it is an enchanting spectacle. [Talking of Jupiter: at Niko-laev] we were graciously invited to watch Jupiter and Saturn through the observatory telescope. I was transported with joy.[1]

At Yalta, where lived a daughter of Stassov's, Sophie Fortunato, whose husband ran an hotel, Mussorgsky had many opportunities to rejoice in sunlight and moonlight and mountains and sea. 'He liked to take the back seat in the big coaches in use in the Crimea' [Mme Fortunato tells us], 'so [as not to be obliged to make con-versation and disturb his mood. The most successful expedition was to Gurzuf.']

In the course of the journey he composed a couple of unimportant piano pieces, inspired by impressions of the Crimea, a piano fantasy, *Storm on the Black Sea*, which he played in public, but never wrote down; and Mephistopheles's *Song of the Flea* from Goethe's *Faust*, one of his least characteristic [songs], but the most widely known. He also remodelled *On the Dnieper*.

On 27th November 1879 Rimsky-Korsakov conducted excerpts from *Khovanshchina* at St. Petersburg [—chorus of the Streltsy, Marfa's song and the Persian dances—and Mussorgsky had to take a number of calls. His] service with the Control department ended on 31st December. He would have been destitute had not friends come to the rescue: first Filippov and others arranged for him to receive a monthly allowance of a hundred rubles to enable him to finish *Khovanshchina,* and shortly afterwards another group added an allowance of eighty rubles a month, stipulating that he was to finish *The Fair*. And his hopes were as high as ever:

I am not down-hearted. My motto, 'Dare! Ahead towards new shores!' remains unchanged. If fate enables me to widen the beaten track and progress towards the vital aims of art, I shall rejoice and triumph. The time for writing at leisure is past: to give one's whole self to the people —that is what is needed now in art. [To Stassov, 16th January 1880.]

Unfortunately, having undertaken to work on the two operas

[1] From letters to the Naumovs.

simultaneously, he got more and more entangled with both and did not succeed in finishing either.

Leonova, too, did her best to help him. She persuaded him to join her in setting up a school of singing. His functions were not only to act as accompanist, but to teach elementary theory and to compose duets, trios and quartets for the use of the pupils (the four attractive arrangements of folksongs for unaccompanied vocal quartet, published posthumously, date from that period). In the summer she invited him to stay at her country house at Oranienbaum. There he worked on *Khovanshchina* and *The Fair*, and also outlined the plan of a Suite for orchestra, harp and piano, on motives from folk tunes collected during his tour.

It seems that at that point he might have had a chance to make good; but his forces were ebbing fast. The allowances he received would have been sufficient to support him in normal circumstances, and his spirit, sustained by illusion, was still strong. He wrote to Stassov on 22nd August [1880]: 'Our *Khovanshchina* is finished, except for the final bit of the last scene'; and the following week:

This very second, I've finished the market scene in *The Fair*. *Khovanshchina* too is advancing. But the scoring—ye gods!—time! Perhaps Mussoryanin will prove faithful to what he has always proclaimed: a new, unexplored road; and perhaps he will discover it.

But death was near. On 3rd February 1881 he attended a performance of *The Destruction of Sennacherib* and appeared on the platform in response to the calls from the audience. The next day he took part in a commemoration of Dostoevsky (who had died on 28th January), extemporizing at the piano a dirge not unlike the chant of the monks in the death scene in *Boris*.[1] On 9th February he accompanied at a concert. Three days later he came to see Leonova:

He was in a appalling state of perturbation; he said he was done for, helpless, and that nothing remained for him but to beg in the streets. I assured him that what little I had I would always share with him. I

---

[1] See Lapshin's article in the Mussorgsky number of *Muzïkalny Sovremennik* (Petrograd, 1917).

succeeded in calming him a little. In the evening we had to go to a party. He played accompaniments. Later on he had a stroke. A doctor, who happened to be present, attended him; and he was able to return home with me. He implored me to allow him to spend the night at my flat.

He slept [the whole night] on a chair. He came to breakfast looking quite cheerful; but suddenly he collapsed. I summoned a doctor, and later his friends; and we decided he should be sent to hospital.[1]

The next day he was taken to the Nikolaevsky Military Hospital, Dr. Lev Bertenson (an old friend and keen admirer of his) securing his admission, on the unofficial suggestion of [his chief], by register/ ing him as 'salaried orderly to the resident doctor Bertenson.' He was unconscious at the time. He was given a private room, made com/ fortable and vigilantly looked after.[2] At first he was delirious most of the time, but soon showed signs of improvement. He was able to chat reasonably, and even began to make plans for the future. Among the friends who came to see him was Repin, who in four sittings [painted] the famous portrait of him, unkempt, haggard, a haunted look in his eyes, which—obviously on account of its pathetic and sensational character—has been far more often reproduced in books, press articles and programmes than any portrait of his normal, healthy self in happier times. Repin has given the following account of the cause of a sudden relapse that hastened his end:

His birthday was nearing.[3] He had been kept on a very strict diet, but the craving for drink remained. He was planning to reward himself for his long spell of patience. Despite rigorous orders, an attendant, in misguided kindness (the whole staff had grown very fond of him), provided him with a full/sized bottle of brandy in view of the birthday celebration. The next day (16th/28th March) when I arrived for the fifth and last sitting, he was no more.

[1 See Leonova's reminiscences printed in the *Istorichesky Vestnik*, April 1891.]

2 Ivanóv, the music critic of the *Novoe Vremya*, having described the accommodation provided for him as miserable and heart/breaking, Borodin, Cui and Rimsky/Korsakov issued a denial and protest which appeared in *Golos*.

3 It will be remembered that Mussorgsky and everybody else with him believed the date to be 16th/28th instead of 9th/21st March.

The end came at 5 a.m. The night nurse's report was that all of a sudden he cried out aloud: 'It's the end! Woe is me!' and expired.

Mussorgsky was buried in the Alexander Nevsky Cemetery, close by the tombs of Glinka and Dostoevsky. In 1895 a monument was erected over his grave.

His friends' first concern was to set his manuscripts in order and entrust them for safe keeping to the Petersburg State Library. Rimsky-Korsakov undertook to put the finishing touches to those requiring completion, [drastically 'revising' them in the process,] and yielded to the temptation to 'revise' *Boris* and [other already completed works, as will be described in the next chapter]. It is often averred that by so doing he saved them from oblivion; but many people hold that, on the contrary, he placed obstacles in the way of their coming into their own. Even nowadays, when the genuine texts are available for performance and study, a number of people are still in favour of the revised versions.

Despite the many ordeals Mussorgsky had to endure, he had not lived an unhappy life. His confidence in his star, his conviction that he was bringing the world a valuable message, sustained him and kept him in good cheer. Although he must have felt his loneliness acutely, he was never without a friend or two in whom to confide. And to the last he kept faithful to his motto: 'Towards new shores.'

CHAPTER VI

SONGS

[THERE is no better way of grasping the essentials of Mussorgsky's art, the stages of its growth to maturity and the changes that overtook it in its prime, than to study his songs. They are a long way from being the whole Mussorgsky, of course; yet they embody more fully than his work in any other single field the elements that constitute his contribution to the art of music. His instrumental music is, as we shall see later, remarkably unequal—some of it, particularly the bulk of the piano music, negligible. Even his operas do not reveal him as completely as the songs. If one had only their somewhat chaotic pages (with the single great accomplishment of *Boris Godunov*) to judge him by, it would be considerably more difficult to place him —or to understand him—as a musical personality than it would be by the unaided light of the songs. For, of the half-dozen or so operas that Mussorgsky actually began to write, to say nothing of those he contemplated writing, only one—*Boris*—was ever completed; the songs are all finished works of art. In the songs we can trace the lyricism of the early *Salammbô* and the uncompromising realism of *The Marriage*, the superb blending of both that produced *Boris*, and the weakening grip and increased lyricism of *Khovanshchina* and *Sorochintsy Fair*. Moreover, in the songs we can trace the beginnings of Mussorgsky's creative career, for one of the two earliest of all his surviving compositions—they date from 1857—is the setting of Grekov's poem, *Where art thou, little star?*]

In its first version, with piano accompaniment, this is altogether delightful and touchingly beautiful.[1] There is a version of 1858 for voice and orchestra [2] which differs from the former one in many important particulars. As a result, when studying the song we have to face a curious problem. We are confronted with two settings of the same text. The points in which the second differs from the first are far too great to be regarded as mere corrections. But the discrepancies are not great enough to be traced back to differences of

[1] See *Years of Youth*, Lamm edition, Moscow, 1931, page 1. The Lamm edition is the only one that gives the full unadulterated texts of all Mussorgsky's works, with all known variants.
[2] Same edition, page 4.

conception (such as gave rise, for instance, to Liszt's two settings of
Goethe's *Wer nie sein Brot mit Tränen ass*). The same problem arises,
in a far more complicated form, with regard to the two versions of
the song *King Saul* (1863) and of certain portions of the second act of
Boris Godunov (1869 and 1871); and, to a lesser extent, with regard
to other songs. What little can be said about *Where art thou, little star?*
will not help much to solve the problem as it concerns that song. In
the orchestral version a middle section has been added. The remainder has been considerably altered, the vocal part is shorn of its
coloratura, the harmonies are changed. The whole is less attractive,
less subtle, less sensitive. Not one of the changes seems to have been
dictated by considerations of orchestral needs or possibilities (of which
Mussorgsky, in 1858, must have known practically nothing); nor
are these changes of a kind which might have been suggested by an
adviser. One is almost tempted to wonder whether Mussorgsky
did not, when composing, occasionally lack decision and consistency, whether he did not remain very much at the mercy of the
inspiration, or whim, or chance of the moment. The doubts are
formidable ones even when one remembers that in the music of his
maturity he showed purpose enough; they are doubts certainly not
to be dealt with casually.

Here are the first few bars of both versions:

It remains for us to examine this early product for forecasts of Mussorgsky's mature style. The examination reveals, apart from any question of spirit, mostly negative signs: a paucity of bold harmonies, abundant use of long values in the vocal parts, a tendency to dwell on one harmony, practically no changes of time-signature and very few rhythmic changes. The positive signs are: the modal character of the song (especially in the first version, which uses a variable scale, D♯ and E♯ alternating with D♮ and E♮), and also one or two 'finger-prints,' of which the most striking is, in the first version, the cadence

derived from Russian folk-music, and used by Mussorgsky, later, in a number of closely interrelated variants.

[Neither version of *Where art thou, little star?* appeared in Mussorgsky's lifetime; indeed the orchestral version was published as recently as 1931; but the first version turned up in Paris in 1909 when Charles Malherbe, archivist of the Opéra, announced that he had acquired from an unspecified source a bound volume containing the autograph manuscripts of seventeen Mussorgsky songs, together with

Mussorgsky's arrangement (1864) for mezzo-soprano and baritone of Luigi Gordigiani's song, *Ogni sabato avrete il lume acceso*. The title-page was inscribed in Mussorgsky's own hand: *Years of Youth. Volume of Songs (from 1857 to 1866)*. Four of these songs had been published in the composer's lifetime: *Tell me why*, substantially in the same form as the Paris version, *King Saul*, *Night* and the *Cradle Song* from Ostrovsky's *Voevoda* (also known as *Peasant Lullaby*) in revised forms, and one, *Kalistratushka*, posthumously by Rimsky-Korsakov. The remaining twelve were quite unknown.

Although these songs have no connection other than the accidental one that the composer lumped them together as juvenilia and, apparently, disowned most of them—for they are not mentioned in any of the lists of his works compiled by himself—they may as well be considered as a group. Some of them need not detain us long. No. 17 is the song of the Balearic slinger from the unfinished opera *Salammbô*, which will be discussed in the next chapter. *What are the words of love to you?* (1860), *But if I could meet thee again* (1863) and *Why are thy eyes sometimes so cold?* (1866) are weakly lyrical efforts without feeling or character; in the first and third songs Mussorgsky is content with conventional accompaniment figures, though the second, while colourless, does bear some of the marks of his peculiar *facture*; and the earlier songs attempt piano epigrams at the end. *Why are thy eyes sometimes so cold?* is decidedly the feeblest of the three. *Tell me why* (1858)—the words of which Karatïgin wrongly attributed to Pushkin—has a little more individuality, and the setting of Koltsov's drinking-song, *Hour of Jollity*, if not strikingly Mussorgskian, it is at any rate characteristically vivid, with suggestions in the piano part of clinking glasses and bubbling wine, and not at all like a conventional drinking-song. Here again, as with *Where are thou, little star?* Mussorgsky wrote two versions, one dated 1858, the other April 1859, hardly differing enough to be considered separate settings, yet sufficiently unlike to demand comment on both. The later version is shorter, a number of bars of instrumental interlude being omitted, and has a considerably simpler piano part; the accompaniment of the earlier one is extremely awkward at the pace ('rather fast'), and the third-and-fourth-finger trills and other details suggest that it was intended to be orchestrated. The more practicable second version, with its

alternative high notes at the end (marked 'for Vasenka'),[1] is just the
sort of copy a composer might make for a friend. But it is much more
than a simplified copy of the first version. Not only is the accompaniment altered, but the melodic line at many points is entirely
different; sometimes—this is an interesting point—only the underlying harmony remains unchanged:

Dynamics are modified too, in one place from *p* to *fff*. Many
of the melodic alterations are obvious improvements: for instance,
the filling-out of the crotchet rest in bar 2 of the voice part in order
to avoid a break in the opening phrase; but one regrets such features
of the 1858 version as the tremendous festive *ff* trill dropped on the
tail of a *pp* passage with an effect not unlike that of the vinous trills
in Act III of Verdi's *Falstaff*.

[1] 'Vasenka' was V. V. Sakharin, a naval lieutenant and an actor-singer
with a remarkable voice, to whom both versions of the song are dedicated.
Balakirev also dedicated a couple of songs to him.

Hour of Jollity is more interesting as another early illustration of Mussorgsky's habit of drastic revision than valuable for its own sake. But a steadily mounting *crescendo* of artistic merit is maintained through the six songs *Sadly rustled the leaves* (words freely adapted from Pleshcheev) (1859), *I have many palaces and gardens* (words by Koltsov) (1863), the so-called *Old Man's Song* (a setting of *An die Türen will ich schleichen* from Goethe's *Wilhelm Meister*) (1863), *King Saul* (adapted from Kozlov's translation of Byron's *Song of Saul before his Last Battle*) (1863), Koltsov's *The wild winds blow* (1864) and *Night* (of which the first version is a setting of Pushkin's *My voice for thee is weak and languid*).[1] *Sadly rustled the leaves* is a beautiful bass song in German rather than Mussorgskian vein; it is conventionally constructed, but well constructed; the only problem it offers is its sub-title, 'a musical narrative,' for that is just what it is not. Having set Pleshcheev in German style, Mussorgsky then proceeded to set the *Harper's Song* from *Wilhelm Meister* in Russian style, for *An die Türen will ich schleichen* bears a family resemblance to the lament of the Chief Priest in Act III of *Salammbô*, written a year later—or possibly three years earlier—which later became the lament of the guilty tsar in *Boris Godunov*. In fact, the *Harper's Song* itself could, so far as musical style is concerned, be easily inserted into the score of *Boris*. Mussorgsky himself was rather pleased with the song, though he does not appear to have made any effort to get it published. 'One place has turned out quite well,' he wrote to Cui. 'The beggar could sing my music without misgiving—so I think.' There is already the true Mussorgsky, trying to find the true musical expression for a beggar. And he not only tries to put the right music in his mouth: he *sees* him mentally, and in the last six bars of the piano part contrives to convey a picture of the old man dragging his weary steps away. The music ends not on the tonic chord (E♭ minor) but on the tonic chord with a lower third added; technically it is a chord of the seventh, but the C♭ and E♭ in the low register of the piano combine to produce a sound almost of indeterminate pitch.

The two romantic Koltsov songs both testify to Mussorgsky's rapidly developing individuality. *I have many palaces and gardens*, a

---

[1] A poem which Rimsky-Korsakov set three years later as his Op.7, No. 1.

robust song in B major with an all-significant coda in slower tempo and an unexpected key (D major), has certain thematic affinities with the Intermezzo in B minor written a year or two before. *The wild winds blow* simply paints a wood, but does it not only with great power —the stormiest parts of the accompaniment sound like a forecast of part of the Revolution scene in *Boris*—but by skilful placing of con-trasts, one of them a very typical example of Mussorgskian cantilena. Like *Sadly rustled the leaves* and the *Harper's Song*, both are written for a bass. *King Saul* and *Night* both exist in two widely different versions. *King Saul*, a fine virile song, rough, wild and full of char-acter, the accompaniment related to that of *The wild winds blow*, is as puzzling as *Where art thou, little star?* for the second version, the only one known till 1923, is incontestably inferior to the first: smooth, tame and far less characteristic; even the tempo is considerably altered. Perhaps the explanation is the same as that of *The Hour of Jollity*— that the first version was an orchestral sketch ('trumpets' are indicated here and there), the second a more practicable reduction for the average pianist. But again one has to regret that Mussorgsky did much more than simplify the original form of the work, and to wonder what his motive was. *Night,* a song in totally different mood, is still more puzzling. Having set Pushkin's poem fairly faithfully, and so much to his own satisfaction that he orchestrated the setting four years later,[1] why did he almost completely rewrite Pushkin and then set this garbled text to music which, with all the changes (similar to those in the cases previously discussed), is still substantially the same? In either version *Night* is a lovely song, and the harmonically bold and beautiful passage that translates the lines about the beloved's eyes 'shining in the gloom of night' is practically the same in both versions, the words only slightly changed, the music altered only enharmonically. An interesting point is the almost-identity of the piano part at the beginning of each version, while the words and vocal line are completely changed. I omit the first two bars of the first version and the opening bar of the second:

---

[1] The full score was first published in volume vii of the Lamm collected edition; it must not, of course, be confused with Rimsky-Korsakov's orchestration of the second version of *Night,* made in 1908.

One can only say, in each of these cases, that the same musical noumenon has been made manifest, perhaps by improvisation, in two different phenomena, neither of which can be regarded as its definitive one, despite the composer's apparent preference for the later and weaker version. And these alternative embodiments of ideas are characteristic of Mussorgsky throughout his career in small things and in great, from the details of a single passage to the 1869 and 1872 versions of *Boris Godunov*.

Only in the case of the *Cradle Song* (1865) from Ostrovsky's *Voevoda* (a play which provided both Tchaïkovsky and Arensky with a subject for operas) do we know of a plausible explanation for the existence of two versions: that the first or longer one, judging by the stage directions inserted ('Dozes. . . . Almost spoken. . . . In her sleep'), was intended for performance in the actual play, the other for independent performance. And here, as it happens, the differences are much less essential than in *King Saul* or *Night*. This peasant lullaby might be regarded as a companion piece to *Kalistrat* (1864), of which the first version, *Kalistratushka,* is actually called 'a study in folk style.' Nekrassov's poem is the reverie of a peasant remembering the lullaby his mother sang over him in the cradle, how she had prophesied: 'Thou shalt be happy, Kalistratushka! Thou shalt live in clover!' and how ironically her prophecy has been fulfilled. The parts where the peasant speaks in his own person are typical of Mussorgsky's flexible, unsymmetrical, lyrical cantilena at its best: for instance, the opening which almost anticipates the 'parrot' episode in *Boris*:

while the quotation from the lullaby is accompanied by an actual Russian folk-tune.[1] With *Kalistrat* begins a whole series of peasant studies. In the list of his works given to Lyudmila Shestakova in 1871 Mussorgsky speaks of it as 'a first attempt at the comic'; there *is* an element of comedy in Kalistrat's ironic philosophy; but on the whole the song is as lyrical as the earlier *Harper's Song* and the Ostrovsky *Cradle Song*.

Kalistrat, like so many of its companions, was left by Mussorgsky in two forms, one for baritone, the other for tenor, but otherwise differing in details rather than essentially. But with it we reach another question. Neither version of the song was published during Mussorgsky's lifetime; indeed the first version came to light only when Paul Lamm brought out his edition of *Years of Youth* in 1931;[2] but the second version was published by Rimsky-Korsakov in 1883 in a much edited form: in fact, a third version. Most people are by this time aware that the generally known version of *Boris Godunov* was drastically 'edited' by Rimsky-Korsakov: changed in melody, harmony, figuration, scoring, so that hardly a bar was left as the composer

[1] Which, as Rimsky-Korsakov tells us in his edition of the song, was afterwards given him by Mussorgsky for his opera *The Maid of Pskov*; in Act II, Scene ii it accompanies the entrance and exit of Olga and her maids.

[2] The Paris edition of 1923 is simply a reprint of the Rimsky-Korsakov version—an unnoticed fact which led Riesemann into a characteristic blunder in his article 'Mussorgskis "Jahre der Jugend"' in *Der Auftakt* (V. Jahrg., Heft 3).

wrote it. It is less generally realized that not only *Boris* but practically all Mussorgsky's works were at some time or other posthumously re-touched or rewritten by Rimsky-Korsakov, and that this editorial work was not limited to the completion of unfinished scores such as *Khovanshchina,* immediately after Mussorgsky's death, plus the edition of *Boris* and the orchestration of certain songs fifteen or twenty years later. Rimsky-Korsakov began his 'editorial' work on his dead friend's completed but unpublished compositions as early as 1883. Many of his emendations are slight and relatively unimportant: re-distributions of chords and the like. A great number are academic 'corrections' of awkward harmony or part-writing: understandable and well-intentioned though wrong-headed. But many others are wilful and indefensible alterations of the composer's own musical substance, made without any editorial indication that the text has been tampered with. It will suffice to show side by side, two short excerpts from Mussorgsky's own second version of *Kalistrat*—for that matter, they are practically identical in his first version—and the same passages in Rimsky-Korsakov's text which for nearly half a century was naturally accepted as the true one:

71

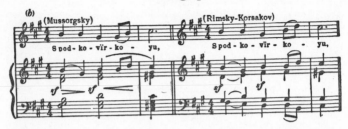

With that example we may leave the whole rather dreary topic, bearing in mind only that the great majority of the Mussorgsky texts in current use are 'doctored' ones. Unless otherwise stated, all quotations in the present volume are from the authentic text of the Russian State edition of the complete works, edited by Paul Lamm.

The two remaining songs in *Years of Youth*—an undistinguished setting of Lermontov's famous *Prayer,* and a curious 'essay in recita-tive,' *The Outcast* (both 1865)—are of slight interest. So are the two Heine songs, *Ich wollt' meine Schmerzen ergössen* and *Aus meinen Tränen,* both written the following year, which were not included in *Years of Youth.* But Mussorgsky's 'years of youth' as a song-com-poser were over by 1866; *King Saul, Night* and *Kalistratushka* can hardly be considered juvenilia, and the eighteen separate songs which, together with the *Nursery* cycle, were written during the next five or six years—the years before and during *Boris*—include most of those on which Mussorgsky's reputation as a song-writer is based. These eighteen may, for convenience, be divided into three classes, nearly equal numerically: the essentially lyrical and romantic songs, the caricatures and other essays in the comic and what we must, also for convenience' sake, call the 'realistic.' Naturally there is no hard and fast division between these classes. *Eremushka's Lullaby* (1868), for instance, though on the whole lyrical, leans towards realism.

At this point it appears necessary to digress in order to define more precisely what is meant by Mussorgsky's 'realism.' It has already been pointed out in Chapter II that 'realism' does not consist in the artist's choice of commonplace subjects, still less in the stressing of commonplace or repulsive elements in his subjects.]

I cannot remember who the first critic was who pointed out that

Zola, contrary to current opinion, was the very reverse of a realist or naturalist. He dealt, it is true, with realistic or naturalistic subjects: but his methods comprised the same amount and kind of rhetorical artifice, over-emphasis, trickery and frippery, as the methods of the worst sort of non-realistic writer. In other words, he dealt, say, with a dirty rag exactly as the idealistic or romantic scribbler might deal with a beautiful silk veil.

The very critical principle which this remark illustrates led me to suggest, many years ago, that the label 'realism' is useful only if it refers to methods of treatment and never to the choice of subjects. Again, Rabelais describing the birth of the river Bièvre is as much a lyric poet as Ovid describing the birth of the fountain Arethusa—the method in both cases being founded on poetic amplification. Endorsing the application of the label 'realism' to Mussorgsky, I attempted to justify it by showing that his methods were simple, straightforward, unadorned and led to a minimum of poetic amplification and of artistic conventionalization—a horrible but unavoidable word—to which I shall presently revert.

Practically at the same moment (1908) Mme Marie Olenin d'Alheim, in the first chapter of her excellent little book *Le Legs de Moussorgski*, gave a slightly different, perhaps more comprehensive and certainly less matter-of-fact definition of Mussorgsky's realism. This, she wrote, is shown firstly in his capacity to suggest the physical aspect, the voice and the very intonation of the characters which his songs embody.

A few bars are enough to make them live in front of us and to show them to us whole. A while ago they cropped up from out the silence; a few sentences, and back into the silence they go: but they will live for ever in our memory, in their full reality.

It is shown secondly in the light which his imagination sheds upon this reality, bringing out and accentuating its entire significance. These two features of Mussorgsky's realism, she adds, 'are not contradictory, but agree and co-operate like two notes at the distance of an octave.'

The crucial point, of course, remains the value of Mussorgsky's music as music pure and simple. As soon as you present Mussorgsky with the whole indefinite content of the label 'realism,' it becomes fatally easy to overlook the purely intrinsic quality and value of his music, saying, for instance: 'It is very effective so far as realistic suggestion is concerned, but as music it is unsatisfactory.'

Exactly the same thing is constantly happening with regard to descriptive and programme music. One cannot help wondering when people will cease to attempt to judge works from the point of view of their author's intentions, not of his actual achievement. Knowing that a composer found inspiration for a work in a 'story,' some of us will insist on judging this work as something quite different from pure music, without ever asking themselves how far from pure music the work actually is. Likewise, knowing that Mussorgsky set out to achieve as faithful and direct as possible an equivalence of the intonations of speech, certain critics will see in his songs merely the copy of the model, not the music—which is as logical as to say that a portrait cannot be a good picture if the painter aimed at achieving a faithful likeness.

This is where the question of the 'minimum of conventionaliza' tion' comes in. We all know what the conventionalized flowers, leaves and tendrils as they appear in architectural and other decora' tions are; so that there is no need to explain the term. Now, if we were to encounter a decorative scheme founded on slightly conven' tionalized, or altogether non'conventionalized representations, we should naturally judge it on the strength of its fitness and beauty, without even asking what the particular degree of conventionaliza' tion happens to be.

In music, conventionalization is very much the same thing as in the decorative arts. It consists in simplification and adaptation to a certain purpose. But music being far more abstract, conventions seem to play a far greater part in it, and are sometimes considered to be the alpha and omega of the art. With many of us, they become a matter of habit; to dispense with them is found impossible, or never dreamed of. Music, then, cannot be real music if it lacks any of the landmarks which proclaim that the conventions have been duly observed. And if it be found that besides certain customary con' ventions being overlooked, the music originates in a descriptive, dramatic or picturesque subject, the case against it is considered complete.

The principle of the 'minimum of conventionalization' as ex‑emplified in the works of Mussorgsky the 'realist' is not the only one which implies defiance of—or rather indifference to—certain con‑ventions. The tale of composers who ignored conventions for reasons that had nothing to do with 'realism' or descriptive intentions would be endless. So that you must be prepared either to make light of conventions or to remain incapable of enjoying music throughout the course of its natural evolution. And if you succeed in ridding yourself of one prejudice, you should experience no difficulty in casting the other aside. Instead of asking yourself how near this or that song of Mussorgsky remains to the actual whine of a beggar or to the actual rude yells of a street arab, you will simply try to feel how these songs stand as music. Then, in all likelihood, you will realize that a song such as *The Ragamuffin*—which is often adduced as a mere instance of crude realism—is really a highly organized, self‑contained, altogether satisfying musical whole.

[This element of minimum conventionalization enters hardly at all into such songs as *On the Dnieper* (1866, revised 1879), the *Hebrew Song* (1867), *The Garden by the Don* (1867), the *Child's Song* (1868) and the *Evening Song* (1871). The last, an extremely simple setting of some verses by Pleshcheev, calls for little comment. Yet, naïve as it is, it repays looking at as well as singing; the voice‑part is limited to the five notes A, B, C♯, D, E, and its centre of gravity lies on the nominal dominant, while the nominal tonic is strangely neglected. Hence the strange charm of a trifle that would otherwise remain quite commonplace. The little *Child's Song* of Mey belongs to the same category and is notable for its ending on a dominant‑seventh chord; the song was originally written with rather fussily irregular barring, which Mussorgsky afterwards reduced to a regular 4–4, only once interrupted, without detriment to the effect. It is one of the songs least altered by Rimsky‑Korsakov, though bar 8 and the penultimate bar were retouched by him harmonically. *The Garden by the Don* is rather more elaborate in texture, though the poetic and musical content place it in the same class. Koltsov's verses[1] about a girl

---

[1] Or rather the mangled remains of Koltsov's poem as Mussorgsky left them. Rimsky‑Korsakov never maltreated Mussorgsky worse than Mus‑sorgsky maltreated his poets.

whom he watches daily from his window, watering her garden, and who once even smiles timidly and spills the water, belong to a type that has inspired many a German composer to simple, sentimental melody, and it is interesting to observe how freshly Mussorgsky has approached them, how without sacrifice of lyrical simplicity and tenderness he has contrived by an unconventional melodic line, unconventional harmony and unconventional piano figuration (though the triplet chords beginning at 'I shall never forget how she sighed' are in a Russian convention deriving from Glinka) to translate the spirit of the poem without adding to it the faintest shade of sentimentality. I would draw special attention to the melodic and harmonic importance of the flattened sixth (occasionally sharpened fifth) of the scale throughout the song, a characteristic of the Glinka school.

But in pure lyrical beauty these songs are overshadowed by the *Hebrew Song*, from Mey's paraphrase of *The Song of Songs* (ii. 1–3) and *On the Dnieper,* Yarema's song from the Ukranian poet T. G. Shevchenko's *Haydamaki* in a Russian translation also by Mey. What attracted Mussorgsky to Hebrew subjects it is impossible to say, but the existence of the attraction is undeniable. The setting of Byron's *Song of Saul* has already been mentioned; in January 1867 Mussorgsky had completed the first version of his choral setting of another of Byron's *Hebrew Melodies, The Destruction of Sennacherib,* and now in June of the same year came the Mey song set to an arabesque, quasi-oriental melody of the type we associate with Borodin or Rimsky-Korsakov rather than Mussorgsky. Indeed that same year Rimsky-Korsakov took another verse of the Mey paraphrase of *The Song of Songs* (v. 2) and set it under the same title, *Hebrew Song,* as his Op. 7, No. 2, with a dedication to Mussorgsky; one or two little melodic patterns are common to both songs and there is probably an interesting story connecting them, if only one could unearth it. Oddly enough, *On the Dnieper* makes a good deal of the freeing of the Ukraine from Poles and *Jews*; the Dnieper is to 'carry the blood of the Jews away to the distant sea.' This song shows Mussorgsky at the height of his lyrical power, and one cannot help regretting that the merely 'interesting' and experimental sides of his song-writing, and artistically worthless jokes like *The Peepshow,* have distracted attention from such a masterpiece as *On the Dnieper*. Shevchenko (1814–61) was an ardent Ukrainian nationalist, whose patriotism got him sent to a penal battalion in 1847, and Yarema's song is a stirring call for a free Ukraine, though Oskar von Riesemann is quite wrong in saying [1] that Mussorgsky's song 'could not be published in Russia during the tsarist régime, owing to difficulties with the censorship.' (It was in fact passed by the censor on 11th May 1888, and published the same year.) *On the Dnieper* is conventional enough to close with a reference to the broad introduction, Yarema's invocation of 'my broad Dnieper.' The main portion of the song is a fiery *allegro*.

In the other setting from *The Haydamaki*, the *Hopak* (1866, revised and orchestrated 1868), as in *Eremushka's Lullaby* (1868, words by Nekrassov), realistic influences slightly modify essentially lyrical conceptions. The one is no more a simple lullaby than the other is a simple dance-song. *Eremushka's Lullaby*, of which the first version was dedicated 'to the great teacher of musical truth, Alexander Sergeevich Dargomïzhsky,' stands in a direct line with *Kalistratushka* and *The Peasant Lullaby* of 1865; a peasant woman broods bitterly over the child's future. And the *Hopak* is another scene from peasant life, with layer beneath layer of characterization. Superficially this is simply a wild, incessant dance of the type suggested by the title; but the incoherent, almost untranslatable words seem to be those of a girl married to an old Cossack to whom she is unfaithful. Yet Mussorgsky's sub-title, 'The *Kobzar's* [2] Song,' and his 'stage-direction,' 'The old man sings and dances,' show that it is not, as most critics have supposed, a woman's song, but the song of a man impersonating a woman.

Gathering Mushrooms (1867) is definitely less conventionalized. Or rather it is another convention devised by Mussorgsky himself and of which he was particularly fond: a rendering of Russian speech in terms of an almost uninterrupted flow of even crotchets. Mey's savagely humorous little poem, spoken by a woman gathering mushrooms with wicked thoughts of their poisonous possibilities, thus becomes a sort of *moto perpetuo* scherzo. The melody, opening

[1] *Mussorgski* (Munich, 1926).

[2] A *kobzar* is a player on the *kobza*, a Ukrainian national instrument.

diatonically, is soon given modulatory twists and underlined by pungent harmonies which, as is proved by the different notation of the two versions in which the song exists:

Sta - ry est, ne spra - vit - sya: Sta - ry est, ne spra - vit - sya:

were conceived quite empirically. (Similar enharmonic changes of notation occur in the different versions of *Eremushkas's Lullaby* and other compositions.) Incidentally, whereas the first version of *Gathering Mushrooms* is marked 'Quietly—don't hurry' and ends *ppp*, the second, which does not differ much in musical substance, is marked 'Rather quickly' and ends *f*.

Gathering Mushrooms is at least partly lyrical in feeling, but in the prototype of Mussorgsky's 'realistic' songs, the famous *Darling Savishna* (1866), conventionalization is reduced to an absolute minimum. The song, for which Mussorgsky wrote his own words, was inspired by an incident seen the previous year. 'As Mussorgsky himself told me at the time, he conceived it while he was in the country with his brother (on the farm at Minkino) in the summer of 1865,' writes Stassov in the 'biographical essay' which he published in the very year of the composer's death.

He was standing once by the window when he was impressed by something going on under his eyes. An unhappy idiot was declaring his love to a young woman who had attracted him; he was pleading with her, though ashamed of his unseemliness and his unhappy condition; he himself understood he could have nothing in the world—least of all the happiness of love. Mussorgsky was deeply impressed; the type and the scene were firmly imprinted on his soul; in a flash there occurred to him the peculiar forms and sounds for the embodiment of the images that were agitating him, but he did not write the song at that very moment; first of all he wrote his

Peasant Lullaby, full of oppressive sadness, and completed and wrote down *Savishna* only after some months.

The 'forms and sounds' are indeed peculiar. Except the first two and last three bars, for piano only, the song consists of an unvaried, uninterrupted flow of crotchets for forty-seven bars in 5–4 time:

The piano reiterates that rhythmic figure, underlining and sup-porting the voice with its crude sonorities, from beginning to end—and breaks off on a $\frac{6}{4}$ chord, *ppp*, which is no more an end than the con-clusion of the *Harper's Song* is. There is no need to insist that in *Savishna* Mussorgsky not only chose a very unusual subject, but treated it in a very unusual way. But two or three points must be made. The whole forty-seven-bar vocal line conveys with extraordinary vividness the rise and fall of the idiot's voice as he pleads, as the piano part almost pantomimically suggests the agitated movements of his hands. Yet this vocal line, if not melodic in the conventional sense, is by no means recitative. As the example above shows, Mussorgsky adopted a genuine musical convention—of one-bar motives—to embody his idiot's babblings. On the one hand, the shape of these motives is not so very far removed from the sing-song motives on three or four notes, endlessly repeated, to which the Russian peasant bards used to recite their interminable *bïlïnï* or narrative ballads (cf. the legend of the Dove Book which Rimsky-Korsakov introduced into *Sadko* and the song about Volga and Mikula which is the origin of the melody to which Misail and Varlaam make their appearance in the last scene of *Boris,* cf. examples on page 188); on the other, the general result is a melodic line hardly less satisfactory than the quintuple *moto perpetuo* scherzo of Borodin's and Rimsky-Korsakov's third Symphonies. In other words, if Mussorgsky discarded all the usual conventions of song-writing, he found another, satisfactory 'minimum' convention of his own.

In *Gathering Mushrooms,* as we have seen, this new convention was infused with a certain element of lyrical feeling. In *The Feast* (1867) it was used, with more varied rhythmic patterns,[1] to convey Koltsov's description of a peasant festival. In *The Orphan* (1868, words by the composer) the note-values are more varied—in *The Feast* the flow of crotchets is varied only by a single minim and interrupted only by one bar's rest—and the pleading of the child-beggar with the 'dear gentlemen, kind gentlemen' leans more definitely to the *bilina* type:

Ba - rin moy mi - len-ky,   Ba - rin moy dob - ren-ky,

In *The Magpie* (1867), of which the text is curiously compounded of two of Pushkin's poems, *A Chattering Magpie* and *Little bells tinkle,* the scherzo-like chatter of the voice part and snap of the accompaniment are twice interrupted by snatches of more lyrical melody at the references to 'the play of the reddish sun-ray and the silver gleam of the snow'; the whole thing is as nonsensical and delightful as a nursery rhyme. Thematically,] except for one contrast in the middle section, all the music is derived from the four-note germ-cell with which the song opens. *The Ragamuffin* (1867, words by the composer) is equally close-knit and might be in form as well as in character an instrumental scherzo as self-sufficient musically and self-explanatory as the scherzo of Borodin's third Symphony [or that of Rimsky-Korsakov's third, already mentioned, which it anticipates still more closely. For the flow of crotchets, though not interrupted as in *Savishna,* is mainly in 5–4 time. While this impression of a street urchin shrieking every imaginable insult at an old woman

[1] In a letter to Rimsky-Korsakov, written immediately after the composition of *The Feast,* Mussorgsky proudly draws attention to the 6–4 plus 5–4 as 'constituting the whole *chic* of this little piece . . . both Russian and, I venture to think, musical.'

remains in the sphere of comic realism, *You drunken sot* (written the year before, also to Mussorgsky's own words) exaggerates the comedy of abuse almost into caricature. Indeed it originated as a joke 'for private consumption' based, as the sub-title tells us, on 'the adventures of Pakhomïch' (Mussorgsky's nickname for Nikolsky) and was never intended for publication.[1] Yet from this comic sketch of a scolding wife Mussorgsky was able a year or two later to borrow a theme ('Oh, how oft did I beseech you, husband? . . . Don't you care for your poor little children? . . .') for one of the most moving passages in *Boris Godunov*: that where the dying tsar tells his son: 'Do not trust the disloyal boyars around you. Watch with the utmost care their secret intrigues with Lithuania. . . .' But the greater part of the song is in the vocal *moto perpetuo* style, though not a very good speci-men of it. One passage is worth quoting as a simple example of Mussorgsky's forthright, unconventional but intensely expressive harmony:

Here the 'nagging' of a pattern in tenths against an unprepared dis-sonant inner pedal, often inexplicable in any technical terms, was evidently discovered empirically by the composer's fingers at the piano.

The Seminarist (1866) and *The He-Goat: a worldly story* (1867) again have words by the composer. Indeed in this particular comic genre it would have been next to impossible for Mussorgsky to find suitable words by any one else. The portrait of the theological student, gabbling his lists of Latin nouns of the third declension and lapsing into amorous reveries about Styosha, the priest's pretty daughter,

[1] It was found by Andrey Rimsky-Korsakov in the Leningrad Public Library in 1925. An English version, *A Song to a Drunkard*, with words by M. D. Calvocoressi, was published by Chappell in 1943.

belongs to the field of comic realism; the parodying of Orthodox church music anticipates the characterization of the vagabond monks in *Boris* and the priest's son in *Sorochintsy Fair*. But *The He-Goat*— the parallel between the wicked, bearded old goat who frightens an innocent girl out of her wits and the wicked, bearded old bride-groom who doesn't alarm her in the least—is satire of a different kind. The point-making is obvious enough: the naïve lyrical melody of the girl, the leaping dotted motive of the voice as it describes the goat, the similar pantomimic figures of the piano part, the 'sarcastic' dis-sonances. Yet the music really adds very little to the words, whereas the comedy of *The Seminarist* is essentially musical.

Two other satirical songs, or rather musical lampoons, are *The Classicist* (1867) and the famous *Peepshow* (1870): interesting enough as specimens of a very rare genus, but of no artistic importance and, to tell the truth, only mildly amusing. Both are directed against enemies of the 'Mighty Handful.' In *The Classicist* Mussorgsky attacks A. S. Famintsïn, the twenty-six-year-old professor of musical history at the Petersburg Conservatoire, a conservative composer and musical pro-German critic who had sneered at Rimsky-Korsakov's early orchestral piece *Sadko*. One version of the song is headed 'In reply to Famint-sïn's remarks on the heresy of the Russian school of music,' the other 'Occasioned by Mr. Famintsïn's musical articles.' The champion of classicism announces, to a collection of late eighteenth-century musical platitudes: 'I am simple, I am clear, I am modest, polite . . . I am a pure classicist.' In an 'agitated' middle section he proclaims his hostility to 'new-fangled contrivances,' to the accompaniment of the 'sea' motive from the offending *Sadko*. 'Their noise and hubbub, their awful disorder alarm me,' he says. 'I see in them the coffin of art. But I . . . I am simple,' etc.

Famintsïn also has a place in the much more ambitious and correspondingly less successful *Peepshow,* beside other enemies of the Balakirev group and the Free School of Music: N. I. Zaremba, director of the Petersburg Conservatory, F. M. Tolstoy, critic and song composer, A. N. Serov, critic and composer of the popular operas *Judith* and *Rogneda,* and the Grand Duchess Helena Pavlovna, foundress and patroness of the Russian Music Society. After an introduction, which in the original version is headed 'I myself' and in which the composer invites the audience to walk up and see the show, he introduces the theorist Zaremba (who was a member of the Herrnhut sect of Pietists) to the tune of 'See, the conquering hero comes,'[1] and explains that he teaches that 'the minor mode is original sin, but the major mode is sin redeemed.' The next victim is 'Fif' (contemptuous diminutive of Feofil, or Theophilus, Tolstoy's Christian name), a fanatical admirer of Italian music; he had recently made himself ridiculous by his enthusiasm for Patti—whose praises he sings here to a banal valse. Then Famintsïn, to the tune of one of his own songs, is described as 'a sorely wounded youth' complaining of a blot on his character which he is trying to wash out: an allusion to a libel action he was then bringing against Stassov. Serov, too, is caricatured to his own music. He is heralded by a fanfare from the finale of Act I of his *Rogneda*. 'There he is! The Titan!' cries the showman, who then—to the accompaniment of other themes from *Rogneda* (the buffoon's song in Act III and the anti-Christian chorus, 'Death to him!' in Act I) alludes—in terms comprehensible only to contemporaries familiar with the chit-chat of musical circles in Petersburg—to Serov's vanity, his propaganda for Wagner, his annoyance at not being given a press seat at the Russian Music Society's concerts, at not having been invited to a dinner to Berlioz and at not being elected a director of that society. *The Peepshow* ends with the appearance of Euterpe (the Grand Duchess Helena Pavlovna) and a 'Hymn to the Muse,' again based on the *Rogneda* buffoon's song in slow tempo. But this final jest completely misses fire; the buffoon's song is really a folk melody and in this form has a real breadth and dignity.

The Peepshow is really a quite unimportant *jeu d'esprit,* the description of which takes up more space than it deserves. But it would be difficult to exaggerate the importance of the *Nursery* cycle (1868–72) (words by the composer),] that set of little gems which contributed so much to establish Mussorgsky's reputation: a unique incursion into the realm of childhood, its physical aspects and its psychology carried out with loving and far-reaching intuition and skill. [The first of the seven songs, *With Nurse,* was also the earliest in date: it was composed in the summer of 1868 when Mussorgsky was at the height of

[1] Stassov, with his habitual inaccuracy, says 'a theme from the oratorio *Samson.*'

his admiration for Dargomïzhsky—the second version is dedicated to him in exactly the same terms as the first version of *Eremushka's Lullaby*—and just before he embarked on *The Marriage,* the high-water mark of his realism, his rejection of all previous musical conventions. This almost phonographic record of a small child begging 'Nanny dear, tell me the story of the awful bogy-man who lived in the wood and ate up naughty children. . . . Or, I know—tell me about the tsar and the tsaritsa who lived in a wonderful palace over the sea . . .' is perhaps Mussorgsky's most uncompromising essay in this style. The even crotchet recitative with its ever-changing time-signatures (7-4, 3-4, 7-4, 3-2, 3-4, etc.) following every inflection of the child's speech in rhythm and pitch, the mainly empirical but always vivid harmonic flicks of pantomimic suggestion (the gnawing of the children's bones, the limping of the tsar, the sneezing of the tsaritsa and so on) combine in the most extreme manifestation of this side of Mussorgsky's genius. The result is so astonishingly novel that Rimsky-Korsakov was shocked into the production of what even he could not pass off as an 'edited' version of the song; his 'free musical rendering' in B flat minor and major, and strict 3-2 pulse, is one of the curiosities of Russian music.

The next four songs of *The Nursery—In the Corner, The Cockchafer, With the Doll* and *Going to Sleep*—date from two years later, the middle of what we may call the *Boris* period. The extreme realism is slightly modified. These songs are very far from conventional; as studies of the child mind—the very injured innocence of the naughty child in the corner; the fright caused by the cockchafer and the wonderment when it falls on its back, wings trembling, and moves no more; the gabbled list of names in the bedtime prayer—they are subtler than *With Nurse*. And they are couched in an idiom that admits a con-siderably greater portion of what we may call normal musical feeling, without sacrifice of acutely sensitive intonation. The lullaby for the doll is even on the border-line of the lyrical, though there is no attempt to stylize the child's muttered crooning as a melody in the ordinary sense; here the blurred drowsy effect of the almost incessant seconds (Db–Eb) in the piano part was obviously suggested, consciously or unconsciously, by the same means—the same notes in the same key—used to the same end in Borodin's song *The Sleeping Princess.*

'The Nursery'

The Nursery was completed in 1872 with *On the Hobby-Horse* and *The Cat 'Sailor'*,[1] accounts of two more typical childhood adventures: the ride, the fall, the quickly dried tears (and the resumed ride which allows a conventional return to the opening music) and the foiling of the cat 'Sailor's' attempt on the cage-bird, at the cost of hurt fingers. Like their predecessors, they perfectly recapture the spirit, the natural attitude of a very young child. That is what differentiates them from practically all the other child music ever written. They are not intended to be sung to children—though probably very young children would enter delightedly into their spirit; they are not the dreams of an adult romantically recalling his childhood; they are such music as a child of five might write if he had the technical equipment of a grown-up. It is this ability to project himself wholly into the skin of human types not only profoundly different from himself but profoundly different from each other—the idiot youth yearning for his darling Savishna, the peasant mother crooning over her baby, the young woman gathering mushrooms with hate in her heart, the street urchin, the great tsar who has done such evil and wished to do such good, the old monk brooding over his chronicles, the young one full of ruthless romantic aspirations, and dozens of others—that make Mussorgsky the great musical dramatist he is. The number of those characters is the measure of his genius. He is the supreme type of the objective, non-egocentric artist, just as Tchaïkovsky is the supreme type of the subjective egocentric, unable to conceive any dramatic character except in terms of himself.

Yet Mussorgsky can be introspective, too, as he shows in his second song cycle *Sunless* (1874). The words of *The Nursery* are his own; for his other two cycles, *Sunless* and the *Songs and Dances of Death* (1875–7), he draws on the rather morbid verses of his friend Golenishchev-Kutuzov. *Sunless* was written during the period of depression occasioned by the hostile and uncomprehending criticisms of *Boris* and by the boredom of the work in the Forestry department, and the subjective pessimism of the six songs of which it consists is almost

[1] These two songs were published posthumously; the *Nursery* cycle, published in 1872, consisted only of the first five songs. According to Stassov two others were projected: *A Child's Fantastic Dream* and *A Quarrel between Two Children.*

unique in Mussorgsky's output. The realistic, pantomimic element, of course, disappears from the musical substance, but the more lyrical feeling and subjective emotion by no means impelled Mussorgsky towards a more conventional type of song. The voice still sings in melodic recitative, approaching most nearly to pure recitative in the second song, *Thou didst not know me in the crowd*,[1] and to pure 'formalized' melody in the beautiful sixth, *On the River*, especially in the passage when the poet 'gazes silently into the deep waters':

But in the first song, *Between Four Walls*, the elements of melody and recitative are perfectly balanced; subtle truth of intonation is ever so slightly stylized, as in *Darling Savishna*, but much more elastically and variedly, by the working out of a rhythmic and melodic pattern all through the song. The quiet statement of the first two bars of the voice part ('narrow, quiet, dear little room') is thus darkened by the sombre thought of the next two ('impenetrable shade') and a moment later warmed by a ray of light ('in my beating heart, an ardent hope'):

---

[1] A song of which the vocal line has some affinity with Borodin's *The False Note* (1868).

ten' bezotv- et - na-ya;Vbyushchemsya serdtse na-dezh-da za - vet - na-ya;

It will be noticed that each of these changes of mood, or rather changes of shade within the same mood, is sensitively underlined by the harmony. Indeed a whole essay might be devoted to the harmony of *Sunless,* though it must suffice here to draw attention to such points as the all-pervading D of *Between Four Walls* (first as pedal, then as inner pedal, always the core of the harmonic structure) and the characteristic appoggiatura harmonies of *Thou didst not know me in the crowd* with its remarkable conclusion of a $\frac{6}{3}$ chord foreign to the key.[1]

Although *Sunless* as a whole must be given a high place in Mussorgsky's work, and a unique place as a document of spiritual autobiography, and although the last three songs—*Boredom, Elegy* and *On the River*—contain some of his finest lyrical melody, one frequently feels the lack of some concrete image serving as a lens to focus the musical emotion in sharp outlines. After all, perhaps the most memorable passages are those in which some such image does help to *préciser* his invention: the 'cloudy night' and the gleaming 'star' at the beginning of the *Elegy* and the clanging 'bell of death' near its end, the deep moonlit waters and 'the distant stars' of *On the River,* and the unforgettable drifting piano figure of *The idle, noisy day is ended,* when the poet 'in imagination turns the pages of lost years, breathing in anew the poison of passionate dreams of spring': [2]

---

[1] The key is D major, the final chord D, F♮, B♭; perhaps Mussorgsky felt the F and B♭ as appoggiaturas unresolved on F♯ and A.

[2] Quoted almost note for note by Debussy in the *Nuages* of his orchestral *Nocturnes* to express a similar mood of melancholy day-dreaming.

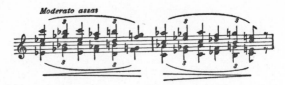

The artistic triumph of the equally sombre *Songs and Dances of Death* (1875–7) is largely due to the fact that each song has this objective, pictorial or dramatic 'lens': in the first [1] the picture of the dying child nursed by its mother, in the second the picture of Death coming to the sick girl at night as a serenading lover, in the third of Death dancing with the drunken *muzhik* who has lost his way in a snowstorm in the forest at night, in the fourth—perhaps suggested by Glinka's *Midnight Review*—of Death, the Great Captain, riding at night over the moonlit battle-field. In each song there is not only a picture, there are characters and action; each is a miniature drama: and whereas the operas Mussorgsky was working on at this period, *Khovanshchina* and *Sorochintsy Fair,* both betray a certain falling off in invention, the *Songs and Dances of Death* have a strong claim to be considered the very cream of Mussorgsky's work as a song composer. Nowhere has he achieved a more perfect fusion of true and subtle declamation with plastic, expressive melody, melting imperceptibly into recitative on the one hand and pure melody on the other, following the inner life of the words, nowhere more vivid and sensitive harmony.

From the structural point of view the *Trepak* is perhaps the most finely wrought of all Mussorgsky's songs. The principal theme is first stated in the fourth and fifth bars of the scene-setting introduction ('the snowstorm weeps and moans') (see page 89), where the left-hand semiquaver motive is derived, as the opening bars of the song show, from the *Dies irae* which is also reflected in bar 2 of the following example, one of the few physical traces of the influence of

[1] The first, that is, in Mussorgsky's own arrangement of the numbers: *Lullaby, Serenade, Trepak, The Field-Marshal.* It was apparently Rimsky-Korsakov who placed the *Trepak* first when he published the set in drastically edited form after the composer's death.

Liszt's *Totentanz* on the *Songs and Dances of Death*, though its spiritual influence is unquestionable.   The gradual transformation of the above into the rhythmic melody of the actual dance:

must be studied in the song itself. But it is impossible not to quote the beginning of the wonderful close, the lullaby that Death sings over the peasant: 'Sleep, my little friend, happy little *muzhik*':

also derived from the two motives of the voice part in the preceding examples.

The *Serenade* is more obvious in its methods; the actual end—the lulling, ever quieter serenade dying away to a silence broken by Death's triumphant cry 'Thou art mine!'—is rather theatrical, and the song falls into two uncorrelated halves: the narrative and Death's song end in different keys. But the dialogue of Death and the mother in the first song is unbearably poignant; here the apparently free and rather amorphous flow of the music is given shape by Death's insidious refrain, half heard when he first appears, then four times repeated with quiet insistence at shorter intervals, the last time in slower tempo closing the song with its wonderful cadence: 'Thou seest, I've lulled him to sleep. Lulla⁄lulla⁄lullaby':

The *Field⁄Marshal*, written two years later than the three other songs, falls into two parts like the *Serenade* (though the transition is much less abrupt) and, like the *Serenade*, is open to the charge of being slightly theatrical. But here the theatricality lies in the idea of the song rather than in its musical embodiment. Actually the music is over⁄

whelmingly effective from the opening battle-painting to the end of Death's grim march, the melody of which, according to Karatïgin, is a Polish revolutionary song, 'Z dymen pozarow.' Four bars from the end occurs one of the most remarkably cacophonous of all Mussorgsky's empirical chord-formations ('Your bones shall *never* leave their graves!'):

though he does not always resolve them appoggiatura-wise as logically as he does here. Needless to say, this chord will not be found in Rimsky-Korsakov's version of *The Field-Marshal*.

Besides *Sunless* and the *Songs and Dances of Death*, Mussorgsky composed two separate songs on words by Golenishchev-Kutuzov: *Forgotten* (1874) and *The Vision* (1877). The earlier, styled 'ballad,' was a forerunner of the *Songs and Dances of Death*—which may, indeed, have arisen from it—inspired by a painting by the famous realistic war-painter, V. V. Vereshchagin: one of his records of the recent campaign in Turkestan exhibited in Petersburg that year, showing the abandoned body of a Russian soldier. (This was one of three pictures so bitterly attacked as anti-patriotic that the painter destroyed them and afterwards suffered a nervous breakdown.) Mussorgsky's 'ballad' is grimly effective, with a 'lullaby' ending anticipating that of the *Trepak*, though in this case the lullaby is the musical symbol of the soldier's wife and baby awaiting his return. But the song is inferior to the *Songs and Dances of Death*. *The Vision* is of little account: it is quite different in style, belonging really to the same group as the five settings of Alexey Tolstoy written the same year: *Not like thunder, trouble struck; Softly the spirit flew up to heaven;* [1] *Pride ;* [2] *Is spinning man's work?; It scatters and breaks.*

None of these is very important. *Pride,* a picture of a pompous, snobbish little parvenu, is amusing but lacks the bite of the earlier satires. It is not particularly realistic, but visual suggestion—here the absurd self-satisfied strut—has, as usual, sharpened Mussorgsky's invention. Lacking that 'lens,' the gently elegiac verse of the other poems failed to focus his musical imagination at all sharply. The flow of even crotchets no longer serves as the vehicle for an idiot's love-making or a street urchin's ribaldry; it now has to convey purely lyrical emotion, to reflect moods of quiet melancholy; and it does this rather inadequately. The piano parts consist either of the ineffective block chords or still less effective tremolo passages. *It scatters and breaks*—a momentary lifting of the cloud of melancholy, which descends again later—is more vigorous and clear in definition. The most nearly Mussorgskian of these Alexey Tolstoy songs is the one in which the composer was able to express his disgust at his office-drudgery: 'Is spinning man's work? . . . Is it for the minstrel to slave at a desk?' But the song is more curious than satisfying.

After *The Nursery* Mussorgsky wrote only three more songs to his own words, *Epitaph* (also known as *Evil Death*; 1874), *The Nettle Mountain* (1874) and *Sphinx* (1875), of which the last was the only one he completed [3] and even that remained unpublished until 1911. All these are in the nature of musical footnotes to Mussorgsky's biography. The only one of artistic value is the *Epitaph* for Nadezhda Opochinina, beautiful and deeply felt if by no means one of his greatest songs. *The Sphinx* is a tribute to another woman friend, Naumov's much-slandered mistress, Marya Kostyurina, and *The Nettle Mountain* was to have been a companion-piece to *The Peepshow*. Before the animals' sanhedrim on the Nettle Mountain the cock (Mussorgsky) is to be arraigned by the crab (the conservative critic and friend of Tchaïkovsky, Hermann Laroche) for crowing too much; the accusation is to be supported by the old blind bear and the rhinoceros

---

[1] Afterwards set by Tchaïkovsky, Op. 47, No. 2 (1880), and Rimsky-Korsakov, Op. 27, No. 1 (1882).

[2] Also set by Borodin after his friend's death.

[3] *The Epitaph* was completed by Karatïgin and published in 1912.

(the violinist Maurer and the double-bassist Ferrero who, it will be remembered, were members of the Opera Committee which rejected the original *Boris*), the marmoset (one Ribatsov, a piano-teacher and conductor), the sloth (Azanchevsky, Zaremba's successor at the Petersburg Conservatory), the manatee (Fedorov, an official of the imperial theatres), the ram (Mussorgsky's old butt Famintsïn), the bug (Soloviev, a minor composer and friend of Serov) and others. But judging by the forty-three-bar fragment which is all that has survived,[1] the humour of the music is extremely feeble; probably Mussorgsky abandoned the thing as a failure.

The tale of his songs is completed by two settings of translations from the German: *The Wanderer*, Pleshcheev's version of Rückert's *Abendlied des Wanderers* ('Wie sich Schatten dehnen Vom Gebirg zum See'; 1878) and the *Song of the Flea* from Strugovshchikov's translation of Goethe's *Faust* (1879). Both are insignificant, and one can only regret that the popularity of the latter has resulted in Mussorgsky's being most widely known as a song composer by one of his least typical works.

The fact that Mussorgsky's career as a song composer ends with inferior work—reflecting the general decline in his powers during the last few years of his life—in no way invalidates his claim to be considered one of the world's great song writers, certainly one of the most original. Mussorgsky was not merely a great innovator in his songs; he was great in achievement; how great we really see for the first time when we stand back and consider] his truly extraordinary versatility and resourcefulness. Even in the realistic group, despite the limitations set by the minimum-of-formalization principle, the styles range from continuous recitative to complex, perfectly shaped and organized song forms. The recitative ranges from the intentional monotone of *Savishna* to the strong contrasts in the *Lullaby* in the *Songs and Dances of Death*, or the free rhapsody of *The Cockchafer*. Elsewhere, we find perfectly rounded-off and balanced arrangements in stanza form or in contrasting sections, with recurring motives on a refrain making for unity (*Peasant Lullaby*, *Kalistrat*).

The function of the piano, too, varies greatly. It may provide an

---

[1] Published in vol. v, part 10, of the complete edition (1939).

accompaniment pure and simple (*Savishna, Hopak, Forgotten,* etc.) or one that aims more specifically at colouring and emphasizing the vocal line (*Epitaph,* most of *The Nursery*); or one whose pantomimic quality suggests attitudes and gestures (*Kalistrat, Eremushka, The Raga-muffin,* etc.). It may also evoke the setting most convincingly (*Trepak, The wild winds blow, On the Dnieper,* etc.). In the *Elegy* in *Sunless* it opens the elusive febrile vistas to which the words allude.

One all-important practical point remains to be made. There exist no traditions for the interpretation of Mussorgsky's music. But one has long been forming which (abomination of abominations!) tends not to interpret it but to regard it as raw material to be worked upon and improved on. This was, let it be repeated, Rimsky-Korsakov's attitude to *Boris Godunov*. But *Boris* will surely vindicate itself, whereas the song repertory stands in great danger. Of late years certain Russian singers have set a nefarious example by introducing gags, changes of tempo and tone, even grunts and hiccoughs, and gramophone recordings exist of these sins against the spirit. How one longs for an antidote! Did there but exist recordings of Mussorgsky's own performances of them (all contemporaries agree they were perfection), of those of Petrov, the great bass whom he regarded as his ideal exponent, of Marie Olenin d'Alheim, whose recitals in 1896 and after were the first steps towards his vindication! But, to turn away from idle dreams, let it be hoped that singers will realize that Mussorgsky's texts are as binding as Schubert's, Schumann's, Fauré's or Ravel's, and that to ignore this truth is to open the road to sheer vandalism.

CHAPTER VII

STAGE WORKS BEFORE 'BORIS'

MUSSORGSKY, so patently preappointed by nature to compose dramatic music, never thought of handling a Russian subject until 1868, except for the projected work 'in three acts, after a Gogol tale' [presumably *St. John's Eve*], mentioned on a slip of paper of 1859. This plan dwindled in 1860 into 'setting one act of Mengden's play *The Witches*'; and the ultimate outcome was the tone-picture *St. John's Night on the Bare Mountain,* in its two forms: orchestral, 1867, and choral, more elaborate, finally set down as part of *Sorochintsy Fair*; both very effective and fit for concert performance. Of all his other [operatic] plans only one, *Boris Godunov,* was carried out to [completion].

[From Mussorgsky's earliest stage-work, *Oedipus in Athens* (1858–61), only one number survives, a choral scene in the temple of the Eumenides. Musically it is not very significant, yet it is interesting for two reasons: because Mussorgsky thought well enough of it to adapt it, as we shall see presently, for insertion in three later works—*Salammbô, Mlada* and *Sorochintsy Fair*—and because it has been the subject of a most remarkable blunder which was not detected even by Paul Lamm in his monumental complete edition of Mussorgsky's works.[1] Both Mussorgsky himself and Stassov spoke—with the cheerful inexactitude common to them—of 'music to Sophocles' tragedy *Oedipus,*' and from that day to this, although the chorus in question was both performed and published, no one noticed that it could not have occurred in either *Oedipus Tyrannus* or *Oedipus Coloneus,* and that it quite obviously was adapted from a well-known Russian tragedy *Oedipus in Athens* (produced in 1804) by a well-known dramatist of the pre-Pushkin age: V. A. Ozerov (1769–1816). Ozerov's play covers the same ground as *Oedipus Coloneus,* but deviates widely from the Sophoclean and traditional account of things. Instead of giving Oedipus and his daughter sanctuary, the Athenians demand his death—at least, the death of a victim—to avert

[1] See his introduction to vol. vi of the complete edition (Russian State Publishing Company, Moscow, 1939).

misfortune from their country; Oedipus, Antigone and Polynices contend for this fate, but finally it is Creon who is, most properly, sacrificed. Mussorgsky's Temple scene does not correspond precisely to any situation in Ozerov (which proves that he was not merely writing incidental music to the play), but stands in as close a relation to Ozerov as do most operas to the plays or novels they are based on. The earliest of the three autograph versions in which the scene survives,[1] and the only one with stage directions, is actually inscribed 'Scene in the temple, from the tragedy *Oedipus in Athens*.' According to the stage direction, which is mis-copied from Ozerov, the scene represents 'the interior of the temple. The temple is divided into two parts; in the farther one are seen an altar and three statues of gods' (*sic*: Ozerov knew that the Eumenides were goddesses). 'The people are gathering in the temple, all in fearful expectation. The priests are finishing the ritual for the taking of the consecrated sword and for the sacrifice.' The orchestra, throughout rather more important than the chorus (which often merely doubles it), begins a rushing figure:

to which the people ejaculate, at first in a hushed *staccato*: 'What will happen to us? How will all this tribulation end? Will the mighty gods accept the victim and redeem us from our affliction? Will innocent blood save us, the sinful?' As this grows in a *crescendo* of fear the priests join in with a powerful invocation to the gods to bless the sacrificial sword. Oedipus enters with Antigone and Polynices; the Chief Priest appears, sword in hand; at the sight of Oedipus the people recoil and cry out in horror. There is a clap of thunder (stroke on the gong) and then in a twelve-bar *adagio* coda in F (Lydian mode) the priests murmur: 'Accept our victim, O ye gods! Have mercy on us!'

[1] Dated '23rd January 1859.' This is the only version for double chorus, male chorus of priests and full chorus of people; in the autograph of 1860 and 1861 the priests disappear, their parts being transferred to the full chorus.

'Oedipus' and 'Salammbô'

It has always been supposed that no more of the Oedipus music has survived. But we know from a letter to Balakirev that during August–September 1860 Mussorgsky wrote two other choruses— an *andante* in B flat minor ('my last mystic outpouring') and an *allegro* in E flat major—both for 'the introduction to Oedipus'; and I would point out that Act III of *Salammbô* opens with a chorus in B flat minor, marked 'Slow,' which leads without a break into another chorus in E flat, marked 'Medium speed.' Moreover, both these choruses are for priests and people; the scene is, in fact, the temple of Moloch. The F minor Temple scene from *Oedipus* was, as we shall see in a moment, transferred to *Salammbô*; is it not reasonable to suppose that these two choruses before the temple of Moloch originated as the choruses, mentioned to Balakirev, in the temple of the Eumenides? The matter becomes doubly interesting when one realizes that the B flat minor chorus contains the themes (cf. examples, pages 102–3) of Boris's monologue in Scene v of *Boris Godunov* and that the E flat chorus (cf. example, page 103) is the original form of the triumphal music of the Pretender in the so-called Revolution scene of the same opera.

Mussorgsky began to compose his *Salammbô* (or *The Libyan,* as he sometimes called it) in December 1863, beginning with Act I, Scene ii, and worked at it fitfully till April–June 1866, when he wrote and orchestrated the 'War Song of the Libyans' for Act I. The libretto—of which, as of the music, only fragments were ever written —was devised by the composer himself. I say 'devised' deliberately, for Mussorgsky not only drew heavily on Flaubert for stage directions, descriptions of scenery, costumes and so on, but pillaged the pages of Zhukovsky, Maykov, Polezhaev and other Russian poets for suitable verses. As Stassov pointed out,

the scenes are full of dramatic movement, almost Meyerbeerian in style, usually representing masses of people at moments of tremendous emotional excitement; scenes with individual characters play an incomparably less important part.

As nearly as one can judge in the absence of a scenario, the action was to have been as follows:

Act I. The Feast of the Mercenaries in Hamilcar's garden as described in Flaubert's opening chapter. The Libyan, Mâtho and the soldiers free the slave Spendius. Appearance of Hamilcar's daughter Salammbô and her lament: 'Ah! pauvre Carthage! lamentable ville!' Both Mâtho and the Numidian prince Narr'Havas fall in love with her. They quarrel but are reconciled.

Act II, Scene i presumably showed the revolt of the mercenaries, led by Mâtho. Spendius's account of the magic power of the *Zaïmph*, the sacred mantle of the moon goddess Tanit, whose chief priestess (according to Mussorgsky though not in Flaubert) was Salammbô. Mâtho and Spendius determine to enter Carthage by secret passages and carry off the *Zaïmph*.

Scene ii. The Temple of Tanit. Salammbô addresses Tanit; worship of Tanit. Mâtho and Spendius carry off the *Zaïmph*. Salammbô gives the alarm. Consternation of the Carthaginians.

Act III, Scene i. The Temple of Moloch. The Carthaginians pray to the giant image of the god to whom they are about to sacrifice children. Salammbô's lament. She resolves to go to the camp of the mercenaries and retrieve the *Zaïmph* from Mâtho's tent.

Scene ii. We know nothing of this scene, but presumably Mussorgsky intended to show Salammbô seducing Mâtho in his tent[1] and carrying off the *Zaïmph*. Possibly also the Carthaginian attack on the camp, the treachery of Narr'Havas, the defeat of the rebel mercenaries and capture of Mâtho.

Act IV, Scene i. Mâtho in the dungeon. The chief priest comes with the pentarchs and priests to pronounce sentence on him.

Scene ii. The priestesses dress Salammbô in wedding garments (she is to marry Narr'Havas)—and then, presumably, the torture and death of Mâtho, and Salammbô's death.

This unfinishable torso of an opera would hardly be worth discussing for its own sake; but it happens to contain many of the musical germs of no less important a masterpiece than *Boris Godunov*.

The music of the first act need not detain us long; only two numbers were written, the incongruously pseudo-oriental song of a young

---

[1] It is impossible to believe that Mussorgsky was not to some extent influenced in his choice of this subject by the parallels with Serov's *Judith*, which had been produced in May 1863, just six months before he began *Salammbô*; but there is no trace of any musical influence.

Balearic slinger, which Mussorgsky included in the already mentioned volume of manuscript songs styled *Years of Youth,* and the choral 'War Song of the Libyans' which in 1877 was given a new middle section, based on part of Mâtho's monologue in the dungeon, and resuscitated as the work we know as *Jesus Navin.*[1] But the second act is important. Salammbô's first prayer is not specially interesting and the music—intended to be played by a small orchestra behind the scenes—that accompanies her silent devotions continues in the same rather weakly lyrical, quite uncharacteristic vein. But when Salammbô softly addresses 'gentle Tanit' the music suddenly sounds familiar; we find ourselves transported from the moonlit catafalque in Hamilcar's Carthage to the great hall in the Kremlin where the dying Boris is praying for his children. As this is only the first of some dozen passages in *Salammbô* that were afterwards transferred to *Boris Godunov,* it is worth while to pause and consider how such transferences were possible, how indeed they could be even considered by a composer with Mussorgsky's yearnings for 'dramatic truth.' To begin with, the musical ideas that are the basis of both Salammbô's prayer to Tanit and Boris's prayer for his children were not simply copied from one scene into the other. The voice parts—in each case superimposed on an orchestral stream of thought containing the essence of the music—are completely different. And this orchestral part was also condensed and purified in *Boris*: four bars of banality cut out, the harmony made simpler and less luscious. Here for instance are two equivalent passages:

(a) Salammbô

Very slowly (half-asleep)

Pri-mi me-nya, pri-mi! K te-be i-du,

Orch.

---

[1] See page 183. It is typical of the Russian, rather than pseudo-Carthaginian, flavour of the *Salammbô* music that this 'War Song' has considerable affinity with the *allegro* portion of the song *On the Dnieper* written the same year.

All the same, the music is *essentially* identical. And there is good reason in the texts why it should be. Boris is praying as he dies; Salammbô is not dying, but she is going to sleep—at the end she goes to sleep—and she is praying. And though the substance of her prayer is very different from Boris's, there are key-words in both which establish a certain connection. She prays that the 'bright form' of the moon goddess may 'keep' her dreams and 'lead them from suffering and evil to love and happiness,' and she ends: 'Hear me, O Tanit! Take me! I go to thee!' Boris prays to God: 'Pour Thy beneficent light on my innocent children . . . with Thy bright wings keep them from woe and evil.' (I am translating as literally as possible, so as to preserve the verbal identities of the two Russian texts). A bright, beneficent image warding off evil: that is the conception common to both passages. And in practically every case, as we shall see, the transference of music from *Salammbô* to *Boris* was similarly justified by identity or near-identity of emotional or dramatic content, an identity made more vivid in several cases by textual parallels. The transferences are never note-for-note and concern the orchestral parts only; they vary considerably as regards the amount of alteration Mussorgsky found necessary, but it is clear that he preferred wherever possible to keep the passages in their original keys (as in the examples above). Study of his emendations of harmony and part-writing is instructive, too.

The choral 'Hymn to Tanit,' sung while Salammbô sleeps, is remarkable for the Berliozian orchestral colour-effects Mussorgsky projected; notably combinations of harp, glockenspiel and piano (four hands), the last being treated purely as an orchestral instrument on these lines:

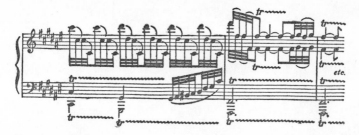

After the appearance of Mâtho and Spendius, who hide behind a pillar, the hymn anticipates the Pretender's love-making in the Fountain scene of *Boris* (the passage beginning "'Tis you alone, Marina'); and the recitative in which Mâtho expresses his wonder at the 'divine, marvellous singing,' a little later, was also used again in the Fountain scene (at the words 'You break my loving heart'). Here, exceptionally, it is difficult to see any real parallel between the two situations, though Mussorgsky might have argued that there is some connection between adoration of a goddess and adoration of a young woman, and that both Mâtho and the Pretender were amorous young men. But the truth is that the music is rather inexpressive and of little value.

The thieves take the *Zaïmph*, awakening Salammbô, and Mâtho tells her he is the leader of the mutinous Libyans, 'the mortal enemy of Carthage,' to the accompaniment of the motive of the Libyan war song from Act I (which is heard once again in the Dungeon scene). Suddenly she notices that he has the *Zaïmph* and calls down curses on his head; instead of fleeing Mâtho stays and, if he could get in a word, would plead his love, but Spendius drags him away by force—all this to music which was later used, with far fewer changes than in most of the borrowings, for the attempted lynching of the Jesuits in the last scene of *Boris*. The music might serve for almost any type of agitated scene, but Mussorgsky had the real pretext of a parallel between Salammbô's cursing of Mâtho and Varlaam's (and the crowd's) abuse of the Jesuits, between Spendius dragging off Mâtho and the crowd dragging off their victims. The score of *Salammbô* makes it clear that the figure:

originated as a 'dragging' motive; it appears each time Spendius tries to get his companion away. As the thieves disappear, Salammbô gives the alarm by strokes on a gong, and under a string tremolo we hear, *pp* and *staccato,* the rushing quavers from *Oedipus in Athens* (see example on page 96). And as the priestesses of Tanit rush in, followed by the populace in general, the whole of that 'Temple scene' is repeated in all essentials, with only changes of detail.[1]

Here, too, there is justification in the dramatic parallel. In both cases the music expresses the agitation and terror of priests (or priestesses) and people in face (or anticipation) of a national calamity. The Greeks demand the death of a victim; the Carthaginians demand the death of the thief. In the hushed *adagio* conclusion—now a little more complicated harmonically, and its Lydian character removed by a sprinkling of B flats—the Greeks pray: 'Accept our victim, O ye gods! Have pity on us!' and the Carthaginians pray: 'Protect us, O Tanit! Save us from woe!'

I have already expressed my view that the great choral scene before the temple of Moloch (Act III, Scene i), which follows this in the score, also originated in the *Oedipus* music. From this music, full of a sense of prostration before an angry and merciless deity, Mussorgsky was able to draw the themes which expressed the gloom and sorrow of his criminal tsar (Scene v of *Boris*):

[1] The *Salammbô* version is closer to the 1861 autograph of the *Oedipus* chorus than to the original conception.

while the innocent music of the children about to be sacrificed to Moloch possibly gave him a hint for the theme that accompanies the boy-tsarevich's geography lesson earlier in the same scene and his appearance in the Death scene. (The Tsarevich Feodor is a child who is to be sacrificed to the Moloch of politics.) When the sacrifice has been completed the priests of Moloch form a procession, singing 'Hail, O Moloch! Hail, O Avenger!':

This is the E flat chorus which I believe to have been originally part of the *Oedipus* music; it was ultimately transferred to the last scene of *Boris,* for the appearance of the troops of the Pretender, the false Dimitry. Again there is a verbal connection, for the troops sing 'Hail, O Tsarevich' (though the chorus parts are entirely different), and it might be argued that the Pretender is also an 'avenger' (he is so called elsewhere in the opera), the avenger of the true Dimitry murdered by Boris. But the essence of the music lies, in both cases, in its triumphant, processional character.

Priests and people move away and Salammbô, emerging from the temple, laments 'Woe to us, woe; in our hearts is sorrow!' the voices of the people, now distant, answer from the Grove of Esch-moûn to a slightly modified version of the example at the top of page 103: 'Protect us. Give us the victory.' Salammbô, after a mystic trance, resolves to go to the Libyan camp and bring back the *Zaïmph*. The people—who have now returned—cry out in horror at the peril of such an adventure, but she is confident in the protective power of Tanit and the *Zaïmph*: 'the foe will be struck with mortal fear.' And as she sings those words the orchestra plays a passage beginning:

which may or may not have originated earlier in the music to Mengden's *Witches* or the projected opera on Gogol's *St. John's Eve*, but which was certainly incorporated three years later in the orchestral piece *St. John's Night on the Bare Mountain*.

From the scene of Mâtho in the dungeon a whole group of themes was transferred to the Duma scene in *Boris*. Mâtho foresees that his enemies will doom him 'to death and shame and torture.' And later the pentarchs come and read his sentence: among other unpleasant details 'his tongue is to be given to the crows to feed on . . . his body itself is to be given to the flames . . . and his accursed ashes thrown to the four winds.' Both these passages are set to music which was used again in *Boris* at the point where the boyars pass sentence on the Pretender: 'Let the scoundrel taste the rack and thumbscrew. And then the gallows . . . on his flesh let crows and ravens feed. Let his body be burnt to ashes . . . and let his accursed ashes be scattered to the wind.' (As this scene does not occur in Pushkin, it is not impossible that Mussorgsky introduced it as a pretext for using an effective piece of music.) And this parallel not unnaturally suggested that the solemn music accompanying the arrival of the priests of Moloch to pass sentence on Mâtho might be used to herald the gathering of the boyars to pass sentence on the Pretender (cf. example at the bottom of page 112). But one other passage common to these two scenes needs a little more explanation. In *Salammbô* it is the orchestral commentary on Mâtho's thoughts of the Numidian king, Narr'Havas:[1] 'Foul traitor! I had you like a woman under my heel and I pardoned you. Pretending to forget the insults at the drunken feast, you long harboured your grudge against me. And secretly sought the alliance of the enemy. And bartered the blood of a thousand brave comrades for the gold of the Carthaginian merchants!' In *Boris* this becomes the orchestral commentary on Shuisky's account of the tsar's hallucinations; he has been spying on his master: 'Pallid, aghast, in cold sweat bathed and quaking, he staggered moaning, oft muttering strange words, wild, unconnected words of terror.' There is obviously

[1] Oddly enough, Mussorgsky also introduced at this point the opening bar of his *Intermezzo,* presumably as a 'Narr'Havas' motive. This was the theme suggested by the spectacle of Russian peasants plunging through deep snow (see page 170)!

no connection between the two texts; the explanation, I suggest, lies in the character of Shuisky. Shuisky, too, is a crafty man who has plotted against Boris under a mask of fidelity. And so the *Salammbô* scene throws light on this curious music, with which Mussorgsky must have intended afterwards to suggest, not Boris's terror, but Shuisky's treachery.

The part of Mâtho's monologue immediately preceding the appear' ance of the priests of Moloch is based textually on a poem by A. I. Polezhaev, a *Song of the Captive Iroquois,* beginning 'I shall die! I shall give my defenceless body to the executioner!' The melody to which it is set here (see example on page 183) was in 1877 adapted, with a good deal of arabesque elaboration, as the middle section (alto solo) of the chorus *Jesus Navin.* The chorus of priestesses consoling Salammbô and dressing her in her wedding garments, the only other surviving fragment of the opera, has lyrical beauty and bears the unmistakable marks of Mussorgsky's invention; but its underlying melancholy—Salammbô is secretly sorrowing for the hated yet loved Mâtho—made it unsuitable for the nearly parallel situation in the Polish act of *Boris Godunov.*

The score of *Salammbô,* fragmentary as it is, shows that Mussorgsky's lyrical vein (or as Rimsky'Korsakov called it, his 'ideal style') was already nearly fully developed quite early in the sixties. But this ideal, lyrical style represents only one side of his genius—which shows itself at its highest only where it is fused, as in *Boris Godunov,* with his realistic, remorselessly 'truthful' style. Before he was fit to write *Boris* he had to exercise himself in that realistic style, and he did so in a work which has absolutely nothing in common with *Salammbô,* which is both dramatically and musically at the opposite pole from it: the setting of Gogol's prose comedy *The Marriage,* of which only one act was completed.[1] *Salammbô* is antique, exotic, romantic tragedy in which individuals are lost amid chorus and *décor*; *The Marriage* is contemporary Russian anti'romantic farce entirely concerned with individuals and with no chorus at all.]

The Marriage is excellent comedy. It does not go very far, but covers the ground well so far as it goes. It deals with a government

[1] The other three acts were composed, not very successfully, by Ippolitov' Ivanov in 1934.

clerk, Podkolessin, who, wishing to get married, has secured the services of a marriage broker, Fekla. Whether he tries to find out if his neighbours are duly interested in his plans, or listens to Fekla describing the advantages of her *parti,* or whether his friend Kochkarev (who in his time has been beguiled by Fekla into marrying, to his everlasting regret) watches to see if he will fall for the line, the first act is very much in the key. It is a comedy of manners, or rather of behaviour. One may take it or leave it, but no good purpose will be served by seeking for what is not there. It is also unlikely that the other acts would have brought new elements into play. So Mussorgsky was probably well advised to give it up as soon as he had found in Nikolsky's suggestion of *Boris Godunov* a better field of inspiration.

The story afforded him plenty of opportunity for brisk, picturesque, realistic dialogue and humorous characterization, without any pretence of psychological depth. The first act shows Podkolessin discussing matters with his loutish valet Stepan, Kochkarev and Fekla.

As he himself put it in his letter [of 15th/27th August 1868] to Rimsky-Korsakov, he had to face 'particularly erratic harmonic conditions,' and rhythmic conditions too. The prose text precluded all possibilities of formalization, not only of the conventional kind (such as those against which he inveighed apropos of *Antar*—see pages 29–30), but even of the most straightforward and legitimate kind; not only in the shaping of motives and phrases, but also in their use and functions in the musical tissue. How to achieve consistency and continuity was a formidable problem. Formal tonal plans and rhythmic periodicity would have stiffened the dialogue and retarded the pace. His solution betokens not only a strong sense of discrimination, but full command of the means selected.

As regards tonal balance, for instance, it will be noticed that although the harmonies are ever shifting, although there is no centre of any duration, and hardly any two successive cadences point in the same direction, no feeling of ambiguity or neutrality ever arises. The ground may be undefinable most of the time, but it remains firm underfoot.

Harmony is the least salient feature: the texture is almost purely linear, chords being used to bring out and reinforce the linear patterns rather than to provide harmonic definition. Intensity and variety are achieved by contrasts of light and shade, pace and accents. Colour proper plays hardly any part in the scheme, which might be said to be one of black and white. There is no suggestion of con-templated special orchestral effects, no exploitation of the particular sonorous properties of the piano, not even of the colours of its extreme registers, which are hardly used. In short, the further we proceed in our survey, the more we realize how perfect an example of economy and restraint we are dealing with.

How secondary a part harmony plays in the scheme is shown by the fact that the composer, who elsewhere avoids stereotypes most carefully, resorts here without a qualm to cut-and-dried formulae such as sequences of diminished sevenths. But he uses them as accents, not as pigments. And the same may be said of the seconds and consecutive seconds that suddenly appear here and there: they naturally fall into place within the black-and-white scheme—one in which not even the colour-begetting properties of tonal contrast are called into play.

As he based his structural scheme neither on tonal relations nor on rhythmic proportions, he had no option but to base it on thematic continuity and interrelations. He was the first Russian to use the *Leitmotiv* principle freely and methodically; and *The Marriage* is the first work in which [we can study his use of it]. The notion must have been suggested to him by Wagner's example; but Liszt's method of theme-transformation influenced him more directly.

All the themes except one are 'characterizing' themes associated with one person, their shape and rhythm being suggested by that person's demeanour, attitudes and gestures; in other words, they are descriptive and pantomimic.

Thus for the loutish Stepan:

For Fekla fussing and bobbing:

or breathlessly chattering:

A brusque run up and down reflects Kochkarev's bull‑in‑a‑china‑shop manners. And in connection with Podkolessin [there is a theme:

suggesting the rhythm of a gesture of helplessness, in addition to] the theme quoted on page 31, the main one of the score, to which a general rather than a pantomimic significance (perplexity: 'to marry or not to marry') may be ascribed. All these themes, plastic, well differentiated, striking yet not obtrusive, are splendid texture‑binding materials: all the more so because, brief as they are, they lend themselves to sub‑division into segments whose origin is unmistakable even when they consist of three or four notes only or, at times, of two.

The treatment of the vocal parts is most interesting. Mussorgsky achieved marvels in the matter of inflections, pitch and pace. Lyricism and expression of the deep emotions were not part of his scheme any more than they were of Gogol's. But within this limit the pregnancy and variety of the dialogue are [remarkable]. Every‑thing is natural and flowing. The music illustrates most of the characteristics of the style of maturity—indeed, all of them, except for certain points of modality, harmony and tonal structure, and for the relation of his idiom to that of Russian folk‑music. The line runs on, rises, falls freely and soberly. Exaggeration and distortion are carefully avoided. Long note-values are never used, and big leaps hardly ever—just occasionally, to provide a touch of emphasis. Never did he carry so far the avoidance of long note-values: practic-ally all the work is done by values ranging from the crotchet to the semiquaver, with additional variety provided by triplets and similar devices. Dotted crotchets are few, and only three instances occur of longer values. Strange to say, there are very few changes of time signature. Yet, when he started work on *The Marriage*, he had already carried out the boldest of his experiments in that direction (and a very successful one) in [the first song of the *Nursery* cycle].

The dialogue proceeds without interruption of any length. The shortest breaks suffice for entrances, stage action and exits (as happens also, comparatively speaking, in *Boris Godunov*). The first scene begins with a six-bar instrumental preamble. Seven bars form the transition to the second, which ends with a four-bar conclusion—not cadential: in fact, it consists entirely of minor seconds in octaves. Three bars usher in the third scene, six bars the fourth. The act ends with a stretch of thirteen bars, in which four of the themes bustlingly follow one another. The unbroken, unswerving motion contributes almost as much to the unity of the whole as its thematic structure does. But, of course, the value of a structure depends, ultimately, upon the [skilful] exploitation of the materials rather than upon its formal merits. In *The Marriage* most of the work is done by the handful of leading motives.

CHAPTER VIII

THE MUSIC OF 'BORIS GODUNOV'

In *Boris Godunov* we have, on the one hand, a group of themes referring to the tsar—these may be called, for short, the 'distress' theme (first heard in the Coronation scene), the 'anger' theme and the 'majesty' theme (both first heard in his great monologue). Then, on the other hand, the theme of Dimitry the tsarevich which, like the 'distress' theme, has its roots in the opening theme of the prologue:

This plain, folk-tune-like, unaccompanied melody, which may have been invented by Mussorgsky, or borrowed more or less textually from Russia's musical lore, constitutes a fitting exordium to the work. It suggests the vast, peaceful setting; it is contemplative, melancholy and resigned enough to stand as an expression of the peasant soul of old Russia; and it lends itself quite well to the quick change leading up to the bustle revealed by the rise of the curtain. [But it is something more than that; it is indeed] actually the embryo of many of the principal themes used in the score. Its function is very similar to that of the 'motto' theme in an instrumental work of the 'cyclic' type. Portions of it, or forms derived from it, are used throughout the various acts, often quite deliberately but at times, no doubt, without conscious intention.

The Dimitry motive is perhaps the most important in the whole score by virtue of the part it plays. Far more than any motive used in relation to Boris himself, it creates a link between the various scenes, reappearing practically in each in some form or other, always with a very relevant purpose, so that its musical relation to the opening tune would suffice to justify our considering this tune as a kind of cyclic 'motto' theme. It first appears in the scene in Pimen's cell, when the murder of the tsarevich Dimitry is mentioned. It accompanies Grigory, the young monk who decides to pose as Dimitry escaped from death, throughout his wanderings; one hears it connected with him in the scene at the inn, during the Polish act, and in the final scene of the people in revolt. We hear it during the scene between Boris and Shuisky, when both the murdered tsarevich and his impersonator are topics of discussion; and again during Boris's hallucination. It affects many forms and colours; it is in turn tragical, poetically mystical, impassioned, sardonic and martial. Here is a quotation from the prelude to the scene at the inn, in which the iteration especially will show how closely it is connected with patterns B and C in the example on page 111 (see notes marked *):

[The 'distress'] motive which underlines the tsar's first appearance (Coronation scene) and, again, his entry in Act II:

is obviously related to the Dimitry motive. The notes are practically the same, only the rhythm is more forcible, and the end is altered for obvious expressive reasons. Intermediate forms occur, which confirm the derivation. A certain pattern [from *Salammbô* (cf. example, page 102)] extensively used in Boris's big monologue:

is connected with pattern A in the opening tune.

In the Duma scene we encounter several elements recalling the same pattern, e.g.:

It is probably a mere coincidence that more than once we should notice a similar pattern in the music underlining Shuisky's crafty utterances. Although distant, the connection between the opening tune and the wild motive whose outbreak marks the climax of the crowd's boisterousness in the final scene:

is plain enough. Again it is quite likely that this is no more than a coincidence. But such coincidences in the music of *Boris* are so numerous that the more one studies the score, the more one doubts that most of them are anything but the outcome of a deliberate purpose. Even if we eliminate all but the most obviously intentional relations, there is no dearth of evidence to show how far-sightedly the opening of *Boris Godunov* was conceived and how skilfully all its possibilities are exploited. [Nor does this account exhaust the *Leitmotiv* material of *Boris*:] we also have accessory themes, notably one for the police officials and one for the rogue monk Varlaam.

The most extraordinary thing is that a score in which the principle of the *Leitmotiv* is turned to so remarkable an account should have been written in Russia in the year 1868. At that time the principle was a novelty, illustrated only in Wagner's works. *The Ring*, which was finally to establish the vogue of the *Leitmotiv* method and render the machinery of the process available to all composers, was not yet published, and Wagner's works were not very widely known in Europe, let alone Russia. Yet the question arises whether Mussorgsky, in this respect, was influenced by Wagner's music or theories. Considering the evidence, we can hardly doubt that he was, although there is in *Boris Godunov* no trace of the slavish imitation or of the mechanical procedure to which the adoption of Wagner's methods led many composers. Let it be remembered that Wagner came to Petersburg as early as 1863; that is, before Mussorgsky had started planning *Boris Godunov*. And five years before, the composer and critic Serov, an enthusiastic admirer of Wagner, had launched upon an energetic campaign of propaganda in his favour.

[But after all the musical fabric of *Boris* exists only as the expression of a dramatic content, and it is time to examine that content a little more closely. It sometimes strikes non-Russian listeners as loosely constructed; as will be shown presently, that is not at all true—yet it must be admitted that the average non-Russian member of the audience lacks one element of connecting knowledge possessed by every Russian member: acquaintance with Pushkin's play, which was the main source of Mussorgsky's libretto.[1] Pushkin's play is itself very different from a conventional, 'well-made' five-act, blank-verse tragedy. Modelled generally on Shakespeare's chronicle plays, it is not divided into acts at all but into twenty-four scenes of varying length, some in prose, but the majority in blank verse:

I. The Kremlin Palace (20th February 1598): Prince Shuisky and Vorotïnsky, neither an enthusiastic admirer of Boris, discuss his refusal to accept the crown.

II. The Red Square: the people lament Boris's refusal; the chief secretary Shchelkalov appears and announces that the boyars and people are to make one more appeal to Boris.

III. The Novodevichy Monastery: the people first weep to order—then obediently acclaim Boris.

IV. The Kremlin: Boris graciously greets the boyars; after his exit Shuisky and Vorotïnsky murmur together.

V. Cell in the Chudov Monastery (1603): the old monk Pimen is writing his chronicle; the young novice Grigory induces him to tell the story of the murder of the young tsarevich Dimitry in 1591.

VI. Palace of the Patriarch: the abbot of the Chudov Monastery informs the Patriarch that Grigory has run away announcing that one day he 'will reign in Moscow.'

VII. The Tsar's Palace: monologue of Boris, weighed down by the misfortunes that have overtaken his family and realm; at the end he betrays his guilty conscience in the matter of the murdered tsarevich by a reference to the visions of 'bloody boys' that haunt him.

VIII. Inn on the Lithuanian border: Grigory in the company of two vagabond monks, Varlaam and Misail; police officers arrive in search of the runaway; Grigory by a ruse escapes.

[1]For a detailed study of the relationship between play and libretto see *Music & Letters*, January 1945.

IX. Shuisky's house: Pushkin (an ancestor of the poet) tells Shuisky that the tsarevich 'Dimitry' (really the runaway Grigory) has appeared in Poland and is gathering Polish adherents and Muscovite malcontents.

X. The Tsar's Palace: Boris with his children, Feodor and Xenia; Shuisky brings the news of the false Dimitry's appearance.

XI. Wisnioviecki's house at Cracow: the Pretender is seen with the Catholic Father Czernikowski, Muscovite refugees and others.

XII. Castle of the Wojewoda Mniszek at Sambor: Mniszek's daughter Marina is being dressed by her women to captivate the Pretender.

XIII. Suite of lighted rooms in the castle: Mniszek, Wisnioviecki and others discuss the Pretender's infatuation with Marina.

XIV. Garden and fountain at night: the Pretender, unable to deceive his beloved, confesses that he is only a runaway monk; Marina—cold and ambitious—goads him into continuing the deception.

XV. The Lithuanian border (16th October 1604): the Pretender and his troops cross into Russia.

XVI. The Duma: the Patriarch tells Boris and the boyars of the blind shepherd whose sight was restored by the relics of the murdered Dimitry; he advises that the remains be brought to Moscow and shown to the people to convince them that the Pretender is a fraud.

XVII. Plain near Novgorod-Seversk (21st December 1604): Boris's troops in flight before the Pretender's.

XVIII. Square before St. Basil's Cathedral, Moscow: Boris has heard the anathema pronounced against the Pretender, but as he comes out of the cathedral he is denounced as a murderer by a simpleton in the crowd.

XIX. Seversk: the Pretender interrogates a Russian prisoner.

XX. A forest (31st January 1605): the Pretender is seen after a lost battle.

XXI. The Tsar's Palace: Boris with his victorious general Basmarov; the tsar is taken ill, takes leave of his son Feodor—commending him to Basmanov and the boyars—and dies.

XXII A tent: Basmanov is persuaded to change sides by an emissary from the Pretender.

XXIII. The Red Square: the people obediently acclaim Dimitry.

xxiv. The Godunovs' house in the Kremlin: Dimitry's followers enter the house; screams are heard; an officer announces that Boris's widow and son have committed suicide; he orders the people to cry 'Long live Tsar Dimitry Ivanovich.' 'The people remain silent.' [1]

The orginal version of Mussorgsky's opera (1868–9) consists of seven scenes.

1. The Novodevichy Monastery: freely based on Scenes ii and iii of Pushkin.
2. The Coronation of Boris Godunov: not in Pushkin but introducing part of Boris's speech in iv.
3. Cell in the Chudov Monastery: equivalent to v.
4. Inn at the Lithuanian border: equivalent to viii.
5. Boris and his children; Boris alone; Boris and Shuisky; the hallucination: based on vii and x.
6. Outside St. Basil's; equivalent to xviii.
7. The Duma and Boris's death: based on xvi and xxi.

In the definitive version (1871–4) [2] more than sixty bars were cut from the end of Scene 1; Scene 2 was included with only minor changes; Scene 3 was both cut and added to; the Hostess's song of the duck was inserted into Scene 4; Scene 5 was almost entirely rewritten and Scene 6 was scrapped. Mussorgsky then inserted two new scenes that constitute the so-called 'Polish act': in Marina's room at Sandomierz (Pushkin's Scene xii with a new character, the Jesuit Rangoni, evolved from Pushkin's quite insignificant Czernikowski) and the garden and fountain of Sandomierz (not Sambor) Castle at night (very freely based on hints from Pushkin's xi, xiii

---

[1] That stage direction, which has become proverbial in Russia, was not Pushkin's but the censor's; in Pushkin's original draft the people obediently hailed the new tsar. In the historical sequel—which was depicted operatically by Dvořák in his *Dimitrij*—the false Dimitry quarrelled with Marina and took as his mistress Boris's daughter Xenia; he was then dethroned and killed by Shuisky, who was in turn dethroned by two other claimants including another false Dimitry who married Marina Mniszek.

[2] The second version was mainly worked out in 1871–2, but further changes—mostly cuts—were made in the vocal score of 1874.

and xiv). The fourth act of the definitive version consists of a slightly cut version of Scene 7, followed by an entirely new scene in the clearing of a wood near Kromy, for which there was no Pushkinian original except the glimpse of the victorious Pretender in xv; Czernikowski here turns up under his own name instead of as 'Rangoni'; the Russian peasants are shown in anarchic revolt; and the simpleton and the urchins who tease him are transferred here from the scrapped 'scene before St. Basil's.']

What strikes us when we consider the original version of *Boris* are its starkness and terseness. It does not, like the later version, afford hearers any opportunity for relief. It pursues its grim course without an instant of intermission, except when the tension is relieved awhile by touches of character-comedy in the dialogue (first and sixth scenes, the people; scene at the inn; Feodor and the nurse at the beginning of the fifth scene). And even at these points, there is nothing (except Varlaam's song, 'By the walls of Kazan, the mighty stronghold') that comes as an intermezzo inducing a halt, however brief, in the action. Every one of these touches is part and parcel of the whole.

A very remarkable feature of the original version (one, indeed, that makes it something unique in the history of lyric drama) is that Grigory never reappears after he has effected his escape into Lithuania and begun his activities as the Pretender. He remains in the background, evoked time after time by references made by Shuisky, by Boris, by the people and by the councillors. And these allusions are made doubly pregnant by corresponding reappearances and transformations of the motive (first example on page 127) first introduced in association with the murdered tsarevich. Hence a particular significance attaches to the fact that this motive (as already explained) is used in connection with both the tsarevich and his impersonator —the two unseen terrors haunting Boris and gradually breaking down his resistance, and the two main factors in what is the real tragedy of Mussorgsky's masterpiece: the fate of Russia.

It will presently be seen that in this original version the Dimitry-Grigory motive is introduced far more forcibly and circumstantially than in the definitive version, and that its reappearances are more numerous and emphatic. And it may be added forthwith that in other respects too the structure of the first version is thematically far tighter than that of the 1874 version. Most of the minor cuts in the latter affect passages in which main themes play a part—a curious fact, which suggests that Mussorgsky's anti-Wagnerian friends and counsellors may have had something to do with the selection of the cuts.

In this matter of recurring motives and in other more important respects nothing could be more instructive than a comparison between the original and definitive versions of the scene in the tsar's apartment. Generally speaking, both contain different music, and very beautiful music; so that if either is set aside there is both loss and gain. For instance, the opening of the scene in the original version, with Feodor studying geography aloud while Xenia, his sister, mourns her dead betrothed, is one of the gems of the score. A passage from it in which the contrasting voices combine in charmingly simple and bold manner may be quoted in evidence:

But against this we find, in the later version, the delightful songs which no lover of Mussorgsky would care to sacrifice.

There are big differences in the monologue of Boris, in his dialogue with Shuisky, and in the final hallucination. At the first blush, when one is accustomed to the later version of the monologue, the music of the earlier version may strike one not only as starker (which is a gain if anything) but as rougher, more angular. One may be disconcerted awhile, as one would be by suddenly encountering any familiar work in altered form. But even then one can hardly fail to realize the pregnancy and force of Mussorgsky's first inspiration. What it lacks in romantic colour and sensational contrasts it more than makes up for in terseness and austere grandeur. The music is founded on one theme only—one of several mutually related themes that accompany Boris—and the Dimitry theme appears towards the end.

The psychological differences between the two versions are most clearly brought out by the Russian critic Igor Glebov:

In the second version, Mussorgsky adopts a more sentimental tone. He shows Boris no longer under an aspect of unmitigated grimness, but as a repentant sinner whom he pities. He accordingly imparts to his music a warm, lyrical quality, touching upon distress, repentance, prayer and qualms of conscience in turn . . . In this second version, the music of the middle section of the monologue is borrowed from his earlier *Salammbô*. The music of the first version was far better suited to the original conception of the whole opera, that of a social and political tragedy, not the tragedy of Boris's conscience. I consider it as more coherent and better thought out.[1]

That chil - dren af-ter death a-ris-ing from their cof-fins,

---

[1] *Towards the Rehabilitation of Mussorgsky's 'Boris Godunov'* (Moscow, 1928).

The music of the dialogue with Shuisky is likewise starker and informed by more numerous thematic reminiscences than in the later version. The differences in technique and spirit may be illustrated by this example, a musically interesting and dramatically very telling use of the Dimitry motive (see above).

This passage, it is true, is exceptional in its insistence upon the theme and in the peculiarity of its handling. In the second version, the corresponding bars are:

In Shuisky's description of the murdered child's body awaiting burial in Uglich Cathedral, Mussorgsky uses the same theme, whereas in the second version he resorts to new, non-thematic materials.

The differences in the music of the final hallucination are primarily accounted for by the fact that the clock with its chimes and puppets is not introduced in the first version. Hence there is no weird phantasmagoria of puppets appearing in a ray of moonlight to heighten the hallucinatory terrors of Boris, and the music remains grim and unadorned instead of expanding into the wonderful evocative symphony of pulsing basses and whirring violins and flickering wood-wind which we find in the second version.

In short—and in a strictly limited sense, for Mussorgsky's methods in *Boris* are always governed by his supreme sense of economy and directness—the first version of the scene is closer to classical restraint and adherence to the unswerving main line; and the second tends towards romantic exuberance and employment of contrasts and of accessory (though not necessarily irrelevant) details.

The scene by the cathedral of St. Basil is altogether admirable. It starts with racy dialogue, which belongs to the very best and most characteristic of Mussorgsky. Here is a quotation from it:

Then comes by way of climax, after the vociferations: 'Down with Boris!'—the big, deeply moving chorus of imploration, from which I give a few bars (see page 124).

The brief meeting of the Tsar and the Simpleton (one of the finest things in Pushkin) is dealt with soberly and stands out in wonderful poignancy. And the artistic value of the remainder of the Simpleton episode is sufficiently proved by the fact that it stood the test of transfer to the Revolution scene, where the final lament makes a worthy

Mussorgsky

ending to the tremendous whole. Both these scenes, dramatically and musically, might well serve as models of well-judged and well-carried out structure: the one, an uninterrupted, splendidly sustained gradation from the entry of Boris (after a short evocation of the tranquil setting of his home surroundings) to his collapse; the other working from the start towards the choral apex and swift dramatic conclusion.

[The cuts made in the 1874 version were in at least two instances decidedly unfortunate: the sixty-odd bars removed from the end of Scene 1 and the excision of the whole of Pimen's description of the murder of the tsarevich in Scene 3. In the original version] the first scene ends, not with the chorus of the wandering pilgrims, but with a discussion characteristically stolid in tone between the people, who express their bewilderment and wonder who the tsar may be whom they are urged to yell for. The police officer interrupts their dialogue and orders them to be at the Kremlin on the morrow, there to await instruction. They accept the inevitable as a matter of course: 'If we must shout, why not shout at the Kremlin? All the same to us.'

The music of this final section is built upon a simple, very telling working-out of the opening motive (example, page 111), which by this reappearance acquires its full significance, and is asserted with the emphasis due to so important a theme. It sets in in A minor following without modulatory transition upon the A flat major of the pilgrims' chorus—a typical instance of the abrupt but apposite changes of key to which Mussorgsky resorts whenever he feels them advisable, to the great distress of his censors—and gradually reverts to C sharp minor,[1] the initial key of the prelude; so that, both thematically and tonally, the structure of the whole scene is perfectly symmetrical and rounded off.

The section is also significant dramatically. It emphasizes an essential point: the indifference and ignorance of the people whose fate hangs in the balance. Igor Glebov points out that the very words, 'No matter where we shout: all the same to us,' predetermine the character and tone of the Coronation scene.

[1] More correctly, C sharp Aeolian; but the questions of modes will be dealt with in the last chapter.

The people hail Boris not willingly, but under compulsion—and, accordingly, in a surly, lifeless way. Shuisky urging them to rejoice is but another incarnation of the police officer with his cudgel in the previous scene. Mussorgsky could very well have written a scene of pure pomp and splendour and unmixed joy, but he did not. Even his choice of the 'official' tune of the *Slava* (Glory) indicates the character he aimed at and achieved—one of constraint. From the beginning to the end of the scene, as Mussorgsky wrote it, there is no progression. The whole scene remains at a standstill, as if frozen.[1]

In the scene in the cell, the narrative by Pimen of the murder of the tsarevich serves to knit the plot (a plot within a plot, as I shall presently show) by stimulating Grigory to action exactly as the second narrative—in front of the tsar and council, that of the miracle accomplished on the tomb of the tsarevich—serves to bring about the final collapse of Boris. Indeed, Mussorgsky's stage directions ('Grigory listens intently; Grigory rises majestically,' etc.) mark the particular significance which he ascribes to it in this respect. And the musical functions of the narrative correspond to this dramatic significance. From the point of view of musical texture, let it be noticed that the main element of the first narrative is:

and that of the second is:

Truly a noteworthy example of adaptation to contrasting ends: on the one hand gloom and tragedy, on the other mystic serenity.

This main element (first example above) undergoes various trans‑

---

[1] Op. cit.

formations in the course of the narrative, and the first form in which the Dimitry motive is introduced:

emanates from it directly. The derivation of this Dimitry motive, from the opening motive and from a motive expressing in a more general way the sombre forebodings of Tsar Boris, has already been referred to (cf. examples, pages 111 and 112).

Mussorgsky's art of preparing, heralding and, if need be, dovetailing themes is as original as it is effective. Throughout the score of *Boris* we can notice seeds that germinate each in due time, brief passages embodying allusions to, or containing germs of, music that will unfold itself later, and playing a part in the extraordinary unity of texture that characterizes *Boris*. We may not perceive these as *Leitmotive* whose reappearances and transformations need be watched: they do their work all the more thoroughly and subtly for that reason. Quite possibly, Mussorgsky was not conscious of every connection that arose as he wrote the music of *Boris*. It is quite admissible that the main elements, at times, just grew out of one another, their mutual relation being as logical, as inevitable, as that of a branch to the root of the tree.

This may or may not be the explanation of analogies such as this: During the Secretary of the Council's speech to the people (Scene i: 'Boris, despite out entreaties, refuses the crown . . .') we hear music

which foreshadows both the character and the actual design of motives that will be extensively used in connection with Tsar Boris; for instance, of

which underlines more especially his preoccupations and fears.

Most of the parts that were transferred from *Salammbô* to *Boris Godunov* are linked with their new surroundings in some similar fashion. But if we did not know that the passages in which these motives occur were taken from *Salammbô*, we could never suspect that they were not originally devised for *Boris*—except perhaps in one instance, the last bars of the tsar's dying prayer, which may appear, especially to those of us who are wise after the event, to stand somewhat stiffly among their surroundings. In every other case, not only the eminent appositeness but the continuity of texture and the thematic relations would preclude the suspicion.

So much for the unity of texture of *Boris*. The unity of structure may be shown in a very few words. The balance and proportions of the structural scheme are almost faultless (if it is admitted that the insertion of the act in Poland—merely a long intermezzo, charming or impressive in parts, but at times, I think, tedious—need not be placed on the debit side of the structural account, then one may strike out the word 'almost'). At the beginning, the people are seen clamouring, by order, for Boris. At the end, the Revolution scene, that soul-stirring conclusion of what is probably the most soul-stirring lyric drama ever written, shows the same people in revolt, hailing the usurper as blindly as they had hailed Boris. Within the compass of this social and political tragedy (to use Glebov's words) is enclosed the tragedy of Tsar Boris, from his first appearance in the Coronation scene (with the words 'My soul is sad; a secret terror haunts me'), and from Pimen's first narrative, to his death, brought about by the shock of Pimen's second narrative as well as by his fear of the ghost that haunts him and of the advancing Pretender. In the initial version the balance is different, but no less perfect. From the people clamouring for Boris, and Boris coming into contact with them after being anointed, the action moves speedily towards the point at which Boris is again in contact with his people, but in an atmosphere of anguish and revolt; and thence towards his death.

The complete version is longer than the primitive version, but makes up for its length by affording opportunities for relaxation and points of repose which, far from breaking or unduly delaying the course of the action, co-operate in it. In the scene in the tsar's apartment, the songs and games are not only delightful in themselves, but serve a definite purpose. They evoke an atmosphere of peace and potential happiness, and impart a particular significance to the sudden irruption of Boris, grim and shaky, furious at seeing the old nurse startled by his appearance. The episode of the parrot is a gem of poesy and music (I can remember a production of *Boris* from which it was cut out, as it usually is; but by way of compensation a special point was made of including in the stage settings a large cage containing a stuffed parrot), and has its function in the display of the psychology of Boris: the noises announcing the parrot's escapade startle him not a little; when his son brings him an account of the humorous happening, he listens with obvious relief.

Stassov, by a piece of careless writing, had established the notion that Mussorgsky, having composed the Revolution scene, had tried placing it alternatively before and after the Death scene. We know by now that Mussorgsky did nothing of the kind. The reversal of the order he adopted produces indeed an appalling anticlimax. It is possible after a fashion—and, unfortunately, all producers of *Boris Godunov* according to the Rimsky-Korsakov arrangement have availed themselves of the possibility. It is likewise possible to place the scene in the cell before the Coronation scene, as was done at Paris in 1908, and perhaps elsewhere—so that (as one critic remarked at the time) one first heard Pimen deploring that a regicide should be holding the throne of Russia, and afterwards witnessed the regicide's coronation. If one overlooks such things as these, if one is mindless of musical fitness and gradation, one may indeed allege that *Boris Godunov* is loosely constructed—especially if a couple or so of the keystones in the structure are knocked out as well. I remember hearing in France the story of an officer who said to a private: 'This button of your tunic is loose.' Upon the private's respectfully protesting, the officer tugged at the button for a minute or so, twisted it, considered matters for a while, and finally, drawing out a pocket-knife, cut the threads, remarking: 'There! you see it *was* loose!' Thus, but not otherwise, is the looseness of *Boris Godunov* demonstrable.

[The full score of *Boris* is practically the only orchestral score of Mussorgsky's own available for study—almost everything else being Mussorgsky-Rimsky-Korsakov, Mussorgsky-Lyadov or even Mussorgsky-Cherepnin—and on that account, if no other, demands fairly detailed analysis. It] is strangely unlike anything of its kind turned out in the nineteenth century. And although at the first glance it might seem that Mussorgsky's methods of choosing and combining timbres could be compared with those practised by some of the younger Frenchmen of to-day (for instance, Darius Milhaud or Honegger), there is no real analogy between the two types of scoring.

Mussorgsky's economy in the matter of timbres appears to verge on parsimony. The setting of *Boris* includes all the usual instruments: 3 flutes (the third occasionally taking up the piccolo), 2 oboes (the second takes up the cor anglais in the third act), 2 clarinets, 2 bassoons, 4 horns, 2 trumpets, 3 trombones and tuba, the strings, timpani, bass drum, side drum (in the third act and the Revolution scene only), tambourine (in the third act only), cymbals (in the third act and the Revolution scene only), gong, a piano in the Coronation scene, a harp in the third act. But many of these (over and above the harp, piano, cor anglais and miscellaneous percussion) are used very seldom.

For instance, there are four scenes out of the nine in the final version of *Boris* in which the piccolo does not appear: the opening scene, the scene in the cell, the scene in Marina's room and the Duma scene with the tsar's death. It is used extensively in the Coronation and Revolution scenes. In the other three it is used only on special occasions: garden music and polonaise in the third act; final stages of the tsar's hallucination in the second act; accompaniment of Varlaam's song, 'By the walls of Kazan,' in the scene at the inn, and in the same scene in the weird and curiously suggestive music connected with Grigory's planning his escape into Lithuania (see example, page 136).

Trumpets, trombones and tuba are used very sparingly throughout the score. The occasions on which the trumpets have to give out melodic patterns, however simple, are very few: a couple of short diatonic descents in the Coronation scene, two bars at the end of the councillors' solemn verdict against the Pretender, and a few bars here and there in the Revolution scene, may be mentioned as exceptions. Otherwise they have little to do except to give out accents, holding-notes or (seldom) brief patterns in repeated notes. In the opening scene they appear only in a few *fortissimo* passages. They are not used in the scene in the cell. In the scene at the inn they have very few notes to play after the end of Varlaam's song, 'By the walls of Kazan.' In the second act they first come in to contribute one touch of colour to the nurse's song, 'The gnat and the flea.' After that they remain silent until used in the accompaniment of the tsar's violent outbreak against Shuisky, and again to underline his perturba, tion upon learning that the Pretender styles himself Dimitry. In the scenes of fury and terror that follow they are used very little. This husbanding of the orchestra's most vivid timbre is particularly characteristic of Mussorgsky's policy of restraint in the use of tone, colours.

The trombones and tuba are used far more freely than the trum, pets, especially for the purposes of dramatic expression, yet with re, markable economy. Neither the tuba nor the third trombone appears during the scene in the cell. The other two trombones have not many notes to play, but are most effective when they come in. The trom, bones and tuba crop up a moment in the prelude to the scene at the inn, but are not heard at all during the course of the scene. In the second act the tuba comes in only during the first vision of the murdered tsarevich, and further when Boris collapses under the agony of his remorse and fears. It is hardly heard during the third (Polish) act, and not at all in the scene of the Duma.

In the opening scene the timpani are used only for the climax of the imploration chorus, for a soft *tremolando* during the chancellor's speech, another at the end of the pilgrims' chorus, and when the music of this chorus is echoed in the ensuing dialogue of the people.[1] In the scene at the inn they appear only for a short while in the accompaniment to the song 'By the walls of Kazan'; in the second act, only when Feodor watches the clock at work and during the final hallucination; in the first scene of the third act (Marina's room) only at the end, to emphasize the Jesuit's threats to Marina. In fact, the timpani—as the whole of the percussion—are used in a way that makes clear Mussorgsky's resolve always to achieve his ends with a minimum of means.

The strings, as may well be expected, are the mainstay—and in this respect due attention should be given to Ivor Glebov's remark

[1] Vocal score, Oxford University Press edition, pages 26–30; this final section is in no other edition.

that when *Boris* is performed there should always be a good number of these in the orchestra despite the general lightness of the setting, which might seem to render a moderate complement permissible. They are used in a very simple manner—e.g. Mussorgsky hardly ever stipulates the use of a particular string or mode of bowing. The violas come very much into prominence. The double basses are often used without the cellos, and often kept silent while the latter give out the bass (at times supported by one or several wind instruments). Generally speaking, they are used rather less than is the current practice.

Of the wind instruments the most prominent are the clarinets, bassoons and horns. All of these are kept very busy. The oboes are treated in a curious manner. Often they are left out for no very obvious reason. It is natural to suppose that the composer wished to husband the characteristic, outstanding timbre which they provide; yet fairly often he uses them to double, very noticeably, the flutes *unisoni* where this doubling does not seem absolutely necessary; or he brings them into prominence somewhat unaccountably—for instance, in the opening prelude the first oboe suddenly appears for four bars, to give out a pattern which is part of an accompaniment entrusted to the strings:

after which appearance the oboes are not heard for quite a long while. But in many instances they are aptly used for definite purposes of coloration or expression, when brightness, pungency and pathos are required.

As will appear from the above remarks, the general scheme is indeed an unusually simple, austere and sombre one, except in parts of the more ornate third (Polish) act. And the austerity is intentional. Mussorgsky was not incapable of achieving bright and even loud colours; but he never resorted to them except when they were needful, and needful from the dramatic point of view rather than from the point of view of music *per se*. Mussorgsky would never have endorsed Rimsky-Korsakov's favourite axiom, 'An opera is, first and foremost, a musical composition,' with all the practical consequences which this axiom entails. Material beauty of texture is for him a means, never an end. Smoothness, mellowness and brilliancy are never aimed at at the expense of fitness. A most convincing instance is afforded by his treatment of the Coronation scene, with reference to which Glebov remarks:

> In *Boris* the coronation proceeds from the crowd's words in the opening scene: 'If we must shout, no matter when we shout.' The people are in-different, merely driven to hail the tsar. Moreover, the coronation is overshadowed with ominous gloom. The character of the music is accordingly bitter and stark, that of the singing 'passive': Rimsky-Korsakov erred particularly deeply when he turned the scene into one of operatic pomp.[1]

There can be little doubt that if a competent judge who knew nothing whatever of *Boris Godunov* was given to read or to hear the Coronation scene in the two versions, he might prefer the more elaborate and richer scoring provided by Rimsky-Korsakov; but the same judge, acquainted with the foregoing scene, and duly realizing the atmosphere of gloom and constraint which needs must pervade the ceremony of the coronation, will surely decide that Mussorgsky struck the right note, whereas Rimsky-Korsakov sacrificed fitness to the ideals of 'musical composition.' And this verdict will be arrived at quite apart from any eventual predilection for sensuous beauty in music—in point of fact, I for one am inclined to set great store by the sensuous appeal of music, and greatly appreciate the appealing qualities of Rimsky-Korsakov's music in Rimsky-Korsakav's own works, where they are never out of place.

Mussorgsky, always conceiving his music in relation to the straight-forward requirements of dramatic expression and dramatic situations, had no use for recipes, however effective they might be, in the matter of scoring or in any other. He often overlooked the most obvious niceties of orchestration. This should not lead us to assume that he was unaware of the possibilities which they afforded: for, indeed, these possibilities are among the very first things that a tyro learns, and inclines to pounce upon whenever the slightest opportunity offers.

[1] Op. cit.

Reading the score, it is impossible not to realize that its aspect here and there suggests a lack of finish. One may have the impression that Mussorgsky did not always think out his music in terms of the orchestra, but orchestrated it piecemeal—perhaps leaving out occa/sionally an instrument or two simply because he did not happen to think of them at the time, as a more practised craftsman would have done automatically. Ninety/nine times out of a hundred the im/pression will be altogether false. Mussorgsky did shun above all things the very semblance, however faint, of automatism in the writing of music (his correspondence teems with utterances to that effect); and now and then he pays the price of this wise prejudice of his—part and parcel of the genius to which we owe *Boris*—by going astray in the matter of some trifling adjustment. But this is the exception; and, as a rule, his orchestration comes off splendidly. The few obvious gaps are easy to remedy, and for the most part seem due to mere oversight on Mussorgsky's part. The editors of the score (of whom Glebov is one, appearing under his real name, Boris Asafev; the other is Paul Lamm) have found it advisable to suggest the addition of a few notes at certain spots (for instance: prologue, full score, page 37; first act, pages 94–6; second act, page 153; fourth act, page 115—all these suggested additions are marked by the use of small type and by footnotes). And to account for the fact that Mussorgsky, when he had the opportunity of judging by results, failed to carry out the emendations himself, we may well imagine him, distressed by the more than casual treatment meted out to his work when it was produced under compulsion, losing heart for a time and neglecting the final touching up of his score during the rehearsal period, which is quite a usual procedure even with far more ex/perienced orchestrators than he, and which would have set matters right.

Apart from these trifles, one may confidently say that it is on reading the score rather than on hearing it performed that one will incline to suspect deficiencies. (Saint/Saëns once wrote that the orchestral effects of Berlioz on paper often seem doomed not to come off, but in practice always come off.) Mussorgsky, Glebov con/cludes, aimed at achieving a supple, mobile, sensitive orchestral setting, as delicately shaded and as alive as the human voices. His ideals called for far more than was provided by the technical resources available in his days; but nevertheless he did not fall very far short of these almost unattainable ideals.

In the plain, austere scheme of *Boris* every orchestral colour stands out in as strong a relief as need be, so that by virtue of his sense of economy and selection he achieves as much as might be achieved by lavishness—and often much more. Subtlety and efficiency are displayed not only in the choice and blend of colours, but in an unfailing sense of values and an almost unfailing sense of tone-volumes (in this last respect let his skill in deciding when to use instruments such as the flutes and double basses be studied with particular care). As examples of remarkably simple and effective combinations I should like to quote (singling out only a few of those that might be adduced without unduly encroaching upon the space available here) the few bars heralding the secretary's address to the people in the prologue—a passage quoted by Glebov as illustrating the 'vocal' and therefore particularly human quality with which the orchestral parts are so often endowed:

the beginning of the working-out section in the coronation music —a very telling instrumental entry, achieved by strikingly simple means:

the curiously suggestive music at the moment when (scene at the inn) Grigory plans his escape while Varlaam, in a semi-comatose state of drunkenness, mumbles a song—this passage contains the patterns in thirds given out by the double basses which is said to have aroused (in the seventies) the indignation of Ferrero, a member of the committee of the imperial theatres who was a professional double bass player:

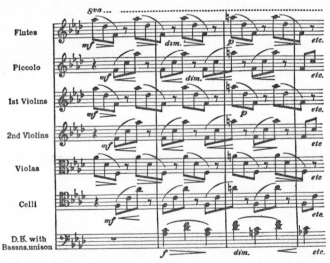

the no less mysterious, stealthy music heard when (second act) the boyar in attendance whispers to Boris that Shuisky and his friends are engaged in plotting:

and the very delightful beginning of Feodor's 'Parrot' song in the same act—the accompaniment being entrusted first to the clarinets and bassoons, then to the flutes and one oboe, then to one flute, the bassoons and the muted first violins leading up to the entrance of the other strings (minus the double basses).

Among particularly fine examples of less restricted, yet equally restrained combinations, one might adduce the hallucination music and the Death scene. The fierce, swift introduction to the Revolution scene is marvellously telling. The third (Polish) act affords ample evidence of what Mussorgsky was capable of achieving on more conventional lines.

Another merit of the scoring, generally considered, lies in the fact that it never compels a singer to yell instead of singing, or to articulate indistinctly. Every syllable of the genuine *Boris* should be heard with perfect clearness. If it is not, the fault will never lie with Mussorgsky. As the orchestra seldom plays alone (for the preludes are very brief, and from one end of the scene to the other there is practically no break in the dialogue), here we have an additional reason for praising Mussorgsky's moderation. Inexpert orchestrators usually err in the other direction, especially when dramatic moments occur.

[Doubtless there will always be some who will prefer] Rimsky-Korsakov's version, the reviser's smoother and more sumptuous orchestration to Mussorgsky's, the honey on the brim of the cup to the potent, unsweetened draught which the cup contains. As Oskar von Riesemann has put it in his book on Mussorgsky: 'Rimsky-Korsakov's re-scoring is the work of a skilled jeweller, by virtue of which many of Mussorgsky's rough, unpolished gems first received their full sparkle and lasting value.' And we all know that jewellery, even in the wrong place, exercises an irresistibly attractive power on certain people. Apart from the question of taste, there is the far more formidable question of habit. And it is a matter not only of the scoring, but of the whole adulterated *Boris* against the genuine one; for we cannot have Rimsky-Korsakov's scoring without his other emendations.

[These emendations—of melody, harmony and rhythm—are similar to those we have already noticed in connection with the songs. But they are far more wholesale, more drastic—except perhaps in the free musical rendering of *With Nurse* in the *Nursery* cycle and one or two of the *Songs and Dances of Death*—and far more notorious, thanks to the fact that they have been debated *ad nauseam* for many years. Moreover Rimsky-Korsakov's alterations were not limited to the musical substance, as in the songs, but extended to the dramatic framework. When he brought out his first 'revision' in 1896, Rimsky-Korsakov not only made slashing cuts—Pimen's narrative, the scene between Boris and his son with the map of Muscovy, the parrot episode, Boris's scene with his son and Shuisky, the episode of the striking clock, the scene between Dimitry and Rangoni and Dimitry's monologue—but reversed the order of the last two scenes so as to end with the death of Boris. In 1908 he produced an edition with the cuts restored but with the last two scenes still in the wrong order, and in addition composed two insets of forty and sixteen bars for the Coronation scene (for the Paris production).][1]

[[1] Thus this unfortunate masterpiece exists in no fewer than five forms: (*a*) the original seven-scene *Boris* of 1868–9; (*b*) the enlarged and reconstructed *Boris* of 1871–2; (*c*) the version of (*b*), cut on the advice of Nápravnik and others, which was performed and published in vocal score in 1874; (*d*) Rimsky-Korsakov's version of 1896; (*e*) Rimsky-Korsakov's version of 1908. Of the available vocal scores the Oxford University Press edition shows (*a*), (*b*) and (*c*), the Chester edition (*c*) and the Bessel edition (*e*). I do not know of a single gramophone record of Mussorgsky's own *Boris*.]

Rimsky-Korsakov's Editing

It has been said that, however great the demerits of the Rimsky-Korsakov revisions may be, they helped to make Mussorgsky's music known and appreciated at a time when the originals would have disconcerted the public. [That was his own view and avowed hope.] The opposite opinion—that no better proof of the vitality of Mussorgsky's music could be found than the fact that it remained significant even after being disfigured; and that but for the revisions, the genuine texts would have been known and appreciated far sooner—has also found support. [For one thing, singers accustomed to the Rimsky-Korsakov versions find it impossible to adapt themselves to the true text.] The truth seems to be that the revisions did serve a purpose in Russia, for whose musicians and musical public the originals were too strong meat. But in France there existed at least a minority of experienced, progressively minded musicians, familiar enough with modern developments to be able to accept Mussorgsky on his own terms. They started vindicating his genius at a time when the garbled texts already in possession of the field stood very much in the way. The vindication would have been easier and speedier had the field been clear.

CHAPTER IX

OPERAS AFTER 'BORIS'

[WITH Mussorgsky's other great historical opera, *Khovanshchina*, the case is somewhat different. *Boris* was a finished work of art, a complete and satisfactory whole in either of its original forms. However good his intentions, Rimsky-Korsakov really had no right to touch it at all. But *Khovanshchina* was never completed, and when Lamm published the vocal score of Mussorgsky's original manuscripts in 1931, although it revealed (as was to be expected) that Rimsky-Korsakov had made innumerable cuts and changes of melody and harmony,] even the most rabid censors of Rimsky-Korsakov as editor of Mussorgsky had to grant that *Khovanshchina*, even if Mussorgsky had finished and scored it, could not have stood the test of performance; and that if Rimsky-Korsakov [in his edition of 1883] did not achieve the impossible task of giving it the continuity and logic which it lacks, he has at least compressed it into a semblance of formal balance and made it possible to produce. [All the same,] in the genuine *Khovanshchina* there are interesting points which were swept away in the process of revision.

[Mussorgsky started collecting materials for *Khovanshchina* at least as early as July 1872, when he sent a list of them to Stassov. After a year he began the composition, though] without any definite plan, building up the libretto piecemeal as he went along. His main idea was to picture the clash between the old régime and the new at a troubled moment in Russian history, [the period 1682–9:] the plot of the Princes Khovansky against the [Romanov dynasty], the annihilation of [one of the congregations of] the Old Believers [who had refused to accept the reforms of the Patriarch Nikon in 1654] and the final triumph of the young Tsar Peter 'the Great' [over both political and religious reaction].

In proportion as he studied all available historical documents, he allowed himself to be swamped by the wealth of facts and particulars which he was ever discovering. In his eagerness to use them all, and also to work out to the full other scenes of his own devising, he lost all sense of proportion and was led to overlook even the most elementary structural requirements. As one of his Russian critics, Karatïgin, has pointed out, he tried to cram into one opera materials whose adequate treatment would have required a whole cycle of operas, more or less similar to Wagner's *Ring*. Eventually, in a desperate attempt to reduce his sketches and plans to order, he found himself compelled to shorten or leave out much of what he had already written, and to give up the idea of tackling certain other scenes. Instead of thereby making good the obscurities and gaps in the action, he increased them; and there is in *Khovanshchina* much that appears unconnected with the drama as a whole, besides not being interesting *per se*. Moreover, he was unable to finish the work: very little of what he had planned for Act v was written (and of that little not all has been preserved); and only a very few portions of the music were scored.

Here is a summary analysis of the work as we now have it. (The Rimsky-Korsakov edition is on the same lines, except for differences expressly pointed out, minor excisions or additions, and differences in the musical texture.)

First Act. At daybreak [in the Red Square] in Moscow, the streltsy, [musketeers, many of them Old Believers, ill-disciplined troops who had originally put the Regent Sophia on the throne, but whose confidence has now been won by Prince Ivan Khovansky,] discuss the brutalities recently committed by them in faction warfare. As they walk away, Shaklovity, [who actually became one of Sophia's chief ministers,] appears and dictates to a public scribe a letter to the regent denouncing Ivan Khovansky and his son Andrey, as plotting to usurp the throne. Then, as the sun rises, the people appear. Seeing a poster stuck on to a pillar, they compel the scribe to read it out to them; it is a proclamation from the throne referring to the punishment of traitors and plotters. (This scene was cut out by Rimsky-Korsakov.) The streltsy march in, led by Ivan Khovansky, who harangues them and orders them to patrol the city. When they are gone, Emma, a Protestant girl, rushes in, pursued by Andrey Khovansky. Marfa, a young woman belonging to the sect of Old

Believers, and a former sweetheart of his whom he has forsaken, intervenes. The scene between them is interrupted by the return of Ivan Khovansky, who, finding Emma attractive, orders his soldiers to seize her. Dosifey, the leader of the Old Believers, appears, rebukes the princes and orders Marfa to lead Emma back to the safety of her home. The act ends on a chant of the Old Believers: 'Lord save us from the evils of this world, crush the power of the Antichrist.'

Second Act. The home of Prince Golitsïn, the counsellor [and lover] of the Regent Sophia. He stands for modern, progressive Russia, as Khovansky for old feudal and Dosifey for old mystical Russia. He is alone, reading letters from the regent and his mother (the reading of the second was cut out by Rimsky-Korsakov), which fill him with evil forebodings. A pastor from the Protestant quarter of the town calls, in order to ask him to protect Emma against Andrey; but on being told that this cannot be done he tries to avail himself of Golitsïn's professed goodwill by asking for leave to build a new church. Golitsïn refuses and shows him out. (The whole scene was suppressed by Rimsky-Korsakov.) The next visitor is Marfa, summoned in order that she may tell the prince his fortune. She foretells disaster and exile. Golitsïn orders his servants to follow her on her way and drown her in the marshes. Then Ivan Khovansky comes in, and there is a quarrel between him and Golitsïn on matters of curtailed privileges. This is interrupted by the advent of Dosifey, and a political discussion takes place. (Both these scenes were much abridged by Rimsky-Korsakov.) Marfa, breathless and frightened, rushes in: she tells how Golitsïn's servants have tried to drown her, and how soldiers of the regent, who were near by, saved her. Hardly has she broken the news of the proximity of the troops, than Shaklovity enters with the news that the Khovanskys have been denounced to the regent as plotters, and will have to appear before her.

This scene was left unfinished. In a letter to Stassov (16th August 1876) Mussorgsky expressed his intention of ending it with a quintet. As this was to be for an unusual combination, contralto, tenor, and three basses, he would require, he said, Rimsky-Korsakov's advice on points of technique. The quintet was never written. Rimsky-

Korsakov provided, by way of ending to the act, a short orchestral epilogue, of which more hereafter.

Third Act. In Moscow, outside the house of the Khovanskys, the Old Believers pass, singing a hymn. Marfa remains behind, alone, and sings of her love for the faithless Andrey. Susanna, an old woman, also an Old Believer, appears and violently upbraids her for her sinful passion. Dosifey intervenes, rebukes Susanna and tries to comfort Marfa. . . .

Let us pause awhile and take stock. We are far into the third act, and have covered nearly two-thirds of the drama—leaving out the instrumental prelude—exactly two hundred pages out of the three hundred and twenty-five of which the score consists. What have we found? The main characters have been introduced and their idiosyn-crasies revealed. Both the political issue at stake and the position between Marfa, Andrey and Emma are made clear. Various indica-tions (to which I have not referred in order not to complicate this synopsis), and skilful suggestions in the atmosphere of the play, have also conveyed the impression that a dire fate threatens the Old Believers.

It is an open question whether we are made to feel interested in what is going to happen next, or whether we remain in a state of passive, rather bewildered expectancy. None of the chief characters, except Shaklovity with his denunciation, has done anything to knit the plot or to forward its progress. The secondary characters—Emma, Susanna, the Pastor—are insignificant in themselves and superfluous from the dramatic point of view. Mussorgsky had planned scenes in which all three were to play more important parts. Rimsky-Korsakov says that he actually composed some of the music for these and played it to his friends; but he never wrote it down.

As regards Marfa and the interweaving of the main plot of the story of her love and sorrows, two views are possible. We may think that Mussorgsky did not succeed in making us feel that she is one of the vital elements in the drama, and not merely introduced in order to relieve the uneventfulness of the general scheme; or, with Robert Godet (in his book *En Marge de Boris Godounof*) we may say: 'A stroke of genius led Mussorgsky to invent Marfa's love-story. . . . In her soul he summed up the conflict between consciousness, super-stition and mystic ecstasy; he shows us this soul as the battle-ground of all the passions which tear her race and are the real prime movers of this collective tragedy.' In either case there will be no doubt that the Marfa scenes contain some of the very finest music in *Khovanshchina* and in Mussorgsky's whole output.

Let it now be noted that as in *Boris,* but to a far greater extent, we are made to feel that the drama is one, not of persons, but of a nation—of Russia, torn by conflicting tendencies and confronted with an unknown future. Khovansky has been shown as brutal, obtuse and self-seeking; his son as a weakling and a slave to passions; Golitsïn as irresolute and callous. Dosifey is merely passive: for him mystic faith is action and renunciation will solve all problems. There seems to be no hope for Russia except at the hands of the unseen regent or the young tsar, both of them unknown quantities in *Khovanshchina.* Mussorgsky had planned a scene in which they were to appear, but we can only surmise how far these scenes would have added to the dramatic logic and interest.

The beautiful aria sung by Shaklovity, who next appears on the stage (for no purpose except to sing it, and then hurl, before dis-appearing, a fresh threat at Khovansky), sums up the position in the words: 'Alas, unfortunate Russia, who hast suffered and still sufferest so much, who shall save thee?'

It is only towards the end of the act, after picturesque and lively scenes between the streltsy and their wives (scenes much shortened by Rimsky-Korsakov), that events proceed more rapidly. The scribe comes with the news that Sophia's soldiers are nearing, and have already massacred many of Khovansky's troops. The streltsy ask Khovansky for orders: he tells them that their fate is in the regent's hands, and advises them to wait in patience.

Fourth Act. Khovansky, in his home outside Moscow, is being entertained by singers and his Persian dancers. He receives from Golitsïn a warning (which he disregards) that danger threatens. Shaklovity comes to tell him that the regent summons him. As he steps out of the room he is dispatched by murderers.

A change of scene takes place [—and historically seven years have passed; the young Tsar Peter is seventeen and by a *coup d'état* he has overthrown his half-sister, the usurping regent. In the square before St. Basil's in Moscow, the same scene as the sixth of the original *Boris*,] the people watch the passing of a carriage in which, by the [young tsar's] orders, [Sophia's lover] Golitsïn is being driven into exile. Dosifey, who knows that disaster threatens the Old Believers and also Andrey Khovansky,[1] feels that the time has come for a collective suicide by fire of his brethren—a last act of faith. Marfa, acting upon his instructions, tries to persuade Andrey that his doom is sealed. He is incredulous and hopes that the streltsy may save him. But as he winds his horn to call them they march in, led by the tsar's soldiers and carrying blocks and axes for their own execution. They kneel down. An officer of the tsar announces that they have been granted a free pardon, and are to return to their homes and keep the peace.[2]

Fifth Act. In a moonlit forest, Dosifey invites the Old Believers to prepare for death. At this point ends the finished draft of the vocal score. Other manuscripts provide sketches for further scenes; they have been set in order by Paul Lamm, and completed by Boris Asafev. First, there is a scene in which Andrey, still in search of Emma, is coaxed by Marfa to resign himself to his fate; then, another in which Dosifey again addresses the Old Believers, who sing a brief chorus of imploration to God. This ends abruptly, and no extant manuscript carries us farther.

From Mussorgsky's letters to Stassov we gather that in 1873 he had intended to write a coloratura chorus to be sung in unison by the Old Believers, which, he said, 'would provide a good contrast with the theme of Tsar Peter's soldiers.' Marfa was to sing an 'incantation to the wind'; and Andrey, standing by the window of a cell in which Emma lay hidden, was to sing a 'nightingale's song' (a love song).

[1 The historical Andrey Khovansky was executed on the same day as his father.]

[2 Mussorgsky seems to have borrowed this incident from the earlier rising of the streltsy. The young Peter executed them wholesale and with great cruelty.]

Then Marfa was to draw him away, and a 'lover's dirge,' or 'love song in death,' was to follow. The music of this last duet was actually composed, and part of it at least sung at concerts given by the singer Darya Leonova; but no trace of it remains. Mussorgsky was greatly pleased with it. In July 1873 he wrote to Stassov:

All the people to whom I have shown it are amazed: nothing like it has ever been done. . . . This duet, with Andrey overcome by terror and helplessly struggling, while Marfa vehemently talks about Emma and suicide by fire, pleases me immensely.

It is not clear whether he intended the drama to end with the collective suicide taking place on the stage, or with the Old Believers marching out to the pyre.[1] In the 1883 edition and its reprints the fifth act, except for the first scene, is practically all Rimsky-Korsakov's work, although the greater part of the music written or sketched for it by Mussorgsky is used.

How does the music compare with that of *Boris*? To answer the question briefly is difficult. It may be said, roughly, that it is carried out on broader and somewhat smoother lines, with fewer bold innovations and a lesser wealth of interesting, pregnant technical details. Here and there it is thinner in texture; and, as a rule, it proceeds at a slower pace, in keeping with the action, which has none of the continuous onward impetus of *Boris*. Certain portions of it are weak, but many others are as telling and original, and as beautiful from the purely musical point of view (that is apart from their value for dramatic purposes or characterization) as anything in *Boris*.

Its dramatic significance is different because its function is not the same. In *Boris* there is always action. The principal characters are doing something or other or tending somewhere or other. They are in motion, and in this motion the music co-operates. In *Khovan-shchina* the only two things which occur on the stage and bear conse-quences shown on the stage are Shaklovity's denunciation and Andrey's pursuit of Emma. The other scenes are illustrative rather than active: chapters from or illustrations to a chronicle rather than

[1 These mass-suicides by fire of congregations of Old Believers actually continued as late as the reign of the Empress Elizabeth (middle of the eighteenth century).]

constituent parts of a drama. In other words, they are, essentially, characterization. And we have plenty of collateral evidence to show that here characterization was Mussorgsky's main object. His correspondence with Stassov teems with explanations as to how he had conceived and intended to portray the characters. Both the Khovanskys are 'stupid.' So is Emma. Shaklovity is 'a characteristic figure, an arch-scoundrel and self-important, but not without a certain grandeur despite his bloodthirsty nature. He has his motif, and an excellent one.' Between Marfa and Susanna Mussorgsky aimed at establishing a strong contrast: 'The one is an unspoilt, strong, loving woman, the other a narrow-minded, heartless old maid, who rejoices in nothing but fault-finding and malevolence.' Even the Pastor is a success, from Mussorgsky's point of view, for the simple reason that the music characterizes him aptly: 'The Pastor scene will please you,' he wrote to Stassov and to Lyudmila Shestakova: 'I have thought out a most physiognomic bit for the pastor.'

All this is in perfect accord with Mussorgsky's motto: 'Not beauty for its own sake, but truth, wherever it be.' But, whereas he usually achieves beauty as well, he sometimes fails to do so. However true to character the tame conventional music, deliberately 'German' in style, which he uses for the Pastor scene may be, it is not good enough in itself to prove as interesting to others as it seems to have been to Mussorgsky himself. Whether the music composed ('in Mozart's style,' Rimsky-Korsakov tells us) for the other scenes in which the pastor appeared was less insignificant we shall never know.

The processes of musical characterization, then, are the first things to consider in *Khovanshchina*; and here comparison with *Boris* provides a useful starting-point. In *Boris* [, as we have seen,] *Leitmotive*, theme transformations and derivations play a big part. In *Khovanshchina* we have only one couple of *Leitmotive*:

the first referring to Khovansky and his streltsy, the second more especially to Khovansky's imperious nature. A few transformations of and derivations from these are to be discovered, but nothing like what we find in *Boris*.

A few themes occur in conjunction with other characters: for instance, Shaklovity, as Mussorgsky himself has informed us, and also Golitsïn. But these are not in any sense *Leitmotive*. The Shaklovity theme does not occur except in the Denunciation scene (unless one chooses to admit that its rhythm was deliberately alluded to at the beginning of the second part of his aria in the third act):

In association with Dosifey there is not even the semblance of a characterizing theme. It is (as in all dramatic music prior to the moment when the notion of characterizing themes cropped up, and a great proportion of the dramatic music written afterwards) by virtue of general qualities—here a tone of austerity, dignity and authority—that the instrumental music associated with him is characteristic.

But it is in the vocal, not the instrumental, parts that the most subtle and remarkable methods of characterization are to be found. Apart from the fact that characteristic delivery and intonation were points to which Mussorgsky gave his utmost care and which play no small part in *Boris Godunov*, the fact is that while composing *Khovanshchina* he was devoting greater attention than ever to questions of melodic design. In December 1876 (one of the two years during which he worked most actively at *Khovanshchina*) he wrote to Stassov:

I feel inclined to prophesy; and what I prophesy is, 'the melody of life, not that of classicism.' I am at work on human speech. With great pains I have just achieved a type of melody evolved from speech: I have succeeded in merging recitative into melody. This type I should like to call 'well-thought-out, justified melody.' Some day, all of a sudden, the ineffable song will arise against classical melody—arise unexpectedly, intelligible to one and all. If I succeed, I shall stand as a conqueror in art—and succeed I must.

Let us turn our attention to the characteristic features in the melody; to the well-thought-out features that are intended to 'justify' it from the particular point of view of characterization.

Andrey, the lovesick weakling, is given, very suitably, nothing but lyrical tunes to sing. Most of these happen to be closely related to folk-tunes. At first, in Act I, we have what might be a Russian dance-tune, with a strong suggestion of Borodin about it. In Act V he sings an actual folk-tune; and no doubt the 'nightingale' song would also have been in the vernacular lyric style.

The music which Marfa sings is also very lyrical in quality, and at times related to folk music (an actual folk-tune is used for her beautiful love song in the third act), but as intense in tone and tragical in character as the Andrey music is shallow. It comprises three melo-dies, of which two refer to her love for Andrey, and her despair, whereas the third is associated with her threatening prophecy to Golitsïn. All three reappear on various occasions. Reappearance of characteristic passages which are not 'themes' (not organic units serving as elements of structure, but organized structures, which can-not be further 'treated' but may be repeated as portions of a general structural scheme, or by way of allusion) is a feature not to be found in *Boris,* but frequent in *Khovanshchina.* The process, well known to older opera composers, may become very conventional and its results tedious, even when it is used for the legitimate purpose of reminiscence. Mussorgsky uses it most aptly not only in Marfa's part, but in those of Golitsïn and Dosifey. For instance not only does the tune of Marfa's prophecy to Golitsïn reappear (in the orchestra) when Golitsïn is being taken into exile, but she sings it again when warning Andrey that death is near. The former instance is one of obvious reminiscence; but in the latter no allusion is intended or effected—the reappearance shows Mussorgsky deliberately using identical music because the character of the musical discourse is identical. And the same explanation fits the reappearances that occur in the parts of Golitsïn, Dosifey and also, occasionally, Khovansky.

One purely instrumental instance of repetition for purposes of allusion, and not characterization, is curious enough to deserve special notice. When Marfa, in Act II, narrating how she was saved by the soldiers, utters the words: 'Glory to Thee, God! They came to my help . . . they are near by,' the motive of the prelude, which was an evocation of Moscow peaceful at dawn, is heard in the orchestra. It is quite logical that this peaceful melody should reappear again to express the relief in Marfa's heart. What is not logical is Rimsky-Korsakov's idea of using it for the instrumental peroration which he supplied for the act. The result may be pretty, but it is far from true to the spirit of the drama: while Marfa's heart is at peace, the other characters on the stage are much perturbed by the news of the advent of the troops. We may safely aver that Mussorgsky would not have ended the act on such an anticlimax.

Let it be remarked, incidentally, that this reappearance of the motive in conjunction with Marfa's words is, so far as I can see, a unique instance in Mussorgsky's output of a repetition for so thoroughly symbolic a purpose—although, of course, it has an expressive value as well as a symbolic.

Certain Russian critics refer to a theme associated with Dosifey. Perhaps they are thinking of a characteristic pattern which often occurs in his utterances—a succession of two falling intervals, generally a fourth and a third, or two thirds, thus:

This is a pattern which Mussorgsky uses very often in music, grave and gay (the Russian critic Lapshin called attention to the fact as early as 1917). It is to be found in the song *The Magpie* as well as in the *Songs and Dances of Death,* in the Dimitry motive in *Boris,* and in the second Khovansky motive (see example (*b*) on page 147). As used in Dosifey's part—especially at the end of phrases—it contributes to the character of dignity, quiet authority and resignation of his utterances. But it would be unreasonable to lay too much stress on this one particular function.

Characteristic melody in Khovansky's part is often achieved by means of energetic ascending patterns. A typical one is:

which is also used for Andrey's horn-call to the streltsy—the last desperate endeavour to assert the power of the Khovanskys.

These brief remarks may suffice to show the lines on which a thorough study of Mussorgsky's methods of characterization should proceed. As regards, more generally, the style and technical idiosyncrasies of the music, few things could be said which could not be said in almost the same words with reference to *Boris*; and to show the differences beyond the resemblances would involve long disquisitions on every single point.

Let it be remarked, roughly, that, as in *Boris,* Mussorgsky resorts freely to modal or irregular scales, but not to so great a variety of them. In the vocal parts he uses wide leaps (of an octave or seventh, for instance) a little more often; and also, but seldom, patterns consisting of the notes of a chord, which are practically never used in *Boris*. The rarity of such patterns is possibly due to the fact that Mussorgsky never inclines to rest long on one harmony. The persistence of the common chord of E major with added sixth throughout the first six bars of the prelude to *Khovanshchina,* without even a changing or passing note, is one of the rare instances to the contrary that can be adduced.

As in *Boris,* changes of time signature are frequent, and neither very long note-values nor combinations of a great diversity of note-values are used. It is a constant feature of Mussorgsky's music (and one doubly worth noting considering the preoccupation with accuracy and subtlety of rhythm and metre which his frequent changes of time-signature reveal) that a small number of note-values should suffice for his purposes. In his vocal parts a dotted minim is rare and anything longer quite exceptional. Minims are not common; most of the work is done by dotted crotchets, crotchets, dotted quavers, quavers and semiquavers, with occasional triplets. Often three of these five note-values are enough: even two may be found almost sufficient—for instance, in Marfa's prophecy to Golitsïn, crotchets and quavers.

It may be added that unusual successions of chords occur, but less often than in *Boris*. The same is true of unusual successions and abrupt changes of keys.

[Before discussing Mussorgsky's last opera, *Sorochintsy Fair,* written at the same time as *Khovanshchina* and likewise left unfinished, we must go back for a moment to a relatively unimportant work—or fragment of a work—on which he worked early in 1872, between the second version of *Boris* and *Khovanshchina*: his share in the collective *Mlada*. For some of the *Mlada* music was to be transferred to *Sorochintsy Fair*. It will be remembered that Mussorgsky was to share the second and third acts of *Mlada* with Rimsky-Korsakov, and he was finally allotted the first part of Act II and the end of Act III: [1] a crowded market scene before the temple of Radegast at Retra, a ninth-century city of the Polabian or Baltic Slavs, followed by a scene in which a number of Polabian princes arrive to consult the auguries—and (in Act III) a fantastic night scene on Mount Triglav in which Chernobog, in the form of a black he-goat, Morena the death goddess and other infernal Slavonic deities celebrate obscene rites. Chernobog attempts to destroy the hero, Prince Yaromir, who is a witness of the scene, but the prince is saved by the cock-crow which announces dawn at the end of the reign of evil.

Mussorgsky's market scene, which was only sketched out for chorus and piano duet, is heralded by a quiet thirty-one-bar prelude in a transposed Mixolydian mode (E major with flattened leading-note). After some unaccompanied choral phrases invoking the help and protection of Radegast comes a crowd scene full of life and colour, with naturalistic and unconventional handling of the chorus in the manner, if not on the level, of the crowd scenes in *Boris*. One of these demands quotation:

Presently a quarrel breaks out between the Polabians and the traders of Novgorod, and they fight with fists. For this fight Mussorgsky proposed to add yet another set of choral parts to the bustling

[1] For a study of the collective *Mlada* as a whole, and an attempted reconstruction of the score in outline, see Chapter VIII of the book of essays *On Russian Music* (William Reeves, 1939).

F minor music (example, page 96) already used in *Oedipus* and *Salammbô*. Forty-eight bars of the orchestral part—revealing certain rhythmic and other modifications—were written out for piano duet, but there the fragment breaks off. Not a note of the new voice parts was put on paper, though the score was laid out for an elaborate triple chorus: women spectators (sopranos and altos in four parts), Polabians (tenors and basses in four parts) and men of Novgorod (tenors and basses in four parts).

The procession of princes and priests consists mainly of variations on a Russian folksong[1] written out for piano duet with indications of the scoring; the trio—the procession of the priests—is based on a theme of Rimsky-Korsakov's in 3–4 time which was to have been used as a 'priests' motive throughout the opera. For the scene on Mount Triglav Mussorgsky recast his orchestral piece *St. John's Night on the Bare Mountain,* adding choral parts for which the librettist provided 'demon language' in the manner of Berlioz's *Faust.* The letter in which Mussorgsky complained to Stassov at having to set such 'senseless words' as 'Sagana, chukh!' has already been quoted from. Unfortunately the manuscript of this second version of *Night on the Bare Mountain* has disappeared, but a good deal of it and part of the market scene at Retra were turned to account in *Sorochintsy Fair,* the comic Ukrainian opera on which Mussorgsky worked more or less simultaneously with *Khovanshchina* and which he left in an even more unfinished state than the historical tragedy of the Old Believers.

Gogol's short story *Sorochintsy Fair,* on which the opera is based, may be summarized as follows:

It is a hot summer day in the Ukraine—Little Russia, as it was often called in tsarist times. (The descriptive opening of the story is one of the outstanding examples of Gogol's rich prose.) On his way to the fair at Sorochintsy[2] is the peasant Solopy Cherevik who hopes to sell his wheat and an old mare; on his wagon rides his eighteen-year-old daughter Paraska and her shrewish stepmother Khivrya. As the wagon crosses a

---

[1] A hauling song, 'A kak po lugu, lugu,' which Mussorgsky found in Balakirev's published collection of folksongs. Tchaikovsky used the same tune in the introduction to the finale of his well-known Serenade for strings.

[2] Gogol's own birthplace, which he oddly miscalls Sorochinets.

bridge, a young *parubok* in a white *svitka*[1] expresses his admiration of Paraska and makes a waggish remark about her stepmother; Khivrya pours out a storm of abuse and he hurls a lump of mud after her, covering her with dirt. But the party continue their way to the hut of Cherevik's *kum* or crony, the Cossack Tsïbul, where they are to stay during the fair. Amid the crowds at the fair Cherevik overhears two men discussing the local bogy-lore; that the place where the fair is held is unlucky, that not far away is an old broken-down shed where a pig-faced devil has been seen looking out of the window, even that the 'red *svitka*' is expected to appear. But before Cherevik can learn what the 'red *svitka*' is, his attention is distracted by the sight of his daughter in the arms of the handsome young *parubok* Grïtsko, who had figured in the bridge incident. With great presence of mind Grïtsko introduces himself as the son of Cherevik's acquaintance Golopupenkov and explains that he and Paraska have fallen in love at first sight and wish to marry. Cherevik is nothing loath, and all three happily make their way to a drinking-booth. However when Khivrya learns that Cherevik has been finding a husband for Paraska, instead of selling his wheat and his mare, she is furious, and he bows before the storm. In the cool of the evening the disconsolate *parubok* is sitting by his wagon, brooding over Cherevik's breach of faith, when he is accosted by a tall gypsy who has been trying earlier to beat down the price Grïtsko has been asking for his oxen; Grïtsko tells him the whole story. 'Will you let me have them for twenty if we make Cherevik give us Paraska?' asks the gypsy. 'If you'll do that,' replied Grïtsko, 'you can have them for fifteen.'

In the *kum's* hut Khivrya is entertaining her youthful lover, the priest's son Afanasy Ivanovich, in the absence of her husband and the *kum* who are to sleep under the wagon to guard it from thieves. Suddenly there is a knock at the door; Khivrya hides her lover behind some lumber on two rafters under the roof. Her husband and daughter and the *kum* with a party of friends come in rather breathlessly; it is now rumoured that the 'red *svitka*' has been seen at the fair, that the devil in pig-form has been searching under the waggons; every one feels it is safer to sleep indoors. Once inside they all feel, or pretend to feel, more at ease, much more at ease than the guilty Khivrya or the wretched youth on the rafters. The drink circulates, the guests grow merrier and Cherevik, who can contain his curiosity about the 'red *svitka*' no longer, demands to know the whole story. The *kum* tells it.

It appears that once a devil was turned out of hell, took up his quarters in

---

[1] Ukrainian words meaning 'young peasant' and 'overcoat' respectively, which will recur often in the tale.

the old shed already mentioned and took to drink. He drank and drank, exhausting first his cash and then his credit till at last he had to pawn his red *svitka*, for a third of its value, to a Jew at Sorochintsy Fair. The devil told the Jew very firmly that he would redeem the coat in a year; but the Jew, delighted with the fine cloth, sold the *svitka* at an outrageous price to some gentleman and denied all recollection of it when the devil came to redeem it at the end of the year. That night the Jew was beaten by pig-faced devils and confessed his guilt, but the *svitka* was not to be found. A gypsy had stolen it from the gentleman and sold it to an old-clothes woman who brought it back to the fair next year. But she found her luck had deserted her; no one would buy from her. She soon guessed that there was something wrong with the *svitka* and, having tried in vain to burn it, slipped it into the wagon of a man selling butter. The man was at first delighted, but presently found that no one would buy his butter; suspecting the *svitka* he cut it up with his axe—but the pieces joined themselves together again. On a second attempt he succeeded in scattering the pieces and fled. But ever since then, each year at fair-time, a pig-faced devil comes grunting round the fair looking for the pieces of his *svitka*. He has now got them all except the left sleeve. . . .

At that moment there is a terrible crash and a *pig's head appears through the broken window of the hut*. Afanasy Ivanovich falls off the rafters in terror and the whole company hides or flies. Cherevik makes for the open country, pursued, as he believes, by one of the devils—actually Khivrya who has fled with the rest; they are both picked up later in the night, half-dead with fright, by gypsies. Next morning Cherevik, who has at last got some sleep in the *kum's* shed, is awakened by his spouse who wants him to lose no more time in selling the mare; hurrying on his ablutions she picks up what she thinks is a towel—and finds it is the cuff of a red *svitka*. That is the first shock to Cherevik's nerves, and worse is to follow. He is accosted by the gypsy who begins chaffing him about the mare. Cherevik pulls at the bridle—and finds instead of his mare a piece of a red *svitka*-sleeve. He flies in terror through the crowd, but the gypsy—who has of course been responsible for all these pranks—raises a cry of 'horse-thief,' and Cherevik finds himself bound hand and foot in a hut in company with the *kum*, on whom a similar trick has been played. Grïtsko now appears, magnanimously forgives the old man his cowardly change of mind and frees the prisoners. Cherevik, overjoyed, goes off to prepare for the wedding. Paraska is sitting alone, in the *kum's* hut, but thinking of her lover and admiring herself in a mirror. She isn't afraid of her step-mother, she tells herself; she begins to step out boldly, then to dance and sing. In come her father and the *kum*, then Grïtsko and a crowd of friends.

Khivrya bursts in angrily to forbid the wedding, but no one listens to her, and the laughing crowd 'forms round her an impenetrable dancing wall.'

That in outline is the story Mussorgsky attempted to turn into an opera. As with *Salammbô* and *Khovanshchina* he did not begin by writing a complete libretto or even a full and detailed scenario, but worked to a rough general idea and wrote the words scene by scene as he went along. The text indeed presented a greater problem than the music. To imitate the contours of Ukrainian folk music might not be impossible: Mussorgsky himself admitted [1] the difficulty of 'mastering all the shades and peculiarities of the melodic contours of Ukrainian speech.' But even before he could seriously try to catch the lilt of spoken Ukrainian, he had to write something that would pass for a Ukrainian libretto: a tolerable compromise between standard Russian and a dialect that differs from it considerably more than broad Scots differs from standard English, a dialect moreover that Mussorgsky is said to have known only slightly. 'As a result,' says Karatïgin,[2] 'the completed parts of the opera are by no means free from musical turns of phrase lacking in definite national char-acter, and the libretto is a rather unpleasing mixture of Great Russian and Little Russian.'

The outline scenario which Mussorgsky roughed out on '19th May 1877, at A.V. and O.A. Petrov's in Petrograd' (now preserved in the Leningrad Public Library) is as follows:[3]

ORCHESTRAL PRELUDE

A Hot Day in Little Russia

ACT I

1. Fair (chorus).

2. Entry of the *Parobok* with comrades (allusion to Parasya and Khivrya).

[1] See page 52.

[2] Article on *Sorochintsy Fair* in the Mussorgsky number of the *Muzïkalny Sovremennik*, Jan.-Feb. 1917.

[3] It will be noticed that his spelling of names and Ukrainian words, which I have followed faithfully, differs sometimes from Gogol's. Kara-tïgin comments on the 'strange words and curious phraseology.'

3. The *Chumak*[1] with Parasya. (Individualization—wheat, beads.)

4. Choral scene of traders about the Red *Svitka*—from which must emerge a scene of four—the *Kum* and the *Chumak*. Parasya and the *Parobok*.

5. After a while, the *Chumak* interferes in the Parasya‑*Parobok* business—recitative scene of the *Parobok's* and *Chumak's* recognition (drinking‑booth). N.B.—The gypsy is witness of this scene from the other side.

6. Entry of Khivrya—scene with Cherevik (the *Parobok*—witness of the scene). Khivrya leads her husband away.

7. The *Parobok's* grief. Appearance of the gypsy (condition of the oxen apropos of Parasya).

8. Little *hopak*. N.B.—? Intermezzo.

Act II

The 'Kum's' Hut

1. Cherevik is asleep. Khivrya wakes him (conversation about business, but more so as to get her husband out of the house).

2. Khivrya's recitatives—cooking—appearance of Afanasy Ivano‑vich. *Duettino*.

3. Entry of every one from the fair. Story of the Red *Svitka*. *Grande scène comique.*

Act III

1. Night. Uproar (with *praeludium*—the gipsy); after the flight from the Red *Svitka,* the *Kum* and Cherevik fall down exhausted. Outcry about the theft of horses and bulls. Arrest of both. Comic conversation of the captives. The *Parobok* to the rescue.

2. The *Parobok's dumka*.

3. It is just light. Parasya comes into the front garden. *Dumka*. Thought of Khivrya—independence—triumph and dance.

4. Cherevik and Parasya—dance.

[1] A *chumak* is a Ukrainian ox‑cart driver; Mussorgsky evidently means Cherevik.

5. The *Kum* and the *Parobok* with laughter—betrothal (talk about Khivrya's cupidity).

6. Finale.

Two points in the rough scenario call for comment. The 'N.B. ? Intermezzo' between Acts I and II refers to Mussorgsky's intention to use the choral version of his 'Bare Mountain' music from *Mlada* as a symphonic interlude in *Sorochintsy Fair*. On the face of it the obvious place for such a 'diabolical' intermezzo would seem to be before Act III, but in a letter to Golenishchev-Kutuzov written three months later than this scenario Mussorgsky says definitely: 'This act,[1] as you remember, follows immediately after the Intermezzo (Sabbath on the Bare Mountain;—it will be called "The *parobok's* dream").' The other point is in Act III, where Mussorgsky must have intended a change of scene before No. 3.

Such was the skeleton which he only partially covered with the flesh and blood of music. Various other composers have tried in various ways to complete the score—Cui in 1915, N. N. Cherepnin in 1923, Shebalin in 1931—while as early as 1904 Lyadov began 'revising' (in Rimsky-Korsakov's sense) and polishing and reorchestrating various separate numbers for concert performance, his treatment of the introduction being particularly drastic. But we are concerned here solely with what Mussorgsky wrote, and as he wrote it.[2]

The introduction, which Mussorgsky himself orchestrated, is headed 'A Hot Day in Little Russia,' as in the draft scenario, but cannot be compared with Gogol's marvellous scene-painting. Indeed it hardly attempts to rival it, for most of the material is taken from passages in the first act which have no connection with hot days or Ukrainian landscapes. Yet it sets the scene well enough. A gracefully indolent clarinet solo, soon picked up by other instruments, leads to a longish passage based on Parasya's first song (see example on page 159); then after a few brief references to the opening tune, in playful imitations, the mood suddenly changes and we hear the vigorous

[1] The second act.

[2] For a discussion of Cherepnin's version of *Sorochintsy Fair*, the only performing version known outside the U.S.S.R., I must refer the reader to a chapter in my book *On Russian Music* (William Reeves, London, 1939).

music of the fair. Among Mussorgsky's sketches for *Sorochintsy Fair* are twenty-seven Ukrainian folksongs, a number of which he introduced into his score, as we shall see presently; although the 'fair' theme is not one of these, it bears a family likeness to a number of Russian folk melodies and may even be one. Then, just as the curtain goes up, we hear the strain on page 152, borrowed from the market scene of *Mlada*. Only the orchestral theme itself is used, of course; the superimposed pedlars' cries and so on are different; but from this theme, much repeated, and others of the same type, Mussorgsky constructs a sort of kaleidoscopic musical mosaic which conveys, as realistically as an opera chorus can hope to convey, the confused impression of a country fair. Small additional choral groups are used: for instance, two tenors in unison represent Jews, three basses gypsies. Each new choral group adds its own thematic contribution; thus a group of *paroboks* and Cossacks enter bawling a folksong,[1] the gypsies have a theme which hints rhythmically at that (see (*a*), page 160) which is to be associated with the one particular old gypsy who plays such an important part in the plot; the girls flirting with the *paroboks* sing the original 'fair' theme of the introduction. But before this Parasya has wandered in with her father and is expressing her naïve wonder at the marvellous ribbons in a melody far more 'instrumental' in nature than one expects from Mussorgsky:

Akh, tya-tya, chtozh e-to za len - tï, chto za di - vo, pros-to za-glyaden'e!

The chorus dies away and the old gypsy comes forward and tells Cherevik, the *kum* and the crowd in general that the place is cursed; two brief passages must be quoted, the opening theme (*a*), which is his motive, and his first reference to the 'red *svitka*' (*b*) since both the ninth drop of the voice and the harmonic progression [2] are always associated with the *svitka*:

[1] According to the scenario there should be an 'allusion to Parasya and Khivrya' here, but Mussorgsky forgot this point.

[2] Karatïgin draws attention (Mussorgsky number of the *Muzïkalny Sovremennik*) to the analogy between these chords and those which accompany Dosifey's reference to 'the fleshly toils of hell' near the end of *Khovanshchina*.

Incidentally the harmonic progression was noted somewhat differently (mostly enharmonic differences) on a scrap of paper marked 'theme of the red *svitka*':

In the meantime Grïtsko has found Parasya and is making love to her; their voices, with the gypsy continuing his tale, blend in a charming though rather 'sketchy' little trio which is suddenly interrupted when Cherevik notices what is going on. Parasya breaks off in the middle of a word. Then follows the scene in which Grïtsko introduces himself, blurts out that he and Parasya are in love and gets Cherevik's consent: the text keeping fairly close to Gogol's dialogue, the music at first based entirely on a Ukrainian folk tune to which Rimsky-Korsakov took such a fancy that he introduced it in *his* Gogol opera, *Christmas Eve*, written some twenty years later. Mussorgsky characteristically seized on Cherevik's stumbling speech for naturalistic treatment, but it is also characteristic of his declining powers that the humour is musically feeble. As the three disappear into a booth, the lively choral fair music is resumed—and the music breaks off.

Mussorgsky left no music for Nos. 6 and 7 [1] of his scenario, though the temptation to insert 'the *parobok's dumka*' as the expression of Gritsko's grief in No. 7 is so overwhelming that Karatïgin,[2] Cherepnin and Shebalin have all succumbed to it—despite the fact that Mussorgsky has placed it as No. 2 in Act III. In compensation we have a comic 'drunk' scene for Cherevik and the *kum* (they 'come out of the booth later in the evening and wander in the twilight, often bumping against various objects,' says the stage direction) which fits nowhere into the sketch scenario but must belong to Act I; Karatïgin was probably right in placing it between 5 and 6. It is broadly humorous and racy, being based almost entirely on three folk tunes: the *kum's* song about the Cossack who went to Poltava, Cherevik's:

Oy, chu-ma-che, do-chu-ma-ko-vav - aya, Chort ma-ta-chiv i och-kur por-vav - aya.

which seems from its appearance in Act II to have been intended as his characteristic motive, and their 'Rududu' duet (another tune which Rimsky-Korsakov borrowed for *Christmas Eve*). And to end the act we have the 'little *hopak*,' or '*hopak* of the merry *parobok*' as Mussorgsky calls it in one manuscript, which is the one number from *Sorochintsy Fair* that every one knows; though every one, perhaps, does not know that its infectious tune is that of yet another Ukrainian folksong. This wholesale employment of actual folk material, in contrast with the merely incidental borrowings in *Boris* and *Khovanshchina,* is one of the most striking features of *Sorochintsy Fair*; one hardly knows whether to attribute it to failing melodic invention or to anxiety to lay on genuine Ukrainian colouring.

After Act II comes the 'intermezzo' which, it will be remembered, was based on the *Bare Mountain* music. It is impossible to say how

---

[1] Among the folksongs noted down by Mussorgsky for us in *Sorochintsy Fair* is one marked '*Parobok*' and beginning 'Oh my oxen,' probably intended for No. 7.

[2] In his edition of Mussorgsky's fragments.

far this third and last version differs from the second, the *Mlada* version, for the score of the latter has been lost. But the chorus parts of the third version must be nearly the same as those written for the second; at any rate the *Mlada* words are preserved in the *Sorochintsy Fair* version. Probably the second and third versions differed only in harmonic details—altered under pressure from Balakirev—and in the addition of the *parobok* theme (see bottom of page 164) at the end. The third version was finished in May 1880 and two or three months later Mussorgsky sent Stassov the following new and more elaborate programme, which may be compared with that of the original orchestral piece of 1867: [1]

THE 'PAROBOK'S' DREAM VISION

The *parobok* sleeps at the foot of a hillock at some distance from the hut where he should have been. *In his sleep appear to him:*

1. Subterranean roar of non-human voices, uttering non-human words.

2. The subterranean kingdom of darkness comes into its own—mocking the sleeping *parobok*.

3. Foreshadowing of the appearance of Chernobog and Satan.

4. The *parobok* left by the spirits of darkness. Appearance of Chernobog.

5. Worship of Chernobog and black mass.

6. Sabbath.

7. At the wildest moment of the sabbath the sound of a Christian church bell. Chernobog suddenly disappears.

8. Suffering of the demons.

9. Voices of the clergy in church.

10. Disappearance of the demons and the *parobok's* awakening.

It should be added that the orchestral work posthumously constructed from Mussorgsky's materials by Rimsky-Korsakov—the composition universally known as 'Mussorgsky's *Night on the Bare Mountain*'—is very much nearer to Mussorgsky's own third version than to his original orchestral piece.

[1] See page 176.

For Act II Mussorgsky composed the music for Nos. 1 and 2 of his scenario and about half of No. 3. The scenes between Khivrya and her husband and between Khivrya and her lover, if musically inferior to the Inn scene of *Boris,* take a high place among Mussorgsky's essays in the comic. To say that the humour is naïve, and its musical expression slight and sketchy, is not adverse criticism, but a definition of the genre. This is peasant farce—and its true musical expression. What makes it particularly remarkable is the extent to which it is constructed from actual folk material. I have not identified as a folk tune Khivrya's love theme:

first heard when she thinks of Afanasy Ivanovich while she does her cooking, though it has some of the characteristic marks of Ukrainian folk music (particularly bars 3 and 4); but when Cherevik starts talking in his sleep and then wakes up, he does it all to the tune shown on page 161, already associated with him in the 'drunk' scene. The dialogue about the sale of the mare is set to a melody that might well be folk, but might equally well be Mussorgsky; but from the point where Khivrya gets angrier (*poco agitato*) both her outbursts and her indolent husband's replies are set to an ingenious patchwork of identifiable folk tunes. And Khivrya's song when she is left alone[1] is constructed from three folksongs. The scene with Afanasy Ivanovich owes most of its humour to the priest's son's ecclesiastical intonations (cf. *The Seminarist* and the drunken monks in *Boris*).

[1] Mussorgsky left this in two forms: a shorter form that can easily be sung as a separate number, published by Bessel in 1886, and a larger one into which are dovetailed the example quoted above and Cherevik's theme see page 161, heard from behind the scene.

The unwelcome return of Cherevik, the *kum* and their friends is accompanied by snatches of a theme:

which Karatïgin regards as a reference to the *hopak* at the end of Act I. Afanasy hides, rapidly muttering 'Lord, have mercy on us,' and the guests crowd in. There follows considerable play with the tune on page 163 and that above, and presently the tipsy ones begin singing the 'Rududu' song, now as a quintet, which is rudely interrupted when the concealed Afanasy knocks over a tin pan and reawakens their superstitious fears. The *kum* begins the tale of the red *svitka,* for which Golenishchev-Kutuzov wrote the words, to one of Mussorgsky's most striking conceptions:

Cherevik at once starts to interrupt, as in Gogol—and there the music tantalizingly breaks off.

The rest of the *Sorochintsy Fair* music consists of a ten-bar fragment for piano, introducing another variant of the theme at the top of this page, marked 'uproar scene,' and evidently intended for the end of Act II, the beginning of Act III or both; the two *dumky* of Grïtsko and his sweetheart for Act III; some unused Ukrainian folk melodies and two unused themes marked 'Sorochintsy gypsies' and 'girls,' which were first published in 1939 in vol. v, part 10, of the complete edition of Mussorgsky's works. Grïtsko's *dumka* in the transposed Phrygian mode (which Mussorgsky oddly writes with two sharps in the signature) is one of his most beautiful melodic inspirations, the phrases of an unaccompanied solo instrument:

being answered by the voice, also unaccompanied except in the middle section. Parasya's *dumka* is less striking, though its melancholy first part is very lovely; the lively tune of the second part, when she admires herself in the mirror and begins to dance, is a *hopak*—and a less infectious one than that in the first act.]

CHAPTER X

INSTRUMENTAL AND CHORAL WORKS

[MUSSORGSKY does not shine as an instrumental composer, least of all in his few and unimportant essays in 'absolute' music. His best instrumental works are those in which his thought has been pre‐cipitated by a visual, best of all by a *moving* image. Neither the nature of his creative ability nor his aesthetic views encouraged him to grapple very seriously with the problems of pure instrumental music. He attempted only two instrumental media, the piano and the orchestra, and numerous musical examples must have already shown in the accompaniments of his songs and the piano versions—in most cases Mussorgsky's own—of the orchestra's share in his stage works that, beyond recognition of the percussive nature of the piano, he had little feeling for pianistic style as such; while the very existence of these piano scores, generally with a minimum of instrumental indication, suggests that Mussorgsky seldom thought originally and directly in terms of the orchestra. That last remark demands some qualification: there is the elaborate 'reduced' score of the 'Hymn to Tanit' in *Salammbô,* in which orchestral colour seems for once actually more important than melodic and harmonic substance; there are the sketches for *St. John's Night on the Bare Mountain,* the projected sym‐phonic poem *Poděbrad* and the completed piano duet version of the procession of princes in *Mlada*—all with indications of projected scoring. Nevertheless it is true, I think, to say that with Mussorgsky, as with many other respectable composers including Schumann and Brahms, orchestral colour was something to be laid on afterwards rather than an integral part of a musical conception.[1] The individual and by no means skilful manner of the laying on has been discussed in Chapter VIII. Still, even if Mussorgsky's piano music often cries out for orchestration and his orchestral music sometimes seems

---

[1] The piano part of *The Marriage* almost defies orchestration.

166

like piano music orchestrated, he yet contrived to give us one considerable orchestral work, *St. John's Night on the Bare Mountain*,
and one quite unique piano work, the *Pictures from an Exhibition*.

Mussorgsky's earliest piano composition, the *Porte-Enseigne Polka*
of 1852, has completely disappeared. The earliest surviving piece,
perhaps even earlier than *Where art thou, little star?* is a *Souvenir
d'enfance*, dated 16th October 1857. According to Stassov it was
written a month or two before Mussorgsky met Balakirev, but as the
most reliable accounts agree in placing that meeting in the summer of
1857, that is unlikely to be true. In any case it would be unwise to
make any deductions from the difference between this empty,
characterless *salon* piece and the expressive but Balakirevian song.
But the principal idea of the *Souvenir* is worth quoting for two reasons:
the conventional 'abstract' music discovered by the amateur composer's fingers at the keyboard is devoid of any specifically childlike
characteristics:

and as far removed as any music could be from the vivid and truthful
transcriptions of the child mind in action that he was to give the world
later in *The Nursery*. And even this early and characterless idea
reveals Mussorgsky's love of pedals.

Of the two piano Sonatas, in E flat major and F sharp minor,
embarked on in 1858, the only traces that have survived—thanks to
their quotation in a letter—are the themes of (*a*) the scherzo,[1] (*b*) the
introduction to the finale, (*c*) the first theme of the finale proper
(*allegro*):

---

[1] Example (*a*) appears to have had a sharp in the key-signature originally,
but Mussorgsky had scratched it through.

They tell us nothing about their composer's evolution, but are worth quoting for the sake of their curiosity. And the Scherzo in C sharp minor, written in November of the same year, is not unattractive. It is in 2–4 time, like the example above, with a really charming and characteristically harmonized trio in 3–4:

I quote from the earlier of the two versions, for, like so many of the songs, the Scherzo exists in two forms (as do several of the other piano pieces); in this case the later is decidedly the better, particularly in the workmanship of the trio, and has a charming little D flat coda based on the trio theme and obviously Balakirevian in inspiration. Not only the bulk of the trio—and the whole of this coda—but the opening of the main section of the scherzo is set over a tonic pedal. The four-bar theme of the scherzo tends to get dwelt on with merciless persistence—a characteristic of Russian instrumental music in general —but the rhythmical monotony is diminished by a pattern of 3 + 2 + 3 bars inserted after three rigid four-bar statements. The piano writing of the more boisterous part of the trio has, particularly in the first version, considerable affinity with the accompaniment of the song *Hour of Jollity,* written the following year; like the trio, the song is in A major with a middle section in F major.

Another Scherzo, actually so called in its first version, is one piece sometimes entitled *Children's Games—Puss in the Corner,* sometimes *Ein Kinderscherz* (first version September 1859, second May 1860). It is a pleasant, insignificant trifle, interesting only as an early essay in pictorialism within the limits of the facile *salon* style. Had it been called simply 'scherzo,' one would accept—or ignore—it as pure music; as it is, one can hear in it something of the rushing and romping of children. Even less significant and more amateurish is the *Impromptu passionné* (*Recollection of Beltov and Lyuba*) (1859) inspired by a love scene in Herzen's novel *Who is to blame?* The only points of interest are that the first two bars of the melody:

faintly anticipate the Dimitry motive in *Boris* (cf. first example on page 127; the likeness is more pronounced in other modifications of the theme) and are later given faintly canonic treatment.

The first movement (*Allegro assai*) of the duet Sonata in C major (1860), though obviously written only as an exercise,[1] is interesting as the only extant composition of Mussorgsky's in sonata form, indeed his only large-scale essay in absolute instrumental music—for which it conclusively demonstrates his inaptitude. The themes are neither typical of Mussorgsky nor promising as material for symphonic treatment; the only interesting feature is the attempt to give the whole thing unity by working a motive from the opening phrase of the subject (*a*) into the second-subject material (*b*) and (*c*):

---

[1] 'Symphonic exercise,' says a note on the manuscript.

But examination of the whole movement[1] is necessary to realize the awkwardness with which the young Mussorgsky handles a classical key-scheme and the emptiness of his would-be academic 'working-out.' The scherzo, the only other movement that seems to have been put on paper, is simply an arrangement of the C sharp minor Scherzo of 1858 transposed to C minor.

In striking contrast with the jejune themes just quoted is that of the *Intermezzo symphonique in modo classico* written the following year:

But although Mussorgsky himself considered this work 'classical' and its principal theme baroque, although the piece has no programme, it was generated in a way that almost invariably evoked Mussorgsky's inspiration in its most individual forms. Stassov has told the story, just as Mussorgsky himself told it to him:

In the winter of 1861 he was in the country with his mother, in the Pskov government, and one beautiful, sunny winter day—a holiday—he saw a whole crowd of peasants crossing the fields and plunging heavily through the snow-drifts; many of them fell down in the snow and then extricated themselves with some difficulty. 'This,' said Mussorgsky, 'was at one and the same time beautiful and picturesque and serious and amusing. And suddenly in the distance appeared a crowd of young women, coming with songs and laughter along a level pathway. This picture flashed into my head in a musical form and unexpectedly there shaped itself the first "stepping up and down" melody *à la Bach*; the jolly, laughing women presented themselves to me in the shape of a melody from which I then made the middle part or *Trio*. But all this—*in modo classico,* in accordance with my

---

[1] Published in vol. viii of the complete edition (1939).

musical preoccupations at that time. And that's how my *Intermezzo* saw the light of day.'

In those few sentences Mussorgsky lays bare the secret of his peculiar creative gift, at least of one of its most important facets: special sensitivity to motor-images and the ability to transmute them spontaneously into musical shapes. Only one word in caution must be said to those who know the *Intermezzo* solely in its original form as a piano solo: they will listen in vain for the trio suggested by the laughing women. That was added in 1867, when Mussorgsky orchestrated the piece:

This second version was also transcribed by the composer for piano solo.[1]

The *Intermezzo* is not equalled in interest by any of the five pieces written during the next twelve years. All five are trifles, and such slight interest as they possess is autobiographical rather than musical. Four of them date from the summer of 1865: the two pieces *From Memories of Childhood* (*Nurse and I* and *First Punishment : Nurse shuts me in a dark room,* the latter a *moto perpetuo* sketch left unfinished and posthumously completed by Karatïgin), both 'dedicated to the memory of my mother' who had just died, a *Duma* (reverie) on a theme by V. A. Loginov, one of the members of the 'commune' in which Mussorgsky was then living, and *La Capricieuse* on a theme by a young pupil of Balakirev's, Count L. L. Heyden. A 'scherzino' entitled *The Seamstress,* written in January 1871,[2] is more pianistic and has a technical neatness unusual with Mussorgsky, but lacks any more substantial quality.

---

[1] Both piano versions are in vol. viii of the complete edition, the orchestral score of the second version in vol. vii, part 5.

[2] Wrongly dated 1880 by Karatïgin, and others who have copied him.

All these trivialities are completely overshadowed by the unique set of *Pictures from an Exhibition* (1874), in which Mussorgsky paid tribute to the art of his dead friend Victor Alexandrovich Hartmann. Mussorgsky has, as it were, left a musical record of a visit to the exhibition of Hartmann's work organized a month or two before by Stassov. Nothing could characterize Mussorgsky's own art more sharply than the complete absence of subjective emotion from a composition directly inspired by a deeply felt personal loss. (The same might be said of the much less important *Memories of Childhood* already mentioned.) He is content to give us his simple, direct musical reaction to each Hartmann design; he has not kept himself out of the music—but he has put himself in only as another visual impression, an objectively seen character strolling from picture to picture.

The 'programme' by Stassov, prefixed to the original edition is as follows:

The introduction bears the title 'Promenade.'

No. 1. 'Gnomus': A sketch [1] depicting a little gnome, clumsily running with crooked legs.

No. 2. 'Il vecchio castello': A medieval castle before which a troubadour sings a song.

No. 3. 'Tuileries. *Disput d'enfants après jeux*': An avenue in the garden of the Tuileries, with a swarm of children and nurses.

No. 4. 'Bydlo': A Polish cart on enormous wheels, drawn by oxen.

No. 5. 'Ballet of unhatched fledglings': Hartmann's design for the *décor* of a picturesque scene in the ballet *Trilby*.[2]

No. 6. 'Two Polish Jews, rich and poor.'[3]

---

[1] Said to have been a design for a nutcracker.

[2] *Trilby* or *The Demon of the Heath,* a ballet with choreography by Petipa, music by Julius Gerber and *décor* by Hartmann, based on Charles Nodier's *Trilby, or the Elf of Argyle,* was produced at the Bolshoy Theatre, Petersburg, in 1871. The fledglings were canary chicks.

[3] The person responsible for rechristening this number 'Samuel Goldenberg and Schmuyle' remains unknown.

No. 7. 'Limoges. *Le marché*': French women quarrelling violently in the market. [1]

No. 8. 'Catacombae': Hartmann represented himself examining the Paris catacombs [2] by the light of a lantern.

No. 9. 'The Hut on Fowls' Legs': Hartmann's drawing depicted a clock in the form of Baba-Yaga's hut on fowls' legs. Mussorgsky added Baba-Yaga's flight in a mortar.

No. 10. 'The Heroes' Gate at Kiev': Hartmann's sketch was his design for city gates at Kiev in the ancient Russian massive style with a cupola shaped like a Slavonic helmet.

It should be added that the 'Promenade' is resumed, in varying lengths and plastically handled, before Nos. 2, 3, 5 and 7 and—more definitely changed—constitutes the second part of No. 8, which in the autograph score is prefaced by the following note: 'N.B.: Latin text: with the dead in a dead language. A Latin text would be suitable: the creative soul of the dead Hartmann leads me to the skulls, invokes them, the skulls shine softly.' Accordingly the published score is inscribed 'Con mortuis in lingua mortua.' No. 9 also calls for some explanation. Baba-Yaga is perhaps the most striking creature of Russian folklore; according to W. R. S. Ralston (*The Songs of the Russian People*) she 'is generally represented under the form of a hideous old woman, very tall in stature, very bony of limb, with an excessively long nose and with dishevelled hair. Her nose is sometimes described as being of iron, as also are her long pendent breasts and her strong sharp teeth. As she lies in her hut she often stretches across from one

[1] In the autograph manuscript the following alternative French texts were afterwards both crossed out by Mussorgsky himself: 'La grande nouvelle: Mr Pimpant de Panta-Pantaléon vient de retrouver sa vache: La Fugitive. "Oui, Maàme, c'était hier.—Non, Maàme, c'était avant-hier.—Eh bien, oui, Maàme, la bête rôdait dans le voisinage.—Eh bien, non, Maàme, la bête ne rôdait pas du tout.—etc.' 'La grande nouvelle: Mr de Puissangeout vient de retrouver sa vache, "La Fugitive." Mais les bonnes dames de Limoges ne sont pas tout à fait d'accord sur ce sujet, parce que Mme de Remboursac s'est appropriée une belle denture en porcelaine, tandis que Mr de Panta-Pantaléon garde toujours son nez gênant—couleur pivoine.'

[2] The autograph score, however, is inscribed 'Sepulcrum romanum.'

corner to the other, and her nose goes right through the ceiling. Her usual habitation is a cottage which stands on fowls' legs, that is, on slender supports. The door looks towards the forest, but when the hut is adjured in the right words it turns round, so that its back is towards the forest and its front towards the person addressing it. . . . When the Baba-Yaga goes abroad, she rides in an iron mortar. This she propels with the pestle, a sort of club, and as she goes, she sweeps away the traces of her passage with a broom.' The Baba-Yaga has also inspired orchestral pieces by Dargomïzhsky and Lyadov, and she plays a prominent part in Rimsky-Korsakov's orchestral *Legend*.

Musically the *Pictures from an Exhibition* show Mussorgsky not at his best, perhaps, but certainly at his most characteristic. The only complete failure is *Il vecchio castello*. The other pieces vary in quality and in pianistic effectiveness (the weakest feature of the set, which cries out for orchestration and has had its cry answered more than once [1]), but broadly speaking the pantomimic numbers—the 'prome-nades,' the darting, pausing, limping gnome, the heavy lumbering *bydlo*—are even more vivid than those which work out musical stylizations of realistic sound: the squabbling children in the Tuileries garden, the chatter of the women in Limoges market. The double portrait of the two Jews, one fat and pompous, the other whining and begging, deserves a place beside the best of the song carica-tures; it is perhaps the *ne plus ultra* of musical characterization—that is, of instrumental characterization without the aid of words except as a title. *The Heroes' Gate at Kiev*, which makes an imposing crown to the work, is most Mussorgskian in the middle: the bell effect reminding one of the Coronation scene in *Boris* and a passage in the introduction to *Khovanshchina*. [2]

Mussorgsky's remaining piano compositions (all dating from 1879–1880) are of little account. The concert tour with Mme Leonova resulted in two pieces both entitled *On the Southern Shore of the Crimea:*

---

[1] Though unfortunately not by Lyadov, who contemplated scoring them in 1903, but never did. His colouring would have been far more Russian than Ravel's is.

[2] An interesting account of Hartmann, with descriptions and reproductions of his pictures, is given in Albert Frankenstein's 'Victor Hartmann and Modeste Mussorgsky' (*Musical Quarterly*, July 1939).

Gkhurzuf by Ayu-Dag (*Yurzuf*). *From notes of travel,* while the second is distinguished by yet another sub-title, *Baydarki Capriccio, baydarki* being Tartar canoes. (The first is often called simply *Gurzuf.*) The middle sections of both pieces are quasi-oriental in character and may be records of actual Crimean folk music heard by Mussorgsky during his visit. *In the Village,* a dance *alla zingara* with a slow and rather beautiful introduction, may be another travel impression. *Méditation : feuillet d'album* and *Une Larme* belong to the small change of *salon* music and lack that fineness of workmanship which alone can make such trifles acceptable.

Mussorgsky's orchestral music is even less in bulk than his piano music. The only really considerable scores he ever completed were the orchestral version of the *Intermezzo in modo classico* already mentioned and the famous and ill-fated *St. John's Night on the Bare Mountain* (both 1867).

The early Scherzo in B flat major (1858) is more classical, less Russian, than the piano Scherzo in C sharp minor, but here too the most characteristic portion is the trio: unmistakably 'school of Bala-kirev.' The *Alla marcia notturna* (1861) has not yet, I think, been published, and the *andante,* scherzo and finale of the projected D major Symphony (1861–2) have all disappeared—unless the four bars of colourless *maestoso molto* in B major and 6–8 time which Mussorgsky quotes in a letter to Balakirev (13th–25th January 1861) are part of the scherzo, which we know to have been in B major.

St. John's Night on the Bare Mountain is another matter. No work of Mussorgsky's has had a more confused history and none is less known; up to the present (August 1945) it has had only a single per-formance in this country—on 3rd February 1932 under Nikolay Malko.[1] Editorial misdating of letters and natural speculation con-cerning possible sketches for the music as early as 1861 (the celebrated but non-existent 'music for Mengden's drama *The Witches*'), if not earlier (the projected opera on Gogol's story *St. John's Eve*), have com-bined to fog even the early history of this music; Rimsky-Korsakov

---

[1] I need hardly remind the reader that the orchestral piece universally known as 'Mussorgsky's *Night on the Bare Mountain*' is an orchestral com-position by Rimsky-Korsakov based on the later version of the *Bare Mountain* music which Mussorgsky prepared for *Sorochintsy Fair.*

in his memoirs and the preface to his *Bare Mountain* score, has contrived to thicken the fog by asserting that the thing 'was first written for piano and orchestra at the beginning of the sixties and soon recast for orchestra only,'[1] but no one else seems to have seen or heard of this version with piano, 'written under the influence of Liszt's *Danse macabre*' (which Mussorgsky could not possibly have heard before March 1866), and there is good reason to believe that it never existed outside Rimsky-Korsakov's notoriously faulty memory. Some of the material (i.e. thematic sketches) may well have originated at the time of the Mengden project and, as we have seen, one fragment of it (cf. example on page 104) was used in 1864 in *Salammbô*. But the first specific reference to actual composition occurs in a letter to Balakirev dated 20th April 1866—a month or so after Mussorgsky had heard the Liszt *Danse macabre*—in which he says definitely: 'I've begun to sketch the witches . . . Satan's journey doesn't satisfy me yet.' And the inscription at the end of the autograph score is equally definite: 'Planned in 1866. Began to write for orchestra, 12th June 1867, finished the work on the eve of St. John's Day, 23rd June 1867, in the Luga District on Minkino Farm.'

Mussorgsky gave this account of the programme of his work in a letter to Nikolsky:

So far as my memory doesn't deceive me, the witches used to gather on this mountain, gossip, play tricks and await their chief—Satan. On his arrival they, i.e. the witches, formed a circle round the throne on which he sat, in the form of a kid, and sang his praise. When Satan was worked up into sufficient passion by the witches' praises, he gave the command for the sabbath, in which he chose for himself the witches who caught his fancy. —So this is what I've done. At the head of my score I've put its content: 1. Assembly of the witches, their talk and gossip; 2. Satan's journey; 3. Obscene praises of Satan;[2] and 4. Sabbath. . . . The form and character of composition are both *Russian and original*.

---

[1] Rimsky-Korsakov says in his memoirs that this orchestral version was left unfinished; he had forgotten the triumphant letters in which Mussorgsky had announced to him its completion.

[2] The third section is actually described on the title-page of the score as 'Black service (*Messe noire*).' Otherwise the programme given in the autograph score agrees exactly with the end of this passage in the letter to Nikolsky.

'St. John's Night on the Bare Mountain'

The original version of the score[1] was first published in 1968. It raises certain problems. For one thing it does not include a passage in 3/4 time:

which the composer had quoted in his letter to Rimsky-Korsakov (see page 20), written only twelve days after the completion of the score; this must have been deleted after 5th July, yet the autograph (which shows no trace of such a deletion) is clearly dated 30th June. One can only conclude that, despite the date, the autograph is in fact a later fair copy. The other excerpt in the letter to Rimsky-Korsakov,

is worth quoting as the original form of a familiar passage in the Rimsky-Korsakov version. It is impossible to determine the relationship between the 1867 score and the lost intermediate version used in *Mlada*, but there are very considerable differences between it and the final version inserted in *Sorochintsy Fair* which was drastically cut and partly rewritten. The original score should certainly be allowed to supersede the Korsakov bowdlerization.

Immediately after the completion of *St. John's Night on the Bare Mountain*, Mussorgsky set about the composition of another major work, a symphonic poem *Poděbrad of Bohemia*, which unfortunately

[1] Recorded by the London Philharmonic Orchestra under David Lloyd-Jones on Philips 6580–053.

he never finished—possibly on account of Balakirev's crushing criticism of its predecessor. Pan-Slav enthusiasm was then at its height in Russia; delegations of Czechs and other Slavonic peoples were visiting Russia, and at a concert in their honour, given in Peters-burg in May, two specially written works had been performed, Balakirev's *Overture on Czech Themes* (later restyled 'symphonic poem, *In Bohemia*') and Rimsky-Korsakov's *Fantasia on Serbian Themes*.[1] Borodin too had in January embarked on a tremendous set of *Sixty Variations on a Czech Theme* for piano, but abandoned the task. Now in July Mussorgsky set about *his* tribute to the Czechs, inspired by a somewhat sketchy impression of the feats of the astute 'Hussite King' George of Poděbrad (reigned 1458–71). All we know of the work is contained in a letter to Rimsky-Korsakov (15th/27th July 1867):

The introductory theme goes like this (slow):

the introduction begins with two series,[2] the second in C sharp minor; after that there is a sort of continuation of this little theme—Slavonic in cantilena, and it ends with a tremolo of all the strings against the orchestra *tutti*; the cres-cendo gradually rises to *ff* (explosion), after which everything gets quieter and quieter. The 'Poděbrad' theme (the introduction depicts the mournful situation of Bohemia, oppressed by the Germans) is as follows (Fairly quick):

---

[1] It was in his notice of this concert that Stassov inadvertently coined the nickname which has stuck to the Balakirev group: 'God grant that our Slavonic guests may never forget to-day's concert; God grant that they may ever preserve the memory of how much poetry, feeling, talent and skill we have in our small but already mighty handful of Russian musicians.' The expression 'mighty handful' (*moguchaya kuchka*) was mockingly seized on by Stassov's enemies; the 'handful' themselves retorted by proudly adopting it.

[2] As does *St. John's Night*. By 'series' Mussorgsky means an entire musical sentence, which is then repeated—Liszt-wise—in another key.

Accompaniment to the theme. The Pope's anger with Poděbrad turns out very energetic and bad-tempered (improvisation only, at present). At the end of the poem, after scurryings on the strings only in the scale of A major *ff* and little Slavonic fanfares of brass, the theme you know (I make it *à la guerra* [*sic*]—Poděbrad—*King*—Slavdom has triumphed) and so the poem begins in F sharp minor and ends in D major:

The themes, particularly the middle one, are Czech in character and may be actual Czech tunes given the composer by Balakirev.

Mussorgsky's only other independent orchestral work is the 'triumphal march,' *The Capture of Kars* (1880). In commemoration of the twenty-fifth anniversary of the accession of Alexander II a 'grand scenic representation' was planned in the Bolshoy Theatre on 19th February/3rd March 1880, consisting of *tableaux vivants* depicting outstanding events of the reign accompanied by music and linked by a dialogue between the Muse of History and the Spirit of Russia. K. Y. Davïdov, the director of the Petersburg Conservatory,[1] approached a number of distinguished composers: Anton Rubinstein, Tchaikovsky, Rimsky-Korsakov, Mussorgsky, Borodin, Cui, Soloviev, Nápravník and others, to provide the accompanying music. Time was short: the commissions were sent out only in January; and although no 'picture' was to last more than seven minutes most of the composers, Mussorgsky included, adapted scores already written for some other purpose, which was just as well, for the 'grand scenic representation' never came off after all. The only composer who really rose to the occasion was Borodin, who produced for it his well-known orchestral piece *In Central Asia*. Mussorgsky, who had

[1] He had succeeded Azanchevsky in 1876.

been commissioned to set the tableau depicting the capture of Kars from the Turks in 1855, simply fished out the 'procession of nobles and priests' from *Mlada,* the main section of which (it will be re-membered) consisted of variations on a Russian folksong, discarded the 'priests' trio and substituted a fresh trio on a Kurdish or Turkish theme. Hence the piece has become popularly known as the *March, with trio 'alla turca'* or even, quite absurdly, as *Marche turque.*

It seems natural to group Mussorgsky's two surviving compositions for chorus and orchestra—both on Old Testament subjects, *The Destruction of Sennacherib* (first version, 1867; second version, 1874) and *Jesus Navin* (roughed out in 1874-5, but finished only in 1877)—with the orchestral works, for they are essentially orchestral music with vocal *obbligati*; the choral parts are seldom independent and, especially in *Sennacherib,* might almost be dispensed with without serious damage to the musical texture. In describing them one has to tell again the old stories of works based on other works and com-positions existing in two quite different forms.[1]

The first version of *The Destruction of Sennacherib* is a setting of a free prose translation, possibly by Mussorgsky himself but more probably by Stassov, of the first three stanzas of Byron's well-known 'The Assyrian came down like the wolf on the fold' from the *Hebrew Melodies.* The first two stanzas are set to vigorous, picturesque music, faintly oriental in character, with a constantly moving crotchet bass: not first-rate Mussorgsky, but characteristic 'romantic' Mussorgsky of the *Salammbô,* pre-*Boris* period. At the beginning of the second stanza (B minor—the main key is E flat minor) one notes a charac-teristic Lisztian figure used in *The Bare Mountain*:

(cf. the finale of the *Faust* Symphony, the *Mephisto Waltz,* etc.).

The music dies away in E flat minor *ppp,* and a hushed setting of the third stanza ('For the Angel of Death spread his wings on the blast') constitutes the middle section of the piece, after which the

[1] Or three if one counts Rimsky-Korsakov's version of the 1867 form of *Sennacherib.*

words and music of the first two stanzas are repeated in their entirety. It was criticism of this middle section:

which Stassov sneered at as 'the indispensable *trio,* in the classical manner . . . an imitation, however unintentional, of western chorales,' which led Mussorgsky to recast the work seven years later. To begin with, he almost completely rewrote the words, preserving only the general sense of the poem and a few Byronic phrases from the opening, just as he had rewritten Pushkin and Byron-Kozlov for the second versions of the songs *Night* and *King Saul.* Nevertheless the music of the first section is essentially unaltered, only minor changes being made in the chorus parts to fit the new text, the time-signature changed from 4–4 to 2–2 and the tempo marking from *Quick* to *Allegretto moderato, alla breve* in the orchestral score and *Allegro giusto* in the vocal score. But instead of the above theme we get some entirely new music which must be amongst the most banal Mussorgsky ever wrote: [1]

[1] It is, moreover, an unmistakable echo in melody and harmony of the chorus 'Hail to Judith, the chosen of Heaven' in the last act of Serov's *Judith.*

dal' - nim khol-mam pro-be - zha - li

describing how 'as the shades of evening hurried over the distant hills Israel prostrated itself in tearful prayer before the face of Jehovah.' The work now ends not with a full recapitulation of the first part, but with a very much shortened version of the music set to new words about the 'shuddering of the children of Baal.'

If *The Destruction of Sennacherib* belongs in spirit and style to the world of *Salammbô*, this world of the ancient East (more specifically the history of the Semitic peoples) which seems to have fascinated Mussorgsky, the companion-piece *Jesus Navin* or *Joshua*—'Jesus' and 'Joshua' are forms of the same name—is literally taken from *Salammbô*. According to the inscription on the score, *Jesus Navin* is 'founded on national songs of Israel' and both Rimsky-Korsakov and Stassov tell how Mussorgsky heard 'the theme of this chorus'—Stassov says 'themes'—sung by Jewish neighbours celebrating the Feast of Tabernacles. The accuracy of these statements is not disproved by the fact that all the material is actually adapted from *Salammbô*: the *Salammbô* themes themselves may be Jewish in origin. Mussorgsky may have argued that the Carthaginians were a Semitic people—though as it happens both themes are sung in the opera by Libyans. But, apart from the fact that the themes are not Jewish in character, it seems a little suspicious that no one has ever said anything about the Jewish origin of any of the *Salammbô* material. The authentic Jewishness is proclaimed only when it is connected with a Jewish subject.

The bass solo (Joshua's call to battle) and male chorus ('Bare thy sword, O Israel'), which together form the first part of the work, are adapted with relatively insignificant alterations from the War Song of the Libyans; the only new feature is the introduction of the Lisztian semiquaver figure quoted on page 180; but the middle section—an alto solo, 'The women of Canaan weep,' rounded off by a brief female chorus—shows more interesting changes. It originated in Mâtho's lament which, it will be remembered, was a setting of a slightly modified version of a poem by Polezhaev:

Ya um-ru —— o-di nok;—— Na po-zor pa-la-cham, vpo-ru-ga- n'e

In *Jesus Navin* this becomes:

Plachut zhe-nï Khana- a - na, sto-nom sto-nut ve-si — Mas-si- fa- va,

which certainly sounds a little more oriental but is, after all, only an ornamental version of the preceding example. The work is rounded off by a repetition of the bass solo in shortened form and the bellicose chorus, in which the women's voices now join.

Of no importance but some slight interest are the little *a cappella* choruses written in 1880 for Darya Leonova's pupils. The four arrangements of Russian folksongs for four-part male chorus—there is a fifth unfinished—are really worth performance; they are quite simple and straightforward but beautifully sympathetic harmonizations. I quote the opening of one of the three-part vocalises for women's voices that have been preserved:

They horrified Rimsky-Korsakov by their 'awful part-writing,' but even here Mussorgsky shows his innate Russianness in such points as the unison cadences, a marked characteristic of Russian folk polyphony.]

CHAPTER XI

MUSSORGSKY'S STYLE AND TECHNIQUE

F. A. POTTLE points out in his *The Idiom of Poetry* (London, 1941) that each sensibility

has an idiom which is perfectly expressive of it; but the sensibility may develop before the idiom is enounced, or the idiom may go on being used conventionally after the sensibility has changed. At the beginning of a shift in sensibility, poets continue to use the old idiom because they know no other. Awkwardly and by half-lights, the new sensibility shows through, striving for more perfect expression. Then, the idiom is enounced. Until it is, a great poetic genius might fumble at expression.

To this we may add that, until listeners have developed the new sensibility and are at ease with the idiom that expresses it, they are bound to fumble for comprehension. Naturally, the innovative artist is ahead of his public. This is what we mean when we say of any one of them that he was born before his time, usually without asking ourselves whether '*his* time' might not have failed to come but for his own contributions to the formation of the new sensibility and idiom.

A new musical sensibility, a sensibility to combinations of sounds and rhythms either novel or long set aside, an awareness of their potentialities in musical art, had begun to crop up with Schubert, Berlioz, Chopin, Schumann and Liszt in western Europe; and in Russia with Glinka. It asserts itself strongly in Mussorgsky, who played an important part in establishing the new idiom and also the new syntax it entailed because it could not fit in with the accepted syntax of the time. His influence made itself felt not only on later innovators such as Debussy and Ravel, but also, through them, on composers who had studied his music but little, if at all: Bartók and Kodály, for instance. In his uphill task of discovering the means of expression he required, he found guidance in his intuition, in the idiosyncrasies of his nature and even in his prejudices—his mistrust of conventions and of theoretical learning, which might lead him to rely on conventional values,[1] in his acquired views on the realistic

[1 One is reminded of Glinka's abandonment of his Ukrainian Symphony because of his inability 'to get out of the German rut in the development.']

184

functions of music; in the native folk music in which, from his earliest childhood, he had been steeped; and, above all, in his auditory sensitiveness and imagination.

That this gift was exceptional in range and subtlety is shown, notably, by the wonderfully original and beautiful harmonies with which his music teems (*Night, The Nursery,* the *Songs and Dances of Death, Sunless, Boris Godunov* provide countless instances); by the aptness and point of the accents and contrasts he achieves by means of harmony; and by his unique capacity for perceiving, and translat-ing into musical inflections, the inflections of human speech—an invaluable asset to a musical 'realist' such as he. Another asset so far as realism is concerned was his strong, keen visual imagination, with its necessary complement, muscular-motor imagination. (For the human eye perceives forms and movements not by a single act of vision, but by a series of displacements of the eyeballs which calls the muscular-motor sense into play.)[1] It enabled him to transpose the rhythms of motions into strikingly effective musical rhythms and patterns, [as has already been described in the previous chapter in connection with the *Intermezzo in modo classico.* But] however graphic pantomimic-descriptive music may be, it is, of course, of artistic value only in so far as it is significant as music pure and simple. When in *Boris Godunov* Pimen in his cell is writing his chronicle:

and where, in *Khovanshchina*, a timorous scribe is hurriedly and anxiously taking down a compromising message:

the music clearly suggests the motions of the writer's hands. But if

[1] The importance of muscular-motor imagination in his make-up, first pointed out in the present writer's book of 1908, is stressed by Lapshin in the Mussorgsky number of the *Muzïkalny Sovremennik* (1917).

its descriptive quality passes unnoticed, or is ignored as irrelevant, we still have adequate, purely musical evocations of austere meditative serenity in the one case, of stealth and trepidation in the other; it would be equally effective in a sonata or a quartet. An uninspired composer might have given us pantomimic patterns no less graphic, yet of no artistic value whatsoever.

The *fons et origo* of Mussorgsky's new idiom, of his harmonies and modal schemes, is to be found in Russia's folk music, and not so much in the solo tunes as in the less known choral songs, which carry us into a harmonic world of their own, unaccountable in terms of western music and often disconcerting to the western ear,[1] but affording a wealth of raw materials to a composer endowed with the right kind of ear and imagination. There is no room for dealing adequately with this point, but a few examples showing the idiosyncrasies of these songs should suffice to illustrate it:

Notice, among other special features, the lack of leading notes, the consecutive fourths and fifths, the unprepared and unresolved sevenths.

In this music Mussorgsky had been steeped since his childhood, and modal music was as natural a language to him as it was to a number of other Russian composers—notably Glinka, Balakirev and Borodin. It would be fatal, however, to deal with the question of modes without taking precautions. As pointed out by Curt Sachs in a most illuminating essay, *The Road to Major*,[2] we must first 'get rid of the obsession that leads to testing all archaic melodies with a modal gauge.' Moreover, it should not be overlooked that 'the old modes have reappeared in modern music only to undergo a

---

[1] These were first studied by Melgunov in the late seventies, and later by Lineva, Kastalsky and many others. Rimsky-Korsakov, in his memoirs, dismisses Melgunov as 'the compiler of a collection of barbarous folksongs.'

[2] *Musical Quarterly*, July 1943.

transformation. Polyphonic and harmonic treatment has lessened their individuality, blurred their melodic contours and other distinctive features.'[1] So it is advisable to speak, not of modes, but of modal scales; and, in order to avoid confusion, to keep to the fixed, simplified nomenclature used in many modern books: mode of C=Ionian; of D=Dorian; of E=Phrygian; of F=Lydian; of G=Mixolydian; of A=Aeolian; and of B=Hypophrygian.

Mussorgsky uses—besides the major, minor and modal scales and occasionally the pentatonic—irregular scales, such as the whole-tone scale; and also what might be termed variable scales: a designation not in general use, but rendered needful by positive facts. The melodic minor scale of western music is a variable scale, the sixth and seventh notes being lower by a semitone when it descends than when it rises. But there are, in the folk music of Russia and of many other countries, scales in which alterations occur now and then, not in accordance with any fixed rule; and it is but seldom that these alterations can be accounted for by attraction towards the next note, or by faulty intonation, or by 'pathetic' intonation.

Here are a few examples. The opening of *Boris Godunov* is in C sharp Aeolian—that is, C sharp minor key, but Aeolian scale; the chorus that follows in F Aeolian, with a few passing-notes, and at one spot a G♭, which introduces a Hypophrygian touch; the Inn scene opens with a three-bar theme in C sharp Phrygian, followed, after a one-bar transition, by a two-bar theme in D Aeolian leading to C major, C sharp Hypophrygian breaking out again three bars farther on. In Xenia's lament, initial version, the first four bars of both periods (Lamm edition, pages 118–19) are an irregular scale, B♭, C♭, D♭, E♭, F, G, B♭, which, with G♭ instead of G, would be B flat Dorian. The 'Kazan' song in the Inn scene is built on two motives: the first in F sharp Phrygian, the second (after an enharmonic modulation) in B flat Aeolian. Typical instances of the variable scales are to be found in the songs *Where art thou, little star?* (first version)—F sharp Aeolian, with D and E now natural, now sharp; *Kalistratushka*—F sharp Aeolian, with B and D occasionally sharp; and *The wild winds blow,* mainly in C sharp Aeolian with occasional D♮ and (in the accompaniment) G♮ and B♯.

[1] Maurice Emmanuel, *Histoire de la langue musicale* (Paris, 1911).

Melodic patterns based on these scales lend themselves to harmonizations that may differ widely without affecting the tonal balance, and to temporary modulations that come as part of the warp and woof, not as shiftings of the centre or as ornamental adjuncts. However elastic and mobile the tonality may be, and even when it is not asserted by any preponderance of the tonic, dominant and subdominant harmonies, and cannot be defined in terms of the old theory, it remains definite and firm under foot.

The harmony ranges from bare fifths and fourths in the archaic style of folk polyphony and church chants, and bare seconds or sevenths, to the richest and most complex chords, further enriched by pedal-points and passing notes, most of which, owing to the elasticity and variability of the scales, become, to all practical intents and purposes, real harmonic notes, and so confirm the modal and tonal schemes instead of blurring them. The selection is intuitive. The harmony that is to come next is hardly ever predetermined. There is no need to stress the point nowadays, for most of these innovations have passed into everyday practice and most of us have learnt to keep our ears and not our technical treatises open; but in Mussorgsky's time it was all very disconcerting.

An especially interesting instance is, in *Boris Godunov*, the song of the vagabond monks. Mussorgsky obtained the tune from the repertory of a folksong singer. It is in F Aeolian, and each note in the harmonization belongs to the chord of the major ninth on E♭ or is a passing note or grace-note, the harmonization ranging from

to

The song ends on the bare fifth F C, and the following chorus suddenly breaks out in F sharp Aeolian.

A comparison with Rimsky-Korsakov's later harmonization of the original folk tune:

will help to realize how brilliant Mussorgsky's treatment is.[1]

He practically never dwells long on one harmony. Exceptions such as a stretch of five bars on the A flat major triad in Salammbô's prayer, the first six bars of the *Khovanshchina* prelude or even the first three in the *andantino* in Boris's dying prayer, are so few as to be negligible. How very mobile his harmony can be is shown by the sequence of the major triads on E, C♯, A, F♯, D♯, G♭, E♭, C, A♭ under a melodic line which is, allowing for enharmony, strongly suggestive of B major, when in Pimen's cell Grigory describes his dream: 'Up an endless stairway I climbed a lofty tower; from the top all Moscow I beheld.'

Another specially interesting instance is the beginning of *Trepak* (*Songs and Dances of Death*), in which the main key, D minor, is introduced via the F major, A minor and F sharp minor triads—a most effective opening, which Rimsky-Korsakov, in his posthumous edition of the work, did away with by transposing it to the main key.

Of all harmonic artifices those that Mussorgsky uses most freely are passing notes and pedal points. He also uses appoggiaturas freely, especially at the beginning of phrases and segments; but he seldom resorts to suspensions or anticipations (see further, page 192). He inclines to use chords for their value *per se* rather than as parts of a harmonic scheme, but does not ignore the fact that this value depends

[1] It is equally instructive to compare his treatment of the beautiful folk tune he uses for Marfa's song at the beginning of Act III in *Khovanshchina* with Tchaïkovsky's in his overture to Ostrovsky's *Storm*.

to a great extent on the context—at the beginning of *Trepak* for instance, the strong contrast between the opening chords and the
appearance, in the main key, of a forecast of the principal theme of
the song is highly significant.

As with the chords, so with the modulations. They may be more
or less prepared or (even when bringing in a far distant key) abrupt.
The above-mentioned leap from F Aeolian to F sharp Aeolian is a
case in point. The bouncing about from key to key in the wild
Revolution chorus opening at this point is particularly noteworthy,
and the effect is tremendous.

Whether prepared or abrupt, the modulations may be founded on
enharmony. When they are, it is never a counsel of despair. Mussorgsky is not infallible, of course; and a few clumsy concatenations
or modulations are to be found here and there in his music. Leaving
aside rough sketches and discarded drafts, we have from his pen one
piece of appalling nonsense: seven bars in the people's chorus in the
St. Basil scene (initial version of *Boris Godunov*) of this nature:

When writing the full score he did away with it, replacing it by
simple, straightforward music, thoroughly in keeping with the rest

of the beautiful chorus. Most of the other instances one might adduce are trifling and call for no more than a little touching up.

Mussorgsky's melodies usually proceed in undulations rather than prolonged motion in one direction. They consist, as a rule, of small or moderate intervals. Intervals bigger than a sixth hardly occur in his mature works except at lyrical or dramatic climaxes or for dramatic (or comic) emphasis. His instrumental themes, and especially the *Leitmotive* in his operas, occupy but a small compass—usually no more than a sixth. He inclines to use only a small number of note-values, ranging from the dotted crotchet to the semiquaver, triplets introducing further variety. Only one minim occurs in the initial version of Boris's monologue. *Savishna* is all in crotchets; *The Feast* likewise, except for one minim. There is no longer value than the dotted crotchet in Marfa's prophetic song (*Khovanshchina*, Act II). There are exceptions, of course: he uses nine values in *Sphinx* and in *The wild winds blow*, eight in the *Serenade* (*Songs and Dances of Death*).

Remembering that he is essentially a composer of vocal music, we should not overlook the fact that the prosody of the texts he sets prescribes certain conditions—predetermining, for instance, whether phrases should start with an upbeat or an accent, have a masculine or feminine ending and so forth. But if we examine those of his melodies that are not devised according to the dictates of prosody, or in the style of vocal melodies (as is the main theme of the prelude to *Sorochintsy Fair*, for instance), we see that they seldom start with an upbeat or have a feminine ending. He prefers to give the voice a 'real' harmonic note (and indeed a repetition of one note rather than a rise or fall), and entrusts the suspensions or appoggiaturas to the accompaniment. Likewise, when an impetus is required at the beginning of a phrase, he usually resorts to an appoggiatura (as often as not in the accompaniment) rather than to an upbeat.

The metre and rhythm of his vocal phrases may be determined by the text or not. In *Savishna* the poetic metre is quintuple throughout, and the music follows it unswervingly. In *The Ragamuffin* triple time is now and then substituted for the quintuple time suggested by the text from end to end. In *Eremushka's Lullaby* the music does not always reflect the 9+7 metre of the words. In *Kalistratushka* the poetic metre does not in the least affect the course of the music, which has many changes of time signature and in which several notes are often given to one syllable.

This last device is one that Mussorgsky seldom uses except for lyrical effects or to reproduce peculiarities of intonation. There is no single instance of it in Pimen's part (*Boris Godunov*) or in that of Boris except at one spot in the arioso in the second version in which he uses music composed for *Salammbô*.

Variety of time-signatures is of all the features of his musical style the only one to have been generally noticed. He uses practically every possible kind of time, asymmetric as well as symmetric; and often several in quick succession. In *With Nurse* (*The Nursery*), the signature changes twenty-four times within fifty-three bars. At the other extreme we have *Savishna,* in breathless quintuple time without a break. Mussorgsky seldom resorts to syncopation. The sole instance of its use on a comparatively big scale occurs in the second half of Act III of *Khovanshchina*.

His realistic purpose accounts for many of these style features, which are in thorough accord with the 'maximum of specificness, minimum of stylization' principle. Especially so, for instance, the scarcity of big leaps, of suspensions, of anticipations, of strong contrasts of note-values, which might so easily lead to declamatory over-emphasis. Bold concatenations and abrupt modulations are eminently suitable for effects of strong, sharp emphasis. So are appoggiaturas. Changes of harmony and of time-signature make for accuracy and pregnancy. The unostentatious treatment of feminine endings, too, [is characteristic].

Passing on to points of structure, we see how the same principles apply. The formal transitions to which he objects spell stylization: one can imagine how feeble the opening of *Trepak* would be with a transition from the F sharp minor chord to D minor. Likewise formal conclusions, unless they serve a specific purpose. The formal conclusion of the Death scene in *Boris* is a significant epilogue, a valuable musical peroration. In the Revolution scene, a similar procedure would have been out of keeping; and Mussorgsky wisely allows the music to die out without even a marked cadence, as also happens in the first scene.

The first act of *Khovanshchina* ends on a discord (the tolling of a cathedral bell). A song may end on a discord (e g. the *Harper's Song* and the *Child's Song*; *Savishna* ends on a bare fourth).[1] It may be in one key throughout, barely touching on other keys in its course, or modulate freely, and perhaps end without reverting to the main key: *Death's Serenade* is in a rather ambiguous F sharp minor, strongly leaning to C sharp minor; but all the main cadences are to A major or minor, the last one minor.[2]

The materials used in the texture may all be derived from the main theme or themes (*Trepak, Death's Lullaby, The Ragamuffin*) or miscellaneous, varying in accordance with the text.

There remains the question of instrumental style. Considering that Mussorgsky was an excellent pianist with a gift for improvisation, it may be said that his writing for the piano is less interesting than might have been expected. Not a feature of it invites special comment. Even in the *Pictures from an Exhibition,* his best work of that order, it is sometimes characterless. On the other hand, in certain of his accompaniments, the writing is remarkably ingenious and effective: *Trepak, Death's Lullaby* and the last three numbers in *Sunless* are cases in point. [His orchestration has already been discussed at length in Chapter VII.]

[1] The piano piece *Nurse and I*, after a full close on the tonic G major, has a brief afterthought suggesting E minor.

[2] There are many instances of ending away from the tonic in Russian folk tunes (and also in Greek folk tunes, among others).

APPENDICES

APPENDIX A

CALENDAR

(Figures in brackets denote the age of the person mentioned during the year in question. Dates are here given in the New Style only: Russian Old-Style dates will be found in the text of this book.)

Year	Age	Life	Contemporary Musicians
1839		Modest Petrovich Mussorgsky born, March 21, at Karevo, government of Pskov, son of Piotr (Peter) Alexeyevich Mussorgsky, a landowner.	Paer (68) dies, May 3. Adam aged 36; Alabiev 52; Auber 57; Balakirev 3; Balfe 31; Berlioz 36; Bizet 1; Borodin 5; Brahms 6; Bruch 1; Bruckner 15; Cherubini 79; Chopin 29; Cui 4; Dargomïzhsky 26; Delibes 3; Donizetti 42; Franck 17; Gade 22; Glinka 36; Goldmark 9; Gounod 21; Halévy 40; Heller 24; Henselt 25; Lalo 16; Liszt 28; Lvov 40; Mendelssohn 30; Mercadante 44; Meyerbeer 48; Moniuszko 19; Offenbach 20; Ponchielli 5; Rossini 47; Rubinstein (A.) 9; Saint-Saëns 4; Schumann 29; Serov 19; Smetana 15; Spohr 55; Spontini 65; Strauss (J. ii) 14; Varlamov 38; Verdi 26; Verstovsky 40; Wagner 26.
1840	1		Tchaikovsky born, May 7.
1841	2		Chabrier born, Jan. 18; Dvořák born, Sept. 8; Pedrell born, Feb. 19.
1842	3		Boito born, Feb. 24; Cherubini (82) dies, March 15;

Appendix A—Calendar

Year	Age	Life	Contemporary Musicians
			Massenet born, May 12; Sullivan born, May 13.
1843	4		Grieg born, June 15.
1844	5		Rimsky - Korsakov born, March 18.
1845	6		Fauré born, May 13.
1846	7		
1847	8		Mackenzie born, Aug. 22. Mendelssohn (38) dies, Nov. 4.
1848	9		Donizetti (51) dies, April 8; Duparc born, Jan. 21; Parry born, Feb. 27; Varlamov (47) dies, Oct.
1848	10		Chopin (39) dies, Oct. 17.
1850	11		
1851	12		d'Indy born, March 27; Spontini (77) dies, Jan. 14.
1852	13	M. is taken to St. Petersburg, where he enters the School for Cadets. *Porte-Enseigne Polka* for piano, his first composition, published.	Alabiev (65) dies; Stanford born, Sept. 30.
1853	14		
1854	15	At the School for Cadets.	Humperdinck born, Sept. 1; Janáček born, July 4.
1855	16		Chausson born, Jan. 11; Lyadov born, May 11.
1856	17	Enters the Preobrazhensky regiment.	Kastalsky born, Nov. 28; Martucci born, Jan. 1; Schumann (46) dies, July 29; Taneiev born, Nov. 25.
1857	18	Meeting with Balakirev (21), Dargomïzhsky (44) and Cui (22)	Elgar born, June 2; Glinka (54) dies, Feb. 15.
1858	19	Begins to study with Balakirev (22). He suffers from a nervous disorder and leaves the regiment.	Leoncavallo born, March 8; Puccini born, June 22.
1859	20	Studies with Balakirev (23) continued. M. visits Moscow,	Ippolitov-Ivanov born, Nov. 19; Lyapunov born, Nov. 30;

Year	Age	Life	Contemporary Musicians
		which greatly impresses him, and composes a choral scene for Ozerov's *Oedipus in Athens*.	Sokolov born, March 26; Spohr (75) dies, Oct. 22.
1860	21	Orchestral Scherzo in B flat major performed. M. again suffers from an illness.	Albeniz born, May 29; Charpentier born, June 25; Mahler born, July 7; Wolf born, March 13.
1861	22	The *Oedipus* scene performed. Liberation of the serfs, with which he is in sympathy, although as a landowner he suffers from it financially, being in fact impoverished. Meeting with Rimsky-Korsakov (17). *Intermezzo in modo classico* (first version) composed.	Arensky born, Aug. 11; Catoire born, April 27; MacDowell born, Dec. 18; Marschner (66) dies, Dec. 14.
1862	23	Two movements of a Symphony in D major composed. M. lives with his brother Filaret (26).	Debussy born, Aug. 22; Delius born, Jan. 29; Halévy (63) dies, March 17; Verstovsky (63) dies, Nov. 17.
1863	24	Stay at Toropets and Volok, spring and summer. At St. Petersburg he lives in a 'commune' with five companions and enters the civil service. Work on the opera *Salammbô* begun.	Mascagni born, Dec. 7.
1864	25	Further work done on *Salammbô*. First representative songs (*Night, Kalistratushka*, etc.).	Grechaninov born, Oct. 25; Meyerbeer (73) dies, May 2; Strauss (R.) born, June 11.
1865	26	Death of M.'s mother. In his distress he plunges into a bout of dipsomania; a serious illness (delirium tremens) ensues.	Dukas born, Oct. 1; Glazunov born, Aug. 10; Sibelius born, Dec. 8.
1866	27	Meeting with Glinka's sister, Lyudmila Shestakova. *Hopak, Darling Savishna, The Seminarist, On the Dnieper* and other songs composed.	Busoni born, April 1; Kalinnikov born, Jan. 13; Rebikov born, June 1.

Year	Age	Life	Contemporary Musicians
1867	28	Leaves the civil service and makes a precarious living by teaching and accompanying. *St. John's Night on the Bare Mountain* (first version) composed. *Hopak* and *Savishna* published.	Granados born, July 29.
1868	29	First song of *The Nursery* cycle composed, also the first act of Gogol's comedy *The Marriage*, which however he carries no further when Nikolsky has given him the idea of an opera on Pushkin's *Boris Godunov*. Summer spent at Shilovo. M. re-enters the civil service in the Forestry Department, in the hope that this will save him from poverty. More songs published.	Bantock born, Aug. 17; Rossini (76) dies, Nov. 13.
1869	30	Goes to live with the Opochinins. Initial version of *Boris Godunov* finished.	Berlioz (66) dies, March 8; Dargomïzhsky (56) dies, Jan.; Pfitzner born, May 5; Roussel born, April 5.
1870	31	Three more songs for *The Nursery* and *The Peepshow* composed. Opera on Spielhagen's *Hans und Grete* projected.	Balfe (62) dies, Oct. 20; Koreshchenko born, Dec. 18; Lvov (71) dies, Dec. 16; Mercadante (75) dies, Dec. 17; Novák born, Dec. 5; Schmitt born, Sept. 28.
1871	32	*Boris Godunov* rejected by the committee of the imperial theatres. M. shares a room with Rimsky-Korsakov (27) and begins the 2nd version of *Boris* there.	Auber (89) dies, May 12; Serov (51) dies, Feb. 1.
1872	33	Remodelling of *Boris Godunov* continued and new opera, *Khovanshchina*, planned. Concert performance of the Coronation born, Oct. 12.	Juon born, March 9; Scriabin born, Jan. 6; Vassilenko born, March 30; Vaughan Williams

Year	Age	Life	Contemporary Musicians
		nation scene from *Boris* given by the Russian Music Society, Feb. 5, but the second version of the work is again rejected by the imperial theatres. *The Nursery* song cycle completed. Work on the collective opera *Mlada*.	
1873	34	Three scenes from *Boris Godunov* produced. New outbreak of dipsomania, from which M. never completely recovers. Rimsky-Korsakov (29) having married, M. shares rooms with Count Golenishchev-Kutuzov (25). Death of M.'s friend, the painter V. A. Hartmann.	Rakhmaninov born, April 1; Reger born, March 19; Cherepnin (N.) born, May 15.
1874	35	*Boris Godunov* published and performed, Feb. 8. Song cycle *Sunless* and suite *Pictures from an Exhibition* for piano composed. First thought of an opera on Gogol's story *Sorochintsy Fair*.	Holst born, Sept. 21; Schoenberg born, Sept. 13; Suk born, Jan. 4.
1875	36	First act of *Khovanshchina* finished and second begun; first three of the *Songs and Dances of Death* composed. Death of Nadezhda Opochinina (53), July 11. *Sorochintsy Fair* temporarily abandoned. Having been expelled from his lodgings, M. takes refuge at the house of Paul Naumov.	Bizet (37) dies, June 3; Glier born, Jan. 11; Ravel born, March 7.
1876	37	Act III of *Khovanshchina* finished and *Sorochintsy Fair* resumed.	Akimenko born, Feb. 20; Falla born, Nov. 23.
1877	38	Alexey Tolstoy songs composed	Dohnányi born, July 27.

Year	Age	Life	Contemporary Musicians

posed and *Songs and Dances of Death* completed with *The Field-Marshal*. Work on *Sorochintsy Fair* continued, mainly during his absence from St. Petersburg in the summer.

1878 39 Association with Darya Leonova (49), who hopes to help him with small engagements. Drunkenness gets hold of him more and more, and he changes to another government department at the suggestion of Stassov (54), who hopes that this may help to cure him. Illness. *Boris Godunov* revived with success.

1879 40 First (concert) performance of the scene in Pimen's cell from *Boris*. Concert tour in the south of Russia with D. M. Leonova (50), with whom he appears as accompanist, solo pianist and composer. Concert performance of excerpts from *Khovanshchina* after his return, Dec. 9.

Bridge (Frank) born, Feb. 27; Ireland born, Aug. 13; Medtner born, Dec. 4; Respighi born, July 9; Scott (Cyril) born, Sept. 27.

1880 41 M. again leaves the civil service and is subsidized by two groups of friends to finish the two operas *Khovanshchina* and *Sorochintsy Fair*.

Bloch born, July 24; Krein (G.) born, Jan. 16; Offenbach (61) dies, Oct. 4; Pizzetti born, Sept. 20.

1881 42 Serious illness. M. is taken to the Military Hospital, Feb. 26. Mussorgsky dies in St. Petersburg, March 28.

Bartók born, March 25; Myaskovsky born, April 20. Akimenko aged 5; Albeniz 21; Arensky 20; Balakirev 45; Bantock 13; Bloch 1; Boito 39; Borodin 47; Brahms 48; Bridge (Frank) 2; Bruch 43; Bruckner 57; Busoni 15;

Catoire 20; Charpentier 21; Chausson 26; Cherepnin (N.) 8; Cui 46; Debussy 19; Delius 19; Dohnányi 4; Dukas 16; Duparc 33; Dvořák 40; Elgar 24; Falla 5; Fauré 36; Gade 64; Glazunov 16; Glier 5; Goldmark 51; Gounod 63; Granados 14; Grechaninov 17; Grieg 38; Holst 7; Humperdinck 27; d'Indy 30; Ippolitov-Ivanov 22; Ireland 2; Janáček 27; Juon 9; Kalinnikov 15; Kastalsky 25; Koreshchenko 11; Krein (G.) 1; Lalo 58; Leoncavallo 23; Liszt 70; Lyadov 26; Lyapunov 22; MacDowell 20; Mackenzie 34; Mahler 21; Martucci 25; Mascagni 18; Massenet 39; Medtner 2; Novák 11; Parry 33; Pedrell 41; Pfitzner 12; Pizzetti 1; Puccini 23; Rakhmaninov 8; Ravel 6; Rebikov 15; Reger 8; Respighi 2; Rimsky-Korsakov 37; Roussel 12; Rubinstein 51; Saint-Saëns 46; Schmitt 11; Schoenberg 7; Scott (Cyril) 2; Scriabin 9; Sibelius 16; Smetana 57; Sokolov 22; Stanford 29; Strauss (J. ii) 56; Strauss (R.) 17; Suk 7; Sullivan 39; Taneiev 25; Tchaikovsky 41; Vassilenko 9; Vaughan Williams 9; Verdi 68; Wagner 68; Wolf 21.

APPENDIX B

CATALOGUE OF WORKS

WORKS FOR THE STAGE

Han d'Islande (projected opera after Victor Hugo's novel) (1856).
Oedipus in Athens (choruses for a projected opera on Ozerov's play) (1858–60).
St. John's Eve (projected opera, after Gogol's story) (1858).
Salammbô (unfinished opera, after Flaubert's novel) (1863–6).
The Marriage (setting of the first act of Gogol's comedy) (1868).
Boris Godunov (after Pushkin's play and Karamzin's *History of the Russian State*) (first version, 1868–9; second version, 1871–2).
Bobïl (*The Landless Peasant*) (projected opera after Spielhagen's novel *Hans und Grete*) (1870).
Mlada (scenes for the second and third acts of the collective opera-ballet) (1872).
Khovanshchina (unfinished opera) (1872–80).
Sorochintsy Fair (unfinished opera, after Gogol's story) (1874–80).
Pugachevshchina (projected opera, possibly after Pushkin's *History of the Pugachev Rising* and his story *The Captain's Daughter*) (1877).

ORCHESTRAL WORKS

Scherzo in B flat major (1858).
Alla marcia notturna (1861).
Andante, Scherzo and Finale of Symphony in D major (1861–2).
St. John's Night on the Bare Mountain (1867).
Intermezzo symphonique in modo classico (orchestral version of the piano piece, with additional trio) (1867).
Poděbrad of Bohemia (projected symphonic poem) (1867).
Triumphal march, *The Capture of Kars* (also known as *March, with trio 'alla turca,'* partly based on the *Procession of Princes* from *Mlada*) (1880).
Transcaucasian Suite (projected work for orchestra with harps and piano) (1880).

CHORAL WORKS

Shamil's March, for soloists, chorus and orchestra (1859).
The Destruction of Sennacherib (after Byron), for chorus and orchestra (first version, 1867; second version, 1874).

Mussorgsky

Jesus Navin (or *Joshua*), for alto and bass soloists, chorus and piano (1874–7).
Three Vocalises for three-part female voices (1880).
Five Russian Folksongs (No. 5 unfinished), arranged for four-part male
  voices (1880).

SONGS

Where art thou, little star? (Grekov) (1857; revised, with orchestral accompaniment, 1858).
Tell me why (anon.) (1858).
Meines Herzens Sehnsucht (anon.) (1858).
Hour of Jollity (Koltsov) (first version 1858; second version 1859).
Sadly rustled the leaves (adapted from Pleshcheev) (1859).
What are words of love to you? (Ammosov) (1860).
I have many palaces and gardens (Koltsov) (1863).
Old Man's Song (also known as *The Harper's Song: An die Türen will ich schleichen* from Goethe's *Wilhelm Meister*) (1863).
King Saul (adapted from Kozlov's translation of Byron) (both versions 1863).
But if I could meet thee again (Kurochkin) (1863).
The wild winds blow (Koltsov) (1864).
Night (after Pushkin) (both versions 1864; first version orchestrated 1868).
Kalistratushka (Nekrassov) (both versions 1864).
Prayer (Lermontov) (1865).
The Outcast: essay in recitative (I.G.M.) (1865).
Cradle Song from Ostrovsky's *Voevoda* (also known as *Peasant Lullaby*) (both versions 1865).
Why are thy eyes sometimes so cold? (*Little One*) (Pleshcheev) (1866).
Ich wollt' meine Schmerzen ergössen (Heine) (1866).
Aus meinen Tränen (Heine) (1866).
Darling Savishna (composer) (1866).
You drunken sot (composer) (1866).
The Seminarist (composer) (1866).
Hopak from Shevchenko's *Haydamaki* (trans. Mey) (1866; revised, with orchestral accompaniment, 1868).
On the Dnieper (*Yarema's Song* from Shevchenko's *Haydamaki*) (trans. Mey) (first version 1866 [lost]; second version 1879).
Hebrew Song (Mey) (1867).
The Magpie (on two poems by Pushkin) (1867).
Gathering Mushrooms (Mey) (1867).
The Feast (Koltsov) (1867).
The Ragamuffin (composer) (1867).

The He-Goat: a worldly story (composer) (1867).
The Classicist (composer) (1867).
The Garden by the Don (Koltsov) (1867).
The Orphan (composer) (1868).
Eremushka's Lullaby (Nekrassov) (1868).
Child's Song (Mey) (1868).
The Nursery (composer): *With Nurse* (1868), *In the Corner, The Cockchafer, With the Doll* and *Going to Sleep* (1870), *On the Hobby-Horse* and *The Cat 'Sailor'* (1872).
The Peepshow (composer) (1870).
Evening Song (ascribed to Pleshcheev) (1871).
Sunless (Golenishchev-Kutuzov): *Between four walls, Thou didst not know me in the crowd, The idle, noisy day is ended, Boredom, Elegy* and *On the River* (1874).
Forgotten (Golenishchev-Kutuzov) (1874).
Epitaph (unfinished) (composer) (1874).
The Nettle Mountain (unfinished) (composer) (1874).
Songs and Dances of Death (Golenishchev-Kutuzov): *Lullaby, Serenade* and *Trepak* (1875), *The Field-Marshal* (1877).
The Sphinx (composer) (1875).
Not like thunder, trouble struck (Alexey Tolstoy) (1877).
Softly the spirit flew up to heaven (Alexey Tolstoy) (1877).
Pride (Alexey Tolstoy) (1877).
Is spinning man's work? (Alexey Tolstoy) (1877).
It scatters and breaks (Alexey Tolstoy) (1877).
The Vision (Golenishchev-Kutuzov) (1877).
The Wanderer (Rückert, trans. Pleshcheev) (1878).
Mephistopheles's Song of the Flea (Goethe, trans. Strugovshchikov) (1879).

Gordigiani's *Ogni sabato* (*canto popolare toscano*), arranged as a duet for mezzo-soprano and baritone (1864).

PIANO WORKS

Porte-Enseigne Polka[1] (1852).
Souvenir d'enfance (1857).
Scherzo and Finale of Sonata in E flat major (lost) (1858).
Sonata in F sharp minor (lost) (1858).

---

[1] Reprinted in *Sovetskaya Muzika*, 1947, No. 2, p. 48.

Scherzo in C sharp minor (1858).

Impromptu passioné (1859).

Ein Kinderscherz (*Children's Games: Puss in the Corner*) (1859; revised 1860).

Allegro and Scherzo of Sonata in C major for piano duet (1860) (the Scherzo is a transposed version of the Scherzo in C sharp minor of 1858).

Preludium in modo classico (lost) (1860).

Intermezzo in modo classico (1861).

Menuet monstre (lost) (1861).

Scherzo of a Sonata in D (lost) (1862) (possibly identical with the lost scherzo of the Symphony in D major).

From Memories of Childhood: Nurse and I and *First Punishment: Nurse shuts me in the Dark Room* (1865).

Duma (*Reverie*) (on a theme by V. A. Loginov) (1865).

La Capricieuse (on a theme by Count L. Heyden) (1865).

Scherzino, *The Seamstress* (1871).

Pictures from an Exhibition, suite (1874).

Fantasy, *Storm on the Black Sea* (lost) (1879).

On the Southern Shore of the Crimea (*Baydarki* and *Gurzuf u Ayu-Daga*) (1879).

Méditation (*Feuillet d'album*) (1880).

Une larme (1880).

Au Village (*Quasi fantasia*) (1880?).

Transcriptions for two, four or eight hands of works by Glinka, Beethoven, Balakirev, Berlioz and himself.

APPENDIX C

Arensky, Antony Stepanovich (1861–1906), Russian pianist, teacher and composer. Studied at the St. Petersburg Conservatoire and later became professor at that of Moscow.

Bortnyansky, Dmitry Stepanovich (1752–1825), Russian church composer. Studied at Moscow and under Galuppi at St. Petersburg, following him to Italy, where he made further studies. After producing operas there, he returned to St. Petersburg and became master of the imperial chapel.

Caccini, Guilio (*c.* 1560–1615), Italian singer, lutenist and composer. He was in the service of the Grand Duke of Tuscany at Florence, visited Paris, wrote short recitative pieces in the new recitative style and later the opera *Euridice* already set by Peri.

Cherepnin, Nikolay Nikolaevich (1873–1945), Russian pianist, conductor and composer. Pupil of Rimsky-Korsakov and others at the St. Petersburg Conservatoire. He became conductor of Belaiev's orchestra and at the Maryinsky Theatre, and in 1908–14 of Diaghilev's Russian Ballet. Father of Alexander Cherepnin, also a composer.

Cui, César Antonovich (1835–1918), Russian composer of French origin; pupil of the Polish composer Moniuszko. He was educated for military engineering and became a professor of fortification; one of the earliest members of Balakirev's circle of nationalist composers, though he seldom followed its principles as a composer and sometimes attacked its members as a critic.

Dargomïzhsky, Alexander Sergeevich (1813–69), Russian composer. He studied music as an amateur and after four years spent in goverment service led the life of a dilettante; but he did much to forward the nationalist Russian school, to whom his setting of Pushkin's *Stone Guest* as an opera served as a model of realistic music-drama.

Davidov, Karl Y. (1838–89), Russian cellist. Studied and first appeared at Leipzig, where he became first cellist in the Gewandhaus Orchestra and professor at the Conservatorium; but he returned to Russia in 1862, becoming first cellist at the Imperial Opera and director of the Conservatoire in St. Petersburg.

Famintsïn, Alexander Sergeevich (1841–96), Russian critic and minor composer. Having studied at St. Petersburg University and at Leipzig, he became professor of history at the St. Petersburg Conservatoire. He was implacably opposed to the nationalist school of composers.

Field, John (1782–1837), Irish pianist and composer. Pupil of Clementi' who took him on his continental travels, including Russia, where he settled as a piano virtuoso and teacher. He was a forerunner of Chopin.

Findeisen, Nikolay Feodorovich (1868–1928), Russian critic. Studied at the St. Petersburg Conservatoire, founded and edited the *Russian Musical Gazette* and wrote a monumental history of Russian music up to the end of the eighteenth century.

Galilei, Vincenzo (1533–91), Italian lutenist, theorist and composer, pupil of Zarlino at Venice. He took part in the discussions that led to the first operas written by the Florentine school and was the father of the astronomer Galileo Galilei.

Glebov, Igor, the pen-name assumed as critic by the Russian composer *Boris Asafiev* (1884–1949). He first studied philosophy and history, but on Rimsky-Korsakov's advice entered the St. Petersburg Conservatoire. He was joint editor with Lamm of the still incomplete edition of Mussorgsky's works.

Golenishchev-Kutuzov, Arseny, Count (1848–1913), Russian amateur poet, distant relative of Mussorgsky.

Gordigiani, Luigi (1806–60), Italian composer. He had a slight connection with Russia by coming under the patronage of the Russian Nikolay Demidov in Italy. He wrote ten operas and innumerable popular songs.

Grekov, Nikolay Porfirievich (1810–66), second-rate eclectic Russian poet. Made numerous translations from English, French, German and Spanish.

Karatigin, Vyacheslav (1875–1925), Russian critic, who devoted most of his work to Mussorgsky.

Kastalsky, Alexander Dmitrievich (1856–1926), Russian composer of church music, pupil of Tchaikovsky and Taneiev at Moscow. He became director of the Synodal School there and after the Revolution took part in the reform of church music and the people's theatres and cultural centres; leading authority on Russian folk-music.

Koltsov, Alexei Vasilivich (1809–42), often called 'the Russian Burns'; son of a cattle-dealer; his poems of peasant life are highly original and unconventional in form and content.

Kozlov, Ivan Ivanovich (1779–1840), a Byronic Russian poet, paralysed and blind in later years; translated a number of English poems.

Kurochkin, Vasily Stepanovich (1831–75), a well-known Russian translator, particularly famous for his versions of Béranger.

Lamm, Pavel Alexandrovich (1882–1951), Russian musical scholar. Studied at the Moscow Conservatoire and began his career as a pianist, but later became director of the State Publishing Department. He was the editor, with Igor Glebov, of the still incomplete critical edition of Mussorgsky's works in their original form.

Laroche, Hermann Augustovich (1845–1904), Russian critic. Fellow student of Tchaikovsky at the St. Petersburg Conservatoire and later professor at that of Moscow. On his return he became critic to several leading newspapers.

Lermontov, Michael Yurevich (1814–41), next to Pushkin the greatest of Russian lyric poets; much influenced by Byron; his novel *A Hero of our Time* is a classic.

Lyadov, Anatol Konstantinovich (1855–1914), Russian composer. Pupil of Rimsky-Korsakov, later professor at the St. Petersburg Conservatoire and attached to the imperial chapel. He was commissioned by the Russian Geographical Society, with Balakirev and Lyapunov, to collect folk-songs in various parts of the country.

Malherbe, Charles Théodore (1853–1911), French musical scholar. He studied law and literature at first, but turned to music and became archivist at the Paris Opéra in 1898. He made a collection of musical autographs.

Malko, Nikolay Andreevich (1883–1961), Russian conductor. Pupil of Rimsky-Korsakov, Glazunov and N. Cherepnin and of Mottl at Carlsruhe. He became professor at the Leningrad Conservatoire and conductor of the Philharmonic Orchestra there.

Melgunov, Julius Nikolaevich (1846–93), Russian pianist and musicologist. Studied at the Moscow Conservatoire, toured as a pianist in Russia and Germany, but later devoted himself to folksong research.

Mey, Lev Alexandrovich (1822–62), a prolific Russian translator of poems in most of the European and classical languages; author of historical dramas, of which *The Maid of Pskov*, *The Tsar's Bride* and *Servilia* inspired operas by Rimsky-Korsakov.

Nápravník, Eduard Franzevich (1839–1916), Czech conductor and composer. Although poor in his childhood, he studied at the Prague Organ School and in 1861 went to St. Petersburg as conductor of a private orchestra, from which position he rose through various appointments at the imperial theatres to the post of chief conductor of the Opera, where he produced four works of his own.

Nekrasov, Nikolay Alexeevich (1821–77), celebrated Russian poet and journalist; co-editor of the famous review *Sovremennik* (*The Contemporary*).

Ostrovsky, Alexander Nikolaevich (1823–86), Russian dramatist; most of his plays, such as the famous *Storm*, are realistic dramas or comedies of contemporary Russian merchant-class life, but his poetic fairy tale *Snow Maiden* inspired incidental music by Tchaikovsky and an opera by Rimsky-Korsakov.

Ozerov, Vladislav Alexandrovich (1769–1816), author of a number of sentimentalized pseudo-classic tragedies (*Fingal, Polyxena, Oedipus in Athens, The Death of Oleg,* etc.) very popular with the Russian audiences of his day.

Patti, Adelina (1843–1919), Italian soprano singer, born in Madrid and first heard at the age of seven in New York, where she reappeared after a period of study in 1859, first visiting London in 1861. She sang with enormous success until 1914.

Pleshcheev, Alexei Nikolaevich (1825–93), humanitarian, idealist Russian poet; arrested in 1849, with Dostoevsky, on a charge of complicity in the Petrashevsky conspiracy; sent to Siberia but pardoned by Alexander II; made many translations from English, French, German and Italian.

Polezhaev, Alexander Ivanovich (1805–38), Russian poet, sent to a penal battalion at the age of twenty for disrespectful allusions to the authorities in a poem written while a student in Moscow University; pardoned when dying of consumption in military hospital.

Riemann, Hugo (1849–1919), German musicologist. Studied at the Leipzig Conservatorium and became lecturer there in 1878, again in 1895, and professor in 1901.

Rimsky-Korsakov, Andrey Nikolaevich (born 1878), Russian musicologist, son of the composer. He attended the universities of St. Petersburg and others abroad, but turned to music in 1913, founding a musical journal and editing another, also editing the memoirs of his father and Glinka, the Mussorgsky documents and Cui's critical writings. He became curator of the musical manuscripts at the Leningrad Public Library.

Serov, Alexander Nikolaevich (1820–71), Russian composer and critic. Studied law and cultivated music while working in the civil service. After a visit to Germany in 1858 he became a passionate Wagnerian and as critic sometimes attacked the Russian nationalist composers.

Shevchenko, Taras Grigorevich (1814–61), Ukrainian poet, author of Cossack epics and lyrics in Ukrainian; sent to a penal battalion in 1847.

Stassov, Vladimir Vassilevich (1824–1906), Russian art critic. Friend and fellow student of Serov at the School of Jurisprudence in St. Petersburg, lived for some time in Italy and became director of the fine arts department of the Imperial Public Library.

Tolstoy, Count Alexey Konstantinovich (1817–75), distant relative of the great novelist; one of the foremost Russian lyric poets; historical dramatist.

APPENDIX D

BIBLIOGRAPHY

Barzel, Charles, 'Moussorgsky.' (Paris, 1939.)

Belaiev, Victor, 'Mussorgsky's *Boris Godunov* and its new version' (trans. S. W. Pring). (London, 1928.)

Calvocoressi, M. D., 'Moussorgsky.' (Paris, 1908; revised and enlarged edition, 1911; English translation, London, 1919.)
'Modest Mussorgsky.' (London, 1956.)

Chiesa, Mary Tibaldi, 'Mussorgsky.' (Milan, 1935.)

Fedorov, V., 'Moussorgsky.' (Paris, 1935.)

Fried, E. L., 'Modest Petrovich Musorgsky: k 100-letnyu co dnya rozh-deniya.' (Leningrad, 1939.)

Glebov, Igor, 'K vosstanovleniyu *Borisa Godunova* Musorgskovo.' (Moscow, 1928.)

Godet, Robert, 'En Marge de Boris Godounof,' 2 vols. (London, 1926.)

Golenishchev-Kutuzov, A. A., 'Vospominaniya o M. P. Musorgskom' (published in *Muzïkal'noe Nasledstvo,* vol. i. Moscow, 1935.)

Handschin, Jacques, 'Mussorgski: versuch einer Einführung.' (Zürich, 1924.)

Karatïgin, V., 'Musorgsky.' (Petersburg, 1922.)

Keldïsh, Y. 'Romansovaya lirika Musorgskova.' (Moscow, 1933.)

Leyda, Jay, and Sergei Bertensson, 'The Mussorgsky Reader.' (New York, 1947.)

Montagu-Nathan, M., 'Mussorgsky.' (London, 1916.)

'M. P. Musorgsky: Pis'ma i dokumenty.' Edited by A. N. Rimsky-Korsakov. (Moscow, 1932.) [1]

'M. P. Musorgsky: Pis'ma k A. A. Golenishchevu-Kutuzovu.' (Moscow, 1939.)

'Musorgsky: *Boris Godunov*—Stat'i i issledovaniya.' (Articles on *Boris* by Victor Belaiev, Igor Glebov, M. D. Calvocoressi, P. S. Kogan, P. A. Lamm, A. A. Khokhlovkina and V. Yakovlev.) Moscow, 1030.)

---

[1] This monumental annotated collection of Mussorgsky's letters, etc., supersedes the earlier separate collections of letters to Balakirev, Stassov, etc. It contains all surviving letters except those to Golenishchev-Kutuzov.

'M. P. Musorgsky: k pyatidesyatiletiyu co dnya smerti. Stat'i i materialy. (Articles by Y. Keldïsh, P. Lamm, Igor Glebov, I. Bryusova, V. Yakovlev, E. Sabelova and M. V. Ivanov-Boretsky, iconography, annotated list of works and full bibliography of books and articles on Mussorgsky in all languages from 1860 to 1928.) (Moscow, 1932.)

'Musorgsky i evo *Khovanshchina*.' (Articles by S. Lopashev, V. Yakovlev and V. Belaiev.) (Moscow, 1928.)

Mussorgsky number of *Muzïkalny Sovremennik*. ('Autobiographical Note' and articles by V. Komarova, I. Lapshin, Andrey Rimsky-Korsakov and V. Karatïgin, and annotated list of works.) (Petrograd, 1917.)

Mussorgsky number of *Sovetskaya Muzïka*. ('Autobiographical Note' and articles by A. Alshvang, G. Khubov, T. Kremlev, V. Protopopov, I. Kubikov, V. Steinpress, Andrey Rimsky-Korsakov, I. Remezov and Mussorgsky's letters to Golenishchev-Kutuzov.) (Moscow, 1939.)

Nilsson, Kurt, 'Die Rimskij-Korsakoffsche Bearbeitung des *Boris Godunoff* von Mussorgskij als Objekt der vergleichenden Musikwissenschaft.' (Münster i/W., 1937.)

Ogolevets, A. S., 'Vokalnaya dramaturgiya Musorgskovo.' (Moscow, 1966.)

Oldenburg-Ermke, Frans van, 'De laatste Herberg: Herinneringen aan Modest Petrovitsch Moussorgsky.' (Rotterdam, 1936.)

Olenine-d'Alheim, M., 'Le Legs de Moussorgsky.' (Paris, 1908.)

Orlov, Georgy, 'Letopis zhizni i tvorchestva M. P. Mussorgskovo.' (Moscow, 1940.)

Orlova, A. A., Trudi i dni M. P. Musorgskovo.' (Moscow, 1963.)

Riesemann, Oskar von, 'Mussorgski' (Monographien zur Russischen Musik: Zweiter Band). (Munich, 1926; English translation, London, 1935.)

Stassov, V. V., 'Modest Petrovich Musorgsky.' (St. Petersburg, 1881.)
——'Stat'i o Musorgskom.' (Moscow, 1922.)

Tumanina, N., 'M. P. Musorgsky: zhizn' i tvorchestvo.' (Moscow, 1939.)

Wolfurt, Kurt von, 'Mussorgskij.' (Stuttgart, 1926.)

INDEX

Index